1st Workshop on Computational Humor (CHum 2025)

Abu Dhabi, United Arab Emirates
19 January 2025

ISBN: 979-8-3313-1361-6

Printed from e-media with permission by:

Curran Associates, Inc.
57 Morehouse Lane
Red Hook, NY 12571

Some format issues inherent in the e-media version may also appear in this print version.

Printed with permission by Curran Associates, Inc. (2025)

For permission requests, please contact the Association for Computational Linguistics at the address below.

Association for Computational Linguistics
209 N. Eighth Street
Stroudsburg, Pennsylvania 18360

Phone: 1-570-476-8006
Fax: 1-570-476-0860

acl@aclweb.org

Additional copies of this publication are available from:

Curran Associates, Inc.
57 Morehouse Lane
Red Hook, NY 12571 USA
Phone: 845-758-0400
Fax: 845-758-2633
Email: curran@proceedings.com
Web: www.proceedings.com

COLING 2025

Proceedings of the 1st Workshop on Computational Humor (CHum)

Editors
Christian F. Hempelmann, Julia Rayz,
Tiansi Dong, and Tristan Miller

January 19, 2025

Association for Computational Linguistics (ACL)
209 N. Eighth Street
Stroudsburg, PA 18360
USA
Tel: +1-570-476-8006
Fax: +1-570-476-0860
acl@aclweb.org

Preface

The impressive recent progress in generative AI has opened up new frontiers for complex tasks that can be thought of as essentially human, including the production or interpretation of humor. For its part, humor research in general has become a mature, interdisciplinary field, both in theoretical advances across disciplines such as psychology, linguistics, and sociology, and in its breadth of purview and empirical support. While much existing research raises the question of whether modern language models can meaningfully contribute to theoretical linguistics, this First Workshop on Computational Humor (CHum 2025) proposes a parallel inquiry: despite their primary focus on engineering objectives, should these models be evaluated for their relevance to humor theory? Specifically, we set out to examine whether they can effectively model humor in alignment with established theoretical frameworks. As such, the workshop aims to foster further work on modeling the processes of humor with current methods in computational linguistics and natural language processing, against the theoretical backdrop of humor research and with reference to relevant corpora of textual, visual, and multimodal materials.

Being more dependent on context and inference than straightforward forms of communication, humor poses particular challenges for probabilistic approaches. For these and other reasons, it has long served as a special field of application for computational linguistics – understanding humor has often been referred to as "AI complete" and as such considered to be a potential test case for Artificial General Intelligence. Humor is approached presumably for this very reason whenever new paradigms arise in NLP, which currently center around large language models (LLMs). However, the study of humor is inherently multidisciplinary, and computational humor systems should therefore integrate insights from multiple disciplines in order to perform effectively. With this in mind, the workshop's keynotes bring together researchers from theoretical linguistics, psychology, and computer science, all of whom have expertise in humor theories. Among the questions raised in the keynotes are how elements of humor theories can be incorporated into LLM-generated text, and whether LLMs can be used to test humor theories.

Although we have chosen to name our event the "First" workshop for computational humor, we must acknowledge the groundwork that has been laid by a number of previous gatherings. These include the Twelfth Twente Workshop on Language Technology joint with the International Workshop on Computational Humour (1996), the Twentieth Twente Workshop on Language Technology, titled The April Fool's Day Workshop On Computational Humour (2002), the 3rd International Workshop on Computational Humor (2012), the 2012 AAAI Fall Symposium Artificial Intelligence of Humor (2012), Dagstuhl Seminar 21362 on Structure and Learning (2021), and the annual panels on Humor and Artificial Intelligence at the International Society of Humor Studies Conferences (2018–). These meetings, sometimes limited to invited contributions, aimed to explore diverse goals, from assessing how modeling humor could contribute to modeling intelligence, to the design of intelligent systems capable of understanding the (theoretical) mechanisms of jokes and collaboratively contributing to their generation. Like us, many of our invited speakers have participated in these previous meetings, making them well positioned to provide insights into the progress and evolution of the field.

CHum 2025 received a total of 28 submissions, which is many more than we could accept for presentation. In the end, we selected eleven papers that we felt most closely aligned with the workshop's interdisciplinary aims. Our selection includes work on advancing the state of the art is humor research by applying current computational models and techniques, as well as more task-focused NLP papers that apply techniques informed by existing humor research.

We would like to thank everyone who submitted a paper to the workshop, as well as the members of our Program Committee for their timely and insightful reviews.

Christian F. Hempelmann, Julia Rayz, Tiansi Dong, and Tristan Miller January 2025

Keynotes

How Many Stochastic Parrots Does it Take to Change a Lightbulb?
Salvatore Attardo, East Texas A&M University

Generally speaking the discussion of humor and AI has centered on questions such as "Does AI have a sense of humor?" or "Does AI understand humor and/or chan it explain it?" or "Can AI produce humor?" More pragmatic projects tend to focus on recognition: "Can AI identify humor/irony/puns/satire?" I find these questions interesting, but up to a point. First, the seem all tinged, more or less consciously, to what we could call the "anthropomorphic AI ideology": the belief that AIs match/reflect/approximate human intelligence and that humor is a folk-metric of performance, a sort of Humorous Turing test: if AIs understand/produce humor then they are truly "human" (for some senses of "be" and "human" to be specified). The character of Data in *Star Trek: The Next Generation* is the standard bearer for this set of beliefs. Second, the idea, to which I shamefully contributed, that humor is "AI complete" and hence if an AI "masters" humor it should thereby be an AGI (Artificial General Intelligence). Third, the current wave of LLMs are essentially black boxes and it is unclear to what extent a black box model counts as an explanation. Having managed to alienate the entire audience of the gathering, I will then proceed to argue that LLMs provide us with an excellent implementation of Trier's (1931) lexical field theory and more broadly of the semantic network postulated by Fillmore, Raskin, Eco and many others. As such they make some aspects of theories of humor testable in a new empirical way.

Unlocking the Punchline: Navigating Humor Computation From Understanding to Generation and Beyond
Liang Yang, Dalian University of Technology

Significant progress has been made in the field of humor computation, including recognition and generation. Despite its promising developments, several challenges still remain in the era of LLMs. In this talk, I will present our recent efforts to address some of them. (1) For understanding, I will discuss the understanding mechanism of large models for humor. (2) For generation, I will introduce how large models generate specific types of humor by integrating humor theory. (3) Finally, I will share our future exploration directions, such evaluation of sense of humor.

The Psychology of Computational Humor
Willibald Ruch, University of Zurich

This keynote will highlight what computational humor needs from research into the psychology of humor, what psychology can gain from requirements and results in computational humor, and where this underappreciated multidisciplinary symbiosis has (not) gone and needs to develop.

Get With The Program! From Talking the Talk to Walking the Walk in Computational Humour
Tony Veale, University College Dublin

LLM-based agents such as ChatGPT exhibit an amiable if superficial wit, and show a skilled ear for mimicry that lets them capture the cadences and attitudes of famous comics. Their auto-regressive generation of continuations to a given prompt makes them especially adept at using the *"yes, and ..."* principle of improv comedy to wring laughs from silly premises. But jokes of the short and snappy variety that are crafted to be retold in many different contexts require an LLM to do more than talk like a comedian. The words and attitudes must be appropriate to a joke, and the text must actually work like a joke too, with an effective logical mechanism that snaps shut on an audience like a mouse in a trap. Although LLMs can do a surprisingly good job of analyzing and explaining jokes, they do a rather poor job of turning this reactive appreciation into a proactive generative ability. In this talk I consider how we might tackle this *understanding vs. generating* gap.

Organizing Committee

Christian F. Hempelmann, East Texas A&M University
Julia Rayz, Purdue University
Tiansi Dong, Fraunhofer IAIS and University of Cambridge
Tristan Miller, University of Manitoba

Program Committee

Adam Jatowt, University of Innsbruck
Alessandro Valitutti, Phedes Lab
Anna Palmann, University of Amsterdam
Anne-Gwenn Bosser, École Nationale d'Ingénieurs de Brest
Bob Mankoff, CartoonCollections.com
Drew Gorenz, University of Southern California
Elena Mikhalkova, European University at Saint Petersburg
Heather Knight, Oregon State University
Joe Toplyn, Twenty Lane Media
Juliette Love, Google DeepMind
Kory Mathewson, Google DeepMind
Kristian Kersting, TU Darmstadt
Larry Lefkowitz, Working Knowledge LLC
Max Petrenko, Amazon
Nathaniel Laywine, York University
Ori Amir, University of Texas Permian Basin
Pelin Cunningham-Erdogdu, University of Texas at Austin
Piotr Mirowski, Google DeepMind
Rada Mihalcea, University of Michigan
Rey Alejandro Gonzalez, Purdue University
Sophie Jentzsch, German Aerospace Center (DLR)
Tatiana Ringenberg, Purdue University
Yi Zhang, Purdue University

Table of Contents

Workshop Program

08:45–09:00 *Opening remarks*
Christian F. Hempelmann, Julia Rayz, Tiansi Dong and Tristan Miller

Keynote 1

09:00–09:45 *How Many Stochastic Parrots Does it Take to Change a Lightbulb?*
Salvatore Attardo, East Texas A&M University

Paper session 1: Multimodal Pathways to Meaning and Memory

09:45–10:05 *The Exception of Humor: Iconicity, Phonemic Surprisal, Memory Recall, and Emotional Associations*
Alexander Kilpatrick and Maria Flaksman

10:05–10:25 *Text Is Not All You Need: Multimodal Prompting Helps LLMs Understand Humor*
Ashwin Baluja

Keynote 2

11:00–11:45 *Unlocking the Punchline: Navigating Humor Computation From Understanding to Generation and Beyond*
Liang Yang, Dalian University of Technology

Paper session 2: Algorithms and Frameworks for Pun Generation

11:45–12:05 *Rule-based Approaches to the Automatic Generation of Puns Based on Given Names in French*
Mathieu Dehouck and Marine Delaborde

12:05–12:25 *Homophonic Pun Generation in Code Mixed Hindi English*
Yash Raj Sarrof

12:25–12:45 *Bridging Laughter Across Languages: Generation of Hindi-English Code-mixed Puns*
Likhith Asapu, Prashant Kodali, Ashna Dua, Kapil Rajesh Kavitha and Manish Shrivastava

Keynote 3

13:30–14:15 *The Psychology of Computational Humor*
Willibald Ruch, University of Zurich

Paper session 3: Explorations in Semantics and Pragmatics

14:15–14:35 *Testing Humor Theory Using Word and Sentence Embeddings*
Stephen Skalicky and Salvatore Attardo

14:55–15:40 *Pragmatic Metacognitive Prompting Improves LLM Performance on Sarcasm Detection*
Joshua Lee, Wyatt Fong, Alexander Le, Sur Shah, Kevin Han and Kevin Zhu

Keynote 4

14:55–15:40 *Get With The Program! From Talking the Talk to Walking the Walk in Computational Humour*
Tony Veale, University College Dublin

Paper session 4: Evaluating and Experiencing Generated Humor

16:10–16:30 *Can AI Make Us Laugh? Comparing Jokes Generated by Witscript and a Human Expert*
Joe Toplyn and Ori Amir

16:30–16:50 *Evaluating Human Perception and Bias in AI-Generated Humor*
Narendra Nath Joshi

16:50–17:10 *The Theater Stage as Laboratory: Review of Real-Time Comedy LLM Systems for Live Performance*
Piotr Mirowski, Kory Mathewson and Boyd Branch

17:10–17:30 *The Algorithm is the Message: Computing as a Humor-Generating Mode*
Vittorio Marone

17:30–17:40 *Closing remarks*
Christian F. Hempelmann, Julia Rayz, Tiansi Dong and Tristan Miller

The Exception of Humor: Iconicity, Phonemic Surprisal, Memory Recall, and Emotional Associations

Alexander Kilpatrick[1] & Maria Flaksman[2]

[1]Nagoya University of Commerce and Business
[2]Otto-Friedrich University of Bamberg

Abstract

This meta-study explores the relationships between humor, phonemic bigram surprisal, emotional valence, and memory recall. Prior research indicates that words with higher phonemic surprisal are more readily remembered, suggesting that unpredictable phoneme sequences promote long-term memory recall. Emotional valence is another well-documented factor influencing memory, with negative experiences and stimuli typically being remembered more easily than positive ones. Building on existing findings, this study highlights that words with negative associations often exhibit greater surprisal and are easier to recall. Humor, however, presents an exception: while associated with positive emotions, humorous words also display heightened surprisal and enhanced memorability.

1 Introduction

There are a number of factors that can influence the memorability of events and stimuli. Two examples of this are probability and emotional valence where highly improbable events and stimuli are remembered with greater clarity (e.g., Ranganath & Rainer, 2003) as are those associated with negative emotions (e.g., Kensinger, 2007). This report documents a meta-study which explores these effects by examining the relationship between phonemic bigram surprisal, emotional valence, and memory recall in American English words. Specifically, it investigates whether humorous words are more surprising and memorable. The findings of this meta-study build upon existing literature by demonstrating that while negative emotional valence generally enhances memory and increases phonological surprisal, humor presents an exception. Despite its positive emotional valence, humor is associated with higher surprisal and recall accuracy. These results provide deeper insights into the interplay between phonological markedness, emotional valence, and memory retention, suggesting that humor may engage unique cognitive processes compared to other emotions. It is important to note that while there are various types of humor (for a review and discussion on how deep learning models might identify them, see Chen & Soo, 2018), the present study focuses on an experiment by Engelthaler and Hills (2017), in which participants rated words highly if they were "amusing or likely to be associated with humorous thought or language (e.g., absurd, amusing, hilarious, playful, silly, whimsical, or laughable)." Consequently, this study adopts a one-dimensional perspective of humor as defined by those ratings.

The negativity bias, the tendency for negative information to have a greater impact on memory than positive information, plays a crucial role in shaping how we recall emotional events. Negative emotions are often remembered with greater accuracy compared to positive or neutral ones (e.g., Baumeister et al., 2001; Rozin & Royzman, 2001; LaBar & Cabeza, 2006), a phenomenon well-documented in psychology and cognitive science. This enhanced recall is primarily attributed to the evolutionary function of negative emotions which can signal potential threats. Learning to avoid negative events is more evolutionarily beneficial than engaging with positive events, leading humans to be primed for remembering and learning from negative experiences. Research by Kensinger (2007) shows that negative emotional content enhances memory retention by fostering greater attentional focus during encoding and retrieval.

Proceedings of the 1st Workshop on Computational Humor (CHum), pages 1–8
January 19, 2025.

Additionally, studies have found that negative events are remembered more vividly due to their emotional salience, resulting in more detailed and accurate recollections (Phelps, 2004; LaBar & Cabeza, 2006). This body of research underscores the cognitive mechanisms behind the superior recall of negative emotions, emphasizing their significance in both personal memory and societal perceptions (Rozin & Royzman, 2001).

Phonemic bigram surprisal, as utilized in this study, is based on Shannon's (1948) Information Theory, which quantifies the amount of information expressed by communication systems. In the context of this study, surprisal is calculated as the negative logarithm (base 2) of the probability of a particular phoneme occurring given the preceding phoneme (*P*), returning a value in bits of information. Phonemic bigram surprisal captures how unexpected a bigram sequence is where unpredictable bigrams carry more information than predictable bigrams. Average surprisal for a word is derived by summing the information for all bigrams and dividing by the total number of bigrams in the word.

$$Surprisal = -log_2 P \qquad (1)$$

Phonemic bigram surprisal has been shown to influence memory recall, as evidenced in a study examining iconicity and surprisal in linguistic processing (Kilpatrick & Bundgaard-Nielsen, 2024). The study demonstrated that words with high surprisal tend to be processed more slowly and less accurately during perception but are more memorable. However, iconic words—which were already known to be easier to process and more memorable (e.g., Sidhu, Vigliocco & Pexman, 2020; Sidhu, Khachatoorian & Vigliocco, 2023)—exhibited higher average surprisal than arbitrary words. Indeed, iconic words tend to evolve towards phonemic predictability and arbitrariness over long periods of time in different stages of de-iconization (Flaksman, 2017). These stages exhibit a stochastic relationship with surprisal whereby words in early, highly iconic stages carry more surprisal than those in later, more arbitrary stages (Flaksman & Kilpatrick, In Press). This relationship between memorability, surprisal and iconicity suggests that while improbable phoneme combinations can create a cognitive disadvantage during processing, this increased effort ultimately enhances retention in long-term memory.

It has also been shown that emotional valence is reflected in phonemic bigram surprisal (Kilpatrick, Under Review). Specifically, negative words are composed of more surprising phoneme sequences, which enhances their retention and suggests that the negativity bias is encoded in languages. This connection between phonemic structure and emotional content provides valuable insights into the cognitive mechanisms underlying memory retention.

Phonemic surprisal could serve as an important additional datapoint in machine learning algorithms focused on emotion and sentiment analysis. By quantifying the predictability of phoneme sequences, phonemic surprisal offers insights into how sound patterns might relate to emotional valence in language. Current sentiment analysis algorithms typically rely on lexical and syntactic features, often overlooking the phonological aspects that could improve model accuracy. This position aligns with earlier research (Kilpatrick, 2023) that explored the utility of iconic associations between phonemes and various emotions and sentiments. In that study, machine learning algorithms were constructed to predict emotions and sentiments using the phonemes in each word. Model feature importance scores revealed that, while it was difficult to distinguish fine-grained emotional differences, general positivity and negativity was stochastically reflected in phonemes. Interestingly, the algorithms constructed to predict negative emotions (Anger, Disgust, Fear, Negative Valence, and Sadness) performed better than those constructed to predict positive emotions (Anticipation, Joy, Positive Valence, Surprise, and Trust), suggesting that iconic negative associations are more robustly reflected in phonemes than positive associations.

Increased surprisal in iconic words represents a form of phonological markedness that goes hand in hand with other observed iconic markedness strategies (Voeltz & Kilian-Hatz, 2001) including the use of phonotactic violations (e.g., *vroom* [vɹum]), non-native speech sounds (e.g., *ugh* [əx]), gemination (e.g., GRRRR! [gr:]), or vowel lengthening (e.g., WHAAT? [wæ:t]). Dingemanse and Thompson (2020) explore the relationship between humor and markedness through the lens of iconicity. They propose that structural markedness is a key factor underlying perceptions of both funniness and iconicity in words. Marked cues function as metacommunicative signals, drawing attention to words as playful and performative. This research suggests that playful and poetic elements are integral to the lexicon, highlighting the intersection of humor and markedness in language. In the context of the present study, this suggests that words with humorous associations should carry more information than those without. Imitative words—particularly ideophones—are expressive and more likely to violate phonological, morphological and syntactic norms (Dingemanse, 2017 Dingemanse & Akita, 2017). As both humorous and iconic words are related to expressivity, this relationship is worth further investigation which we attempt in the present study. For example, we expect humorous words like *booby* (M=4.07), *waddle* (M=4.05) or *gaggle* (M = 3.82) to have higher average surprisal than words like *torture* (M= 1.26), war (M= 1.34), or *casket* (M= 1.38), where numbers in parentheses represent humor Likert averages. However, this prediction is at odds with the finding that words with negative associations carry more information because humor is typically associated with positive valence. This study seeks to reconcile these seemingly contradictory observations.

This study builds on prior research investigating the relationship between phonemic surprisal, emotional valence, and memory, with a particular focus on how humor functions within this framework. While previous findings have highlighted the role of negativity bias in enhancing memory recall (Kilpatrick, Under Review), humor presents a unique case of a positive emotional valence associated with high surprisal. By examining words rated for their humor, we aim to determine whether the cognitive mechanisms that enhance memorability in negative valence also apply to humor, and how these effects differ between iconic and non-iconic words.

2 Method

Data here: https://shorturl.at/2SXvO. Phonemic bigram surprisal was calculated by cross-referencing the SUBLEX-US corpus (Brysbaert & New, 2009) with the CMU Pronouncing Dictionary (Weide, 1999) to obtain phonemic transcriptions and frequencies. A more detailed explanation of this process is provided in the above link. This combined dataset was then cross-referenced with existing datasets to provide morpheme counts (Sánchez-Gutiérrez, 2018) and parts of speech (Brysbaert, New, & Keuleers, 2012) because number of morphemes and word classification have been shown to influence surprisal (Kilpatrick & Bundgaard-Nielsen, 2024). Iconicity ratings were obtained from an existing experiment (Winter et al., 2023) where American English speakers were asked to provide Likert scale ratings to words according to how much they "sound like" their meaning. The memory recall data comes from a pre-existing psycholinguistic experiment (Cortese, Khanna, & Hacker, 2010) which involved the training of 120 undergraduate students on a list of words in one experimental session and the testing of their recall accuracy in a second session within the same week.

This study draws from three existing experiments for the emotion data. Firstly, there are ten emotions—Anger, Anticipation, Disgust, Fear, Joy, Negative, Positive, Sadness, Surprise, and Trust—taken from the NRC Emotion Lexicon (Mohammad & Turney, 2013) where American English-speaking participants were asked to provide binary responses to words according to whether they associate each word with a particular emotion. The NRC_Valence (Mohammad & Turney, 2013) variable also comes from the NRC emotion lexicon while G_Valence (Scott et al., 2019) comes from the Glasgow Norms which was collected from English speaking participants in Scotland and is included to explore potential crossover into other variants of English. Lastly, the Humor variable comes from an online study (Engelthaler & Hills, 2018) where English-speaking participants were asked to rate how humorous words are on a 5-point Likert scale. In that study, participants were asked to rank words where at one end of the scale, words are "dull or unfunny" and at the other, "absurd, amusing, hilarious, playful, silly, whimsical, or laughable" (Engelthaler & Hills, 2018). The original study made no distinction between different types of humor and there is no way to disentangle differences between, irony, sarcasm, dark humor, or wordplay. No samples were excluded from the models except in the case of missing data. That is, words like *glimmer*, *whisper*, and *crunch*, are iconic, but are not particularly humorous nor are they seemingly associated with emotional valence. Despite not carrying said associations, they were included in the following analyses.

The emotional response variables are measured using three distinct types of scales. For emotions from the NRC emotion lexicon, such as Fear, responses are measured on a binary scale, where participants rate the presence or absence of a single emotion from 0 (neutral) to 1 (fearful). On the other hand, the humor dataset presents a one-tailed continuous scale represented by averages of Likert responses from 1 (neutral) to 5 (humorous). Lastly, the valence variables are assessed on a two-tailed scale, where ratings range from 1 (negative) to 7 (positive), with 4 representing a neutral emotional state. This scale accounts for both positive and negative valence, capturing a bidirectional emotional response. That noted, there is undoubtedly some measure of bidirectionality in other variables, particularly the Negative and Positive variables from the NRC emotion lexicon.

This data is used in two series of multiple linear regression models. The first series is designed to explore the relationship between emotions—which are included as the dependent variables—and average bigram surprisal (Average_Surprisal) which is included alongside iconicity ratings (Iconicity_Rating), phonemic length (Phoneme_Length), morphemic length (Morpheme_Length), and parts of speech (PoS) categories. Here, we predict that those emotions associated with positivity (e.g., Anticipation, Joy, Positive, Surprisal, and Trust) will carry less information than those associated with negativity (e.g., Anger, Disgust, Fear, Negative, and Sadness). We predict that this pattern will be exhibited more robustly in the Valence variables due to their bi-directional nature. Humor--or at least words assigned high humor ratings in Engelthaler & Hills, (2018)—is predicted to carry more information despite being typically associated with positivity. In the second series of models, the emotion variables are included as independent variables, and the results of the memory recall experiment are included as the dependent variables. Here, we predict that same pattern whereby negative emotions will exhibit a positive correlation with memory recall, even when average bigram surprisal is taken into consideration. Again, we expect Humor to buck this trend and exhibit an increased memory recall accuracy.

3 Results

Firstly, to test the assumption that humor has a generally positive association, we ran two simple linear regression analyses, using Humor ratings (Engelthaler & Hills, 2018) as the dependent variable and valence ratings (NRC_Valence and G_Valence) as the predictor variables. In both models, valence was a significant predictor of humor, indicating a positive correlation between Humor and positive valence ($p < 0.001$ in both models).

Variable	**G_Valence**	**NRC_Valence**
(Intercept)	28.03***	37.22***
Average_Surprisal	**-2.11***	**-4.51*****
Iconicity_Rating	**-5.32*****	**-10.31*****
Phoneme_Length	0.37	-0.18
Morpheme_Length	1.31	-1.24
PoS_Adverb	1.61	2.89**
PoS_Determiner	0.41	0.029
PoS_Interjection	-0.05	0.87
PoS_Name	-0.18	2.40*
PoS_Noun	1.70	5.37***
PoS_Number	1.337	0.904
PoS_Preposition	-0.22	0.45
PoS_Pronoun	0.45	1.54
PoS_Unclassified	0.28	0.14
PoS_Verb	-1.48	0.74

Table 1: Results of the two valence models. Asterisks denote significance (* $p < 0.05$, ** $p < 0.01$, *** $p < 0.001$).

Two models were constructed using the two-tailed valence variables from the NRC emotion lexicon and the Glasgow norms (Table 1) as dependent variables. Both exhibited a significant negative effect of both average surprisal and iconicity ratings revealing that negative valence is associated with both increased surprisal and iconicity. In other words, words associated with negative valence are made up of more unpredictable bigrams and negative valence is more robustly expressed than positive valence in iconic associations.

Following this, a series of multiple linear regression models were constructed using the one-tailed emotion variables from the NRC emotion lexicon (Table 2) as dependent variables. These models show a general trend whereby negative emotions carry more average surprisal. Important to note here is that this was only significant with Disgust, which exhibited a significant positive correlation, and Anticipation and Joy which exhibited significant negative correlations. Almost

	Negative Emotions					Positive Emotions				
	Anger	Disgust	Fear	Negative	Sadness	Anticipation	Joy	Positive	Surprise	Trust
(Intercept)	-1.305	0.043	-0.909	0.251	0.447	3.298***	2.718**	7.781***	-2.732**	6.267***
Average_Surprisal	**0.247**	**2.574***	**-0.69**	**1.543**	**0.085**	**-3.029****	**-1.989***	**-1.926**	**0.902**	**-1.523**
Iconicity_Rating	**6.495*****	**5.499*****	**7.169*****	**9.963*****	**4.062*****	**0.804**	**2.749****	**-3.43*****	**6.431*****	**-5.886*****
Phoneme_Length	3.181**	1.416	2.593**	2.911**	1.057	1.277	1.679.	4.395***	3.436***	2.854**
Morpheme_Length	0.685	0.347	0.611	1.847.	3.142**	0.668	-0.689	0.481	-1.399	0.179
PoS_Adverb	-2.606**	-2.539*	-2.148*	-3.869***	-1.294	-0.019	-0.759	-1.353	1.132	-0.989
PoS_Determiner	-0.301	-0.441	-0.312	-0.696	-0.335	-0.23	-0.306	-0.533	-0.163	-0.255
PoS_Interjection	-1.391	-0.893	-1.393	-0.197	-1.367	0.586	-1.012	0.149	0.469	-0.384
PoS_Name	-1.45	-2.683**	-0.18	-3.909***	-1.657.	-0.553	-0.442	-1.651.	-1.444	0.257
PoS_Noun	-2.205*	-7.132***	0.745	-9.067***	-3.462***	0.378	-3.275**	-7.027***	0.176	0.556
PoS_Number	-1.163	-1.621	-1.15	-2.623**	-1.398	-0.918	-1.1	-2.278*	-0.54	-1.213
PoS_Preposition	0.798	-1.517	-1.112	-1.118	-1.288	-0.881	-1.065	-0.708	-0.577	-1.192
PoS_Pronoun	-0.414	-0.554	-0.431	-0.917	-0.455	-0.39	-0.469	-0.879	-0.212	-0.477
PoS_Unclassified	-0.55	-0.792	1.645	-1.212	-0.555	2.488*	-0.433	1.228	-0.368	-0.188
PoS_Verb	1.704.	-6.244***	-0.269	-3.253**	-1.014	2.619**	-1.759.	-4.875***	1.616	1.242

Table 2: Results of the models run using the one-tailed NRC emotion variables. Asterisks denote significance (* p < 0.05, ** p < 0.01, *** p < 0.001).

Variable	Humor
(Intercept)	38.202***
Average_Surprisal	3.125**
Iconicity_Rating	18.006***
Phoneme_Length	-1.368
Morpheme_Length	-6.374***
PoS_Adverb	-0.813
PoS_Interjection	1.497
PoS_Name	-0.768
PoS_Noun	2.449*
PoS_Number	-1.823
PoS_Preposition	0.593
PoS_Verb	-1.386

Table 3: Results of the humor model. Asterisks denote significance (* p < 0.05, ** p < 0.01, *** p < 0.001).

all variables demonstrated a positive correlation with iconicity ratings except for Anticipation which was not significant and Positive which revealed a significant negative relationship with iconicity ratings.

Humor was also tested as a dependent variable (Table 3). Despite being associated with positive valence, it exhibited a significant positive relationship with average surprisal. Humor was also found to be a significant predictor of iconicity ratings where high humor ratings correlated with high iconicity. In another way, words associated with humor like *oomph* (Humor = 3.93; Average Surprisal = 6.26; Iconicity = 6.92) are made up of unpredictable bigrams and are iconic while words that are not associated with humor like *cancer* (Humor = 1.46; Average Surprisal = 3.62; Iconicity = 2.83) are less surprising and less iconic.

Variable	G_Valence	NRC_Valence
(Intercept)	29.581***	15.168***
Valence	**-1.009**	**-5.154*****
Average_Surprisal	**4.899*****	**7.098*****
Iconicity_Rating	1.707	2.582**
Phoneme_Length	-2.833**	-2.645**
Morpheme_Length	-2.345*	-3.637***
PoS_Adverb	-0.347	-0.973
PoS_Interjection		0.371
PoS_Name	2.581**	2.64**
PoS_Noun	6.666***	5.657***
PoS_Number	-1.774	0.481
PoS_Preposition	-0.936	-1.034
PoS_Verb	-7.083***	-10.398***

Table 4: Results of the two memory/valence models. Asterisks denote significance (* p < 0.05, ** p < 0.01, *** p < 0.001).

All models thus far were then reconstructed except the emotions were included as an independent variable and the dependent variable for each model was the memory recall accuracy results. First, we reconstructed the valence models (Table 4) and found that negative valence was associated with improved memory recall; however, this relationship was only significant in the NRC emotion lexicon model ($p < 0.001$). For both models, increased average surprisal was associated with increased memory recall.

The pattern between negative valence and memory recall was also exhibited in the models constructed using the NRC emotion lexicon emotions (Table 5). Here, Disgust, Fear, and Negative were significant predictors of increased memory recall while a significant negative correlation was observed between positive

	Negative Emotions					Positive Emotions				
	Anger	Disgust	Fear	Negative	Sadness	Anticipation	Joy	Positive	Surprise	Trust
(Intercept)	29.556***	29.71***	29.569***	29.615***	29.511***	29.662***	29.442***	29.697***	29.515***	29.444***
Emotion	**1.348**	**5.729*** **	**1.392**	**3.346*** **	**2.074***	**-2.787** **	**0.887**	**-2.842** **	**-2.282***	**-0.578**
Average_Surprisal	**5.495*** **	**5.191*** **	**5.464*** **	**5.377*** **	**5.503*** **	**5.436*** **	**5.505*** **	**5.489*** **	**5.526*** **	**5.485*** **
Iconicity_Rating	**2.098***	**1.832.**	**2.083***	**1.71.**	**2.107***	**2.154***	**2.214***	**2.017***	**2.357***	**2.131***
Phoneme_Length	-3.801***	-3.946***	-3.832***	-3.926***	-3.812***	-3.753***	-3.754***	-3.631***	-3.656***	-3.734***
Morpheme_Length	-4.209***	-4.108***	-4.199***	-4.149***	-4.214***	-4.19***	-4.197***	-4.247***	-4.293***	-4.228***
PoS_Adverb	-1.699.	-1.661.	-1.7.	-1.657.	-1.688.	-1.607	-1.741.	-1.665.	-1.719.	-1.689.
PoS_Interjection	0.251	0.305	0.252	0.174	0.259	0.23	0.245	0.221	0.394	0.241
PoS_Name	2.084*	2.162*	2.027*	2.165*	2.133*	2.078*	2.084*	2.002*	2.095*	2.077*
PoS_Noun	2.15*	2.555*	2.121*	2.467*	2.258*	2.09*	2.174*	1.895.	2.09*	2.133*
PoS_Number	0.009	0.063	0.009	0.056	0.021	-0.018	0.009	-0.045	-0.01	-0.004
PoS_Verb	-10.183	-9.798***	-10.165	-9.975***	-10.092***	-10.087***	-10.146***	-10.297***	-10.14***	-10.136

Table 5: Results of the models run using the memory recall results and the one-tailed NRC emotion variables. Asterisks denote significance (* $p < 0.05$, ** $p < 0.01$, *** $p < 0.001$).

emotions, Anticipation, Positive, and Surprise. In all models, high average surprisal was a significant predictor of high memory accuracy.

Lastly, the humor model was reconstructed (Table 6). It revealed that humor follows the same pattern as negative emotions, where words associated with humor are recalled with greater accuracy than humorless words.

Variable	Humor
(Intercept)	15.168***
Humor	**17.628*** **
Average_Surprisal	**5.371*** **
Iconicity_Rating	**-4.625*** **
Phoneme_Length	-2.203*
Morpheme_Length	-1.402
PoS_Adverb	-1.949.
PoS_Interjection	-0.053
PoS_Name	1.872.
PoS_Noun	3.563***
PoS_Number	1.474
PoS_Preposition	-1.437
PoS_Verb	-5.353***

Table 6: Results of the humor model. Asterisks denote significance (* $p < 0.05$, ** $p < 0.01$, *** $p < 0.001$).

4 Discussion

In this study, we explore the hypothesis that humor may be linked to high phonemic bigram surprisal and improved memory recall. High phonemic bigram surprisal, plays a role in cognitive processing (Kilpatrick and Bundgaard-Nielsen, 2024) where words with higher surprisal are more difficult to process but also more likely to be recalled in memory tasks. Negatively valanced words are both more surprising and more memorable (Kilpatrick, Under Review), suggesting that the negativity bias is encoded in language. Humorous words follow this exact trend despite being—at least stochastically—associated with positive valence. In the present study, we explored this contradiction and seek to explain why humorous words behave like negative words despite being generally positive.

The findings that humor follows the same patterns as negative valence suggests that humor may exploit similar cognitive mechanisms. Just as negative stimuli demand attention and leave a lasting impression, humor, which often subverts expectations or highlights absurdities, may trigger heightened cognitive engagement through surprise or incongruity. While both humor and negativity utilize elements of unpredictability, humor diverges in its social function. Suls's Two-Stage Model (1972) for the Appreciation of Jokes provides a useful framework for understanding this. In the first stage, the punch line of a joke is surprising, incongruous, and may be perceived as threatening due to its unexpected nature, eliciting a response akin to the cognitive engagement seen with negative stimuli. In the second stage, the listener resolves the incongruity, leading to a sense of relief and the recognition of humor, which ultimately results in a positive emotional response. This aligns with our findings that humor, while engaging cognitive processes similar to those of negative stimuli, also embodies a transition from initial surprise to positive social outcomes, such as connection and bonding. Unlike negative stimuli, which may trigger responses tied to alertness or threat, humor's playful disruption fosters a social and positive emotional environment.

Dingemanse and Thompson's (2020) work further illuminates these dynamics, proposing that structural markedness, including phonological markedness, underpins perceptions of both humor and iconicity. This aligns with our findings that humor and negative valence share cognitive engagement mechanisms, suggesting that both types of words are marked in ways that enhance memorability. Playful and performative elements like increased surprisal or other markedness strategies inherent in humorous language may interact with the cognitive mechanisms associated with negativity bias, drawing attention to their phonological structure and making them more memorable. Surprisal serves as an objective measure of phonological markedness by quantifying the predictability of linguistic units based on their transitional probabilities within a given context. Unlike subjective judgments that can vary among speakers or listeners, surprisal provides a statistical framework for assessing the complexity of markedness in iconic words. Words or sounds that exhibit higher surprisal values are often those that are less predictable, indicating a higher degree of markedness. This objective measure allows researchers to analyze the cognitive processing of language without relying on potentially biased human assessments. In the context of humor and sentiment analysis, surprisal might play a role in detecting subtle shifts in emotional and cognitive states, such as humor or irony, which often elude traditional sentiment analysis models. By incorporating surprisal, humor models can better capture deviations from predictability, signaling the incongruity and surprise inherent in humor. Integrating phonological surprisal with existing humor-processing frameworks may lead to more sophisticated models that account for the context-dependent nature of humor, paving the way for more nuanced and context-aware humor analysis.

Future research should investigate languages other than American English which might reveal cross-linguistic patterns. If the patterns observed in this study are observed in other languages, then this would suggest that they are innate, rather than cultural, further enhancing our understanding of the interplay between language, emotion, and cognitive processing. Another direction of research is differentiating different types of humor: (1) humor based on use of highly colloquial language highly saturated with iconic words (as words from the original study of Engelthaler & Hills (2018), (2) farcial humor or comedy of situation (e.g., Shakespeare's *Much Ado about Nothing*) where ridiculous dramatic situations fall into category of "highly improbable events" discussed in Ranganath & Rainer (2003), or (3) dark humor and sarcasm (which is a mixture of negativity (see above) and low probability, both of which should, theoretically, increase memorability.

In conclusion, our findings suggest that negativity bias is reflected in the phonological surprisal of words, with negatively valenced words comprising more improbable sequences of sounds and demonstrating greater memorability. Interestingly, humor subverts this trend, exhibiting both increased surprisal and memorability, highlighting its unique role in language.

Acknowledgments

We wish to thank the researchers who made their data publicly available so that we could conduct this analysis. This project was funded by the Japan Society for the Promotion of Science (# 20K13055).

References

Baumeister, R. F., Bratslavsky, E., Finkenauer, C., & Vohs, K. D. 2001. Bad is stronger than good. Review of general psychology, 5(4), 323-370.

Brysbaert, M., & New, B. 2009. Moving beyond Kučera and Francis: A critical evaluation of current word frequency norms and the introduction of a new and improved word frequency measure for American English. Behavior Research Methods, 41(4):977-990.

Brysbaert, M., New, B., & Keuleers, E. 2012. Adding part-of-speech information to the SUBTLEX-US word frequencies. Behavior Research Methods, 44:991-997.

Chen, P. Y., & Soo, V. W. 2018. Humor recognition using deep learning. In Proceedings of the 2018 conference of the North American chapter of the association for computational linguistics: Human language technologies, 2, 113-117.

Cortese, M. J., Khanna, M. M., & Hacker, S. 2010. Recognition memory for 2,578 monosyllabic words. Memory, 18(6), 595-609.

Dingemanse, M. 2017. Expressiveness and system integration: On the typology of ideophones, with special reference to Siwu. In STUF. Language Typology and Universals 70(2). 363–384.

Dingemanse, M. & Akita, K. 2017. An inverse relation between expressiveness and grammatical integration: on the morphosyntactic typology of ideophones, with special reference to Japanese. Journal of Linguistics, 53(3). 501–532.

Dingemanse, M., & Thompson, B. 2020. The playful nature of language: Humor, iconicity, and structural markedness. Language, Cognition and Neuroscience, 35(9), 1133-1150. https://doi.org/10.1080/23273798.2020.1752716.

Engelthaler, T., & Hills, T. T. 2018. Humor norms for 4,997 English words. Behavior research methods, 50, 1116-1124.

Flaksman, M. 2017. Iconic treadmill hypothesis: the reasons behind continuous onomatopoeic coinage. In M. Bauer, Angelika Zirker, Olga Fischer, and Christine Ljungberg (eds.) Dimensions of Iconicity [Iconicity in Language and Literature 15]. 15–38. Amsterdam: John Benjamins.

Flaksman. M. & Kilpatrick, A. In Press. Against the tide: How language-specificity of imitative words increases with time (as evidenced by Surprisal). In M. Flaksman and P. Akumbu (eds.) SKASE Journal of Theoretical Linguistics.

Kensinger, E. A. 2007. Negative emotion enhances memory accuracy: Behavioral and neuroimaging evidence. Current Directions in Psychological Science, 16(4):213-218.

Kilpatrick, A. (2023). Sound Symbolism in Automatic Emotion Recognition and Sentiment Analysis. In P. L. Villagrá, & X. Li (Eds.), Proceedings of the International Workshop on Cognitive AI 2023 co-located with the 3rd International Conference on Learning & Reasoning.

Kilpatrick, A. (Under Review). The Negativity Bias is Encoded in Language.

Kilpatrick, A. & Bundgaard-Nielsen R, L. (2024). Decoding Informativity and Iconicity in American English. Proceedings of the 19th Australasian International Conference on Speech Science and Technology.

LaBar, K. S., & Cabeza, R. 2006. Cognitive neuroscience of emotional memory. Nature Reviews Neuroscience, 7(1), 54-64. https://doi.org/10.1038/nrn1825.

Mohammad, S. M., & Turney, P. D. 2013. NRC emotion lexicon. National Research Council, Canada, 2, 234.

Phelps, E. A. 2004. Human emotion and memory: Interactions of the amygdala and hippocampal complex. Current Directions in Psychological Science, 13(3), 102-105. https://doi.org/10.1111/j.0963-7214.2004.00293.x.

Ranganath, C., & Rainer, G. 2003. Neural mechanisms for detecting and remembering novel events. Nature Reviews Neuroscience, 4(3):193-202. https://doi.org/10.1038/nrn1052.

Rozin, P., & Royzman, E. B. 2001. Negativity bias, negativity dominance, and contagion. Personality and Social Psychology Review, 5(4), 296-320. https://doi.org/10.1207/S15327957PSPR0504_2.

Sánchez-Gutiérrez, C. H., et al. 2018. MorphoLex: A derivational morphological database for 70,000 English words. Behavior Research Methods, 50:1568-1580.

Scott, G. G., Keitel, A., Becirspahic, M., Yao, B., & Sereno, S. C. 2019. The Glasgow Norms: Ratings of 5,500 words on nine scales. Behavior Research Methods, 51, 1258-1270.

Shannon, C. E. 1948. A mathematical theory of communication. Bell System Technical Journal, 27(3), 379-423.

Sidhu, D. M., Vigliocco, G., & Pexman, P. M. 2020. Effects of iconicity in lexical decision. Language and cognition, 12(1), 164-181.

Sidhu, D. M., Khachatoorian, N., & Vigliocco, G. 2023. Effects of Iconicity in Recognition Memory. Cognitive Science, 47(11), e13382.

Suls, J. M. 1972. A two-stage model for the appreciation of jokes and cartoons: An information-processing analysis. The psychology of humor: Theoretical perspectives and empirical issues, 1, 81-100.

Voeltz, F. F., & Kilian-Hatz, M. (Eds.). 2001. Ideophones. John Benjamins Publishing Company. https://doi.org/10.1075/tsl.45.

Weide, R. 1998. The Carnegie Mellon pronouncing dictionary. Release 0.6.

Winter, B., et al. 2023. Iconicity ratings for 14,000+ English words. Behavior Research Methods, 1-16.

Text Is Not All You Need:
Multimodal Prompting Helps LLMs Understand Humor

Ashwin Baluja
Northwestern University
baluja@u.northwestern.edu

Abstract

While Large Language Models (LLMs) have demonstrated impressive natural language understanding capabilities across various text-based tasks, understanding humor has remained a persistent challenge. Humor is frequently multimodal, relying not only on the meaning of the words, but also their pronunciations, and even the speaker's intonations. In this study, we explore a simple multimodal prompting approach to humor understanding and explanation. We present an LLM with both the text and the spoken form of a joke, generated using an off-the-shelf text-to-speech (TTS) system. Using multimodal cues improves the explanations of humor compared to textual prompts across all tested datasets.

1 Introduction

Despite remarkable advances in Natural Language Processing, particularly with Large Language Models (LLMs), the computational understanding of humor remains an elusive goal. Humor operates on multiple levels simultaneously, drawing on cultural context, current events, common sense, phonetic nuances, and rhythm to evoke a comedic response (Bucaria, 2004; Attardo and Pickering, 2011; Warren et al., 2021). Recent studies have focused on analyzing the performance of large language models for understanding cultural norms (Hendrycks et al., 2021a,b), knowledge of current events (White et al., 2024), and common sense reasoning (Zellers et al., 2019; Shao et al., 2024). Yet, the unique challenge posed by computational humor, requiring a combination of all these tasks and information often conveyed through audio, has received comparatively little attention.

A fundamental aspect of verbal humor, particularly evident in puns, lies in linguistic ambiguity. Puns rely on homographs (words that are spelled identically with different meanings) and heterographs (words that are spelled differently but pronounced the same) (Miller et al., 2017). Traditional text-based LLMs, constrained by their token-based processing architecture, struggle to capture these subtle linguistic features that yield essential clues into understanding a joke's underlying mechanics.

Our approach builds on prior research into humor understanding abilities present in LLMs (Xu et al., 2024) and demonstrates significant improvements over baseline textual prompting strategies for humor explanation. Our analysis examines both macro-level performance across humor datasets and micro-level effects through investigation of the model's internal representations and effects of text-to-speech (TTS) parameters.

2 Related Work

LLM-based humor classification. In Wu et al. 2024, pre-trained language models, from early BERT-like models to modern LLMs like LLaMa-3, were fine-tuned or prompted using Chain-of-Thought (CoT) and few-shot strategies for humor classification. Similarly, in Xu et al. 2024, CoT and few-shot example prompting were used for punchline detection and humor explanation. In both, humor specific examples for fine-tuning proved beneficial for humor understanding.

Fused multimodality features. Most directly related to our work, several studies have developed multimodal features for humor detection (Hasan et al., 2021; Aggarwal et al., 2023). Each has improved the performance of their task by incorporating non-text information into a fused representation, validating the importance of other multiple modalities. In contrast to our approach, these studies were conducted using BERT-like models and required training from scratch. We propose a simpler approach that does not require training and is fully compatible with pre-trained LLMs.

Training on paired modality datasets. In domains outside of humor, copious research has been

Proceedings of the 1st Workshop on Computational Humor (CHum), pages 9–17
January 19, 2025.

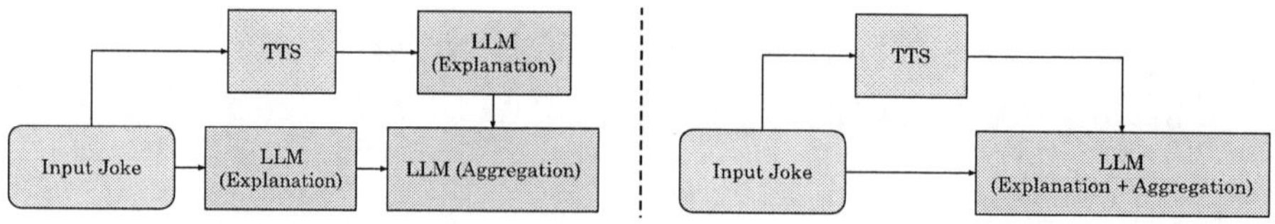

Figure 1: Multimodal prompting strategy overview. Left - separate text and audio explanations are generated, then aggregated. Right - combined text and audio are processed together for a single explanation. Aggregation refers to prompting intended to ensure a coherent output that does not represent the multiple input modalities.

conducted using datasets with multiple representations of the same items. These have been critical to the creation of multimodal language models. For example, LLaVa, a vision+language model, used detailed captions of images to generate question and response pairs from a language-only LLM in order to train a vision-adapter (Liu et al., 2023).

3 Methods

We propose using multimodal (text + audio) prompts and audio synthesis to improve a model's ability to capture the phonetic elements essential to understanding humor, specifically puns. The framework, shown in Figure 1, has two key components: generating audio from text and a prompting strategy that combines both the audio and text into a single prompt.

3.1 Audio generation

The most effective comedians rely on not only their material but also on carefully controlled and exaggerated cadence changes, volume and tonality of their words, as well as myriad more nuanced features. For replicability and breadth of trials, we use a simple, reproducible approach: text-based jokes are first converted into audio using **OpenAI's tts-1-hd**, an off-the-shelf text-to-speech (TTS) model. This procedure is broadly applicable and does not require existing audio datasets or the collection of human speech. This method will be directly compared to only using text-based prompting on a diverse set of large data sets. Note that no additional ground-truth information (e.g., emphasis or timing), is provided to the LLM.

3.2 Prompt configuration

Each prompt is composed of general task definitions, chain-of-thought reasoning prompting, examples (for few-shot, in-context learning), and both input modalities (Fig 2).

Definitions and Instructions: Each prompt begins with a concise definition of puns versus non-puns, accompanied by instructions for humor detection. The instructions request that the model identify whether the input is a pun or not. We explicitly *did not* ask for an explanation at this point; Xu et al. 2024 found this helps reduce hallucinated evidence of non-existent puns.

Few-Shot Examples and chain-of-thought: Each prompt includes examples; this improved performance (Brown et al., 2020). As suggested by (Xu et al., 2024), each example included chain-of-thought reasoning along with the detection result. In total, each prompt included six examples of pun explanation pairs, including both homographic and heterographic puns, selected from each dataset tested. Including few-shot examples also ensured a consistent output tone, making the results more directly comparable with ground-truth human provided explanations.

To obtain an *explanation* of what makes the joke funny and why, we use prompts that encourage chain-of-thought reasoning (Xu et al., 2024). In this configuration, the reasoning for why a pun was detected as a pun or non-pun is used directly as the explanation. This format guides the model to accurately understand the task while avoiding biasing it towards interpreting the input as a pun.

Multimodal Aggregation: In our multimodal setup, both text and audio are provided to the LLM. Two approaches were tested. First, to mitigate the chances of the LLM exclusively using either the text or the audio, we ran two parallel explanation processes. Each only had access to a single modality. Then, an aggregation prompting step was run, combining the two outputs into the final, single, output (Figure 1-Left).

Second, we provided both the audio and text to the model within a single prompt (Figure 1-Right). In both setups, the prompt was carefully crafted to instruct the LLM to actively *avoid discussing the source modality that it used* to answer. This was required as the target explanations in the datasets do not have any reference to modality (as they only

```
Definition of a pun
Instructions
        detect whether pun or non-pun,
        describe why,
        don't address modality
Examples
        joke text, joke detection, reasoning
        ... x 6
==============================
Input joke
Input audio
```

Figure 2: Multimodal prompting strategy where the LLM has both audio and text passed in at once.

had text). We found that the latter method outperformed the first; it will be used going forward. More details are in the ablation experiments.

4 Experimental Setup

4.1 Datasets

We evaluate our multimodal prompting approach using three datasets.

SemEval 2017 Task 7: This set contains 810 & 647 puns (homographic & heterographic), and 1077 non-puns. It contains human annotations: noting the pun-word and the spelling or definition of the pun-word in both interpretations of the pun. Additionally, this set contains human explanations: each pun has a human-provided, sentence-form explanation (Miller et al., 2017).

Context-Situated Puns: This consists of 821 & 1739 puns (homographic & heterographic) with human annotations (Sun et al., 2022). It has the same pun-word and spelling/definition annotations as SemEval. It does not contain human explanations.

ExplainTheJoke: This broad collection of jokes was scraped from the `ExplainTheJoke.com` website, containing 350 jokes. This dataset does not have human annotations. Instead, each entry has human explanations in paragraph-form, which themselves have high variability in style, length, quality and accuracy (theblackcat102).

4.2 Models

For generating explanations, we utilized Gemini-1.5-Flash (Gemini Team, 2024). At the time of the study, only the Gemini family of models offered API-based audio input, and Gemini-1.5-Flash offered the best balance between performance and affordability. This allowed us to effectively leverage the multimodal prompts central to our study, ensuring that the model could process auditory cues alongside textual data.

To avoid human biases in evaluating the quality of the generated free-form text explanations, a separate LLM was used. Recently, using LLMs as *judges* have been assessed favorably (Zheng et al., 2024). Further, the presence of structured annotations for both pun datasets gave the judge ground-truth, so that it did not rely on its own understanding of the joke; details are provided in the next section.

We chose GPT-4o (OpenAI, 2024) as the judge. We did not use Gemini-1.5-Flash or Gemini-1.5-Pro to avoid potential biases from using the same model family for generation and evaluation. Additionally, at the time of our research, GPT-4o was the strongest available model (Chiang et al., 2024).[1]

5 Results

We present our results on the three datasets. Interestingly, there is a wide disparity in the *understanding* and *detection* of humor using LLMs. While previous studies have shown close to saturated results in the simpler problem of *detecting* humor (Xu et al., 2024), an LLMs explanation of the humor is often incorrect. Our results demonstrate the improvements in *understanding* that are possible with multimodal inputs.

5.1 SemEval

To evaluate our system, Gemini-1.5-Flash's generated explanation for each pun was paired with the human-provided explanations from the dataset. The judge, GPT-4o, was then asked to output whether explanation 1 was better than explanation 2, explanation 2 was better than explanation 1, or whether both explanations were of equal quality. The full judging prompt is included in Appendix A.1.2. This process was repeated twice - once for baseline textual prompting, and once for multimodal prompting, where the LLM was provided with both the text and audio. The judge was provided with the annotations each time, ensuring that the judgement considered the ground truth meaning. Win rate is reported as percent of times the model's explanation was preferred over the human's.

[1]The final score was based on pairwise comparisons of each test sample. However, LLM-as-a-judge has been found to have strong positional bias, *a priori* preferring the first element in each pair. To account for this, we run pairwise comparison twice, swapping the order of each pair. Final win rates are determined by averaging swapped and un-swapped win rates (Zheng et al., 2024; Wang et al., 2024).

	Heterograph		Homograph	
	Win %	Tie %	Win %	Tie %
Baseline	47.76	5.64	68.89	8.40
with audio	**51.74**	4.56	**72.59**	6.36

Table 1: Results for SemEval comparing baseline and multimodal prompting vs. human explanations.

Table 1 shows that incorporating audio significantly improves performance over baseline across both homographs and heterographs. Performance increased in both by approximately 4%.

5.2 Context-Situated Puns

Unlike the previous dataset, with no human explanations available, we cannot compare each LLM output to a human baseline. Instead, we compare the LLM outputs (created with and without audio input) directly with each other. To ensure that the judge-LLM is given the correct context, the annotations that were provided in the dataset are also given as input. Here, win-rate is reported as the percent of times the result of one prompting strategy was preferred over the other.

	Heterograph		Homograph	
	Win %	Tie %	Win %	Tie %
Baseline	33.87	29.65	35.08	28.08
with audio	**36.49**		**36.85**	

Table 2: Results for Context-Situated Puns dataset comparing baseline vs multimodal prompting.

As shown in Table 2, the addition of audio cues again provided improvements in both homographic and heterographic cases.

5.3 ExplainTheJoke

Here, we evaluated the model's ability to generate detailed joke explanations in domains outside of puns. As this dataset lacked detailed annotations and only included inconsistent-quality explanations, we attempted to generate a more normalized explanation by first asking GPT to summarize the provided human explanations. This summary was then used as the relevant context to the judge-LLM. The remainder of the evaluation proceeded in the same manner as the Context-Situated Puns; we performed pairwise comparison directly between the results of baseline and multimodal prompting.

Table 3 reveals that even with jokes that are not puns, using the mutli-modal prompting improves performance. While phonetic ambiguity likely explains many of the performance gains for the previously studied datasets, these results suggest that other more nuanced effects are successfully conveyed by including audio.

	Win %	Tie %
Baseline	12.81	71.75
with audio	**15.44**	

Table 3: Results for ExplainTheJoke dataset comparing baseline vs multimodal prompting.

5.4 Analysis

Due to space constraints, details of our three analyses are in the Appendix. Summaries are provided here. First, in an ablation study, we tested various details of multimodal prompting, finding that pure audio-only prompting performs far worse than pure textual prompting (Appendix A.3). Second, we analyzed whether incorporating audio genuinely preserved phonetic ambiguity. Through a detailed examination of the logits of an LLM transcribing puns, we observed that the model assigned significant probability to both potential spellings of the pun-word (*e.g.*, "weight" vs. "wait"), indicating that the phonetic cues *were* captured in its internal representations (Appendix A.2). Finally, we explored the sensitivity to voice parameters, but found no significant evidence that variations in voice type systematically affected the results (Appendix A.4).

6 Conclusion and Future Work

In this study, we demonstrated that incorporating auditory cues into multimodal prompts significantly improves Large Language Models' ability to understand and explain humor, particularly in cases involving phonetic ambiguity. Our approach, leveraging readily available APIs and open-source models, offers a straightforward yet effective enhancement to existing LLM capabilities.

There are several avenues for extending this research. A deeper study into the effects of voice characteristics on humor interpretation could reveal how tone, pitch, or speaker identity affects comedic understanding. Although our TTS-based approach was effective, it did not capture nuances like timing and rhythm that human recordings may convey. Finally, the addition of video analysis may reveal the speaker's facial expressions and other essential cues for humor.

7 Limitations

Prompt Sensitivity: The success of our multimodal prompting approach depends heavily on prompt design. LLMs, particularly those using the Gemini architecture, are highly sensitive to the phrasing and structure of prompts. Small variations can lead to significant differences in output quality, necessitating extensive tuning to optimize performance. This reliance on precise prompt crafting limits the scalability and generalization of the approach to new tasks.

Nuances Beyond Phonetic Ambiguity: While our method demonstrated improved understanding of phonetic ambiguity in humor, it falls short in capturing more nuanced comedic elements such as timing, cadence, and rhythm. Our TTS-based approach does not fully convey the subtleties of real human speech, which are critical for interpreting humor beyond wordplay. This limitation suggests the need for richer audio models or the integration of additional modalities, such as video, to capture non-verbal cues.

Evaluation Challenges: Our evaluation relied on automated LLM-based judging, which, while efficient, may not fully capture the nuanced quality of humor explanations. Future studies should incorporate more robust evaluation strategies, such as human assessments, or using stronger models as they are released, to better gauge the effectiveness of these approaches in real-world scenarios.

8 Ethics Statement

Large Large Language Models can produce offensive and incorrect statements. In the process of explaining comedy, they may frequently encounter harmful stereotypes and offensive content. Both correct and incorrect explanations can result in an LLM outputting potentially hurtful answers. It is advisable for users to exercise caution and avoid prompting the LLM with potentially offensive jokes, so as to avoid the output perpetuating incorrect stereotypes. This work is released with the intent of research purposes only.

References

Sajal Aggarwal, Ananya Pandey, and Dinesh Kumar Vishwakarma. 2023. Multimodal sarcasm recognition by fusing textual, visual and acoustic content via multi-headed attention for video dataset. In *2023 World Conference on Communication & Computing (WCONF)*, pages 1–5.

Salvatore Attardo and Lucy Pickering. 2011. Timing in the performance of jokes. *HUMOR*, 24(2):233–250.

Tom Brown, Benjamin Mann, Nick Ryder, Melanie Subbiah, Jared D Kaplan, Prafulla Dhariwal, Arvind Neelakantan, Pranav Shyam, Girish Sastry, Amanda Askell, Sandhini Agarwal, Ariel Herbert-Voss, Gretchen Krueger, Tom Henighan, Rewon Child, Aditya Ramesh, Daniel Ziegler, Jeffrey Wu, Clemens Winter, Chris Hesse, Mark Chen, Eric Sigler, Mateusz Litwin, Scott Gray, Benjamin Chess, Jack Clark, Christopher Berner, Sam McCandlish, Alec Radford, Ilya Sutskever, and Dario Amodei. 2020. Language models are few-shot learners. In *Advances in Neural Information Processing Systems*, volume 33, pages 1877–1901. Curran Associates, Inc.

Chiara Bucaria. 2004. Lexical and syntactic ambiguity as a source of humor: The case of newspaper headlines. *HUMOR*, 17(3):279–309.

Wei-Lin Chiang, Lianmin Zheng, Ying Sheng, Anastasios Nikolas Angelopoulos, Tianle Li, Dacheng Li, Hao Zhang, Banghua Zhu, Michael Jordan, Joseph E. Gonzalez, and Ion Stoica. 2024. Chatbot arena: An open platform for evaluating llms by human preference. *Preprint*, arXiv:2403.04132.

Gemini Team. 2024. Gemini 1.5: Unlocking multimodal understanding across millions of tokens of context. *Preprint*, arXiv:2403.05530.

Md Kamrul Hasan, Sangwu Lee, Wasifur Rahman, Amir Zadeh, Rada Mihalcea, Louis-Philippe Morency, and Ehsan Hoque. 2021. Humor knowledge enriched transformer for understanding multimodal humor. In *Proceedings of the AAAI conference on artificial intelligence*, volume 35, pages 12972–12980.

Dan Hendrycks, Collin Burns, Steven Basart, Andrew Critch, Jerry Li, Dawn Song, and Jacob Steinhardt. 2021a. Aligning ai with shared human values. *Proceedings of the International Conference on Learning Representations (ICLR)*.

Dan Hendrycks, Collin Burns, Steven Basart, Andy Zou, Mantas Mazeika, Dawn Song, and Jacob Steinhardt. 2021b. Measuring massive multitask language understanding. *Proceedings of the International Conference on Learning Representations (ICLR)*.

Chris Hua. 2024. Gazelle v0.2.

Haotian Liu, Chunyuan Li, Qingyang Wu, and Yong Jae Lee. 2023. Visual instruction tuning. In *NeurIPS*.

Tristan Miller, Christian Hempelmann, and Iryna Gurevych. 2017. SemEval-2017 task 7: Detection and interpretation of English puns. In *Proceedings of the 11th International Workshop on Semantic Evaluation (SemEval-2017)*, pages 58–68, Vancouver, Canada. Association for Computational Linguistics.

OpenAI. 2024. Gpt-4o system card. *Preprint*, arXiv:2410.21276.

Minghao Shao, Abdul Basit, Ramesh Karri, and Muhammad Shafique. 2024. Survey of different large language model architectures: Trends, benchmarks, and challenges. *IEEE Access*, pages 1–1.

Jiao Sun, Anjali Narayan-Chen, Shereen Oraby, Shuyang Gao, Tagyoung Chung, Jing Huang, Yang Liu, and Nanyun Peng. 2022. Context-situated pun generation. In *Proceedings of the 2022 Conference on Empirical Methods in Natural Language Processing*, pages 4635–4648, Abu Dhabi, United Arab Emirates. Association for Computational Linguistics.

theblackcat102. Theblackcat102/joke_explaination - datasets at hugging face.

Peiyi Wang, Lei Li, Liang Chen, Zefan Cai, Dawei Zhu, Binghuai Lin, Yunbo Cao, Lingpeng Kong, Qi Liu, Tianyu Liu, and Zhifang Sui. 2024. Large language models are not fair evaluators. In *Proceedings of the 62nd Annual Meeting of the Association for Computational Linguistics (Volume 1: Long Papers)*, pages 9440–9450, Bangkok, Thailand. Association for Computational Linguistics.

Caleb Warren, Adam Barsky, and A. Peter McGraw. 2021. What makes things funny? an integrative review of the antecedents of laughter and amusement. *Personality and Social Psychology Review*, 25(1):41–65. PMID: 33342368.

Colin White, Samuel Dooley, Manley Roberts, Arka Pal, Ben Feuer, Siddhartha Jain, Ravid Shwartz-Ziv, Neel Jain, Khalid Saifullah, Siddartha Naidu, Chinmay Hegde, Yann LeCun, Tom Goldstein, Willie Neiswanger, and Micah Goldblum. 2024. Livebench: A challenging, contamination-free llm benchmark. *Preprint*, arXiv:2406.19314.

Shih-Hung Wu, Yu-Feng Huang, and Tsz-Yeung Lau. 2024. Humour classification by fine-tuning llms: Cyut at clef 2024 joker lab subtask humour classification according to genre and technique. In *Working Notes of the Conference and Labs of the Evaluation Forum (CLEF 2024). CEUR Workshop Proceedings*, pages 1933–1947.

Zhijun Xu, Siyu Yuan, Lingjie Chen, and Deqing Yang. 2024. "a good pun is its own reword": Can large language models understand puns? *Preprint*, arXiv:2404.13599.

Rowan Zellers, Ari Holtzman, Yonatan Bisk, Ali Farhadi, and Yejin Choi. 2019. Hellaswag: Can a machine really finish your sentence? In *Proceedings of the 57th Annual Meeting of the Association for Computational Linguistics*.

Lianmin Zheng, Wei-Lin Chiang, Ying Sheng, Siyuan Zhuang, Zhanghao Wu, Yonghao Zhuang, Zi Lin, Zhuohan Li, Dacheng Li, Eric P. Xing, Hao Zhang, Joseph E. Gonzalez, and Ion Stoica. 2024. Judging llm-as-a-judge with mt-bench and chatbot arena. In *Proceedings of the 37th International Conference on Neural Information Processing Systems*, NIPS '23, Red Hook, NY, USA. Curran Associates Inc.

A Appendix

A.1 Prompts

These prompts are based on those used in (Xu et al., 2024), modified for use with multimodal prompting

A.1.1 Explanation

The prompts used for generating explanations are shown in Figure 5.

A.1.2 Judging

The prompts used for judging are shown in Figure 6.

A.2 Phonetic Ambiguity

In order to test whether phonetic ambiguity is preserved by including an audio version of the joke, we directly analyze the logits of a transcription task. Following the same pattern as in the joke explanation task, we convert the text to audio using OpenAI's tts-1-hd model. As publicly available LLM APIs do not provide logit outputs, we use (Hua, 2024), an open-source model available on Hugging Face.

As a simplified task, we converted the word, "Where," to audio, and asked the LLM to transcribe the file. If phonetic ambiguity is preserved, the model would output homophones for "where" as highly probably alternatives. As shown in A.2, this is the case: "wear," "ware," "here," and "there," are all present in the top ten highest probabilities.

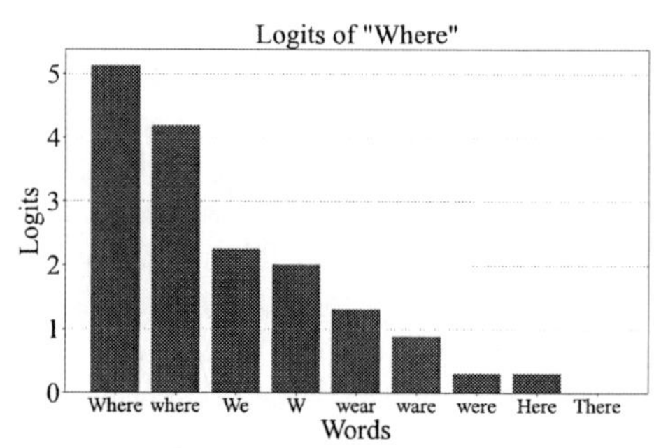

Figure 3: Logits of transcribing an audio file containing the word, "Where".

Further, we test the logits in a realistic pun scenario. We tested on the pun, "Patience is a heavy weight," where the pun-word is "weight," and the alternate spelling is "wait." As shown in A.2, "weight" and "wait" are the top two tokens with the highest probability. Notably, "weight" is a close third; this is not contradictory to the claim that including audio preserves the ambiguity of a pun. Although the pun had two intended interpretations of the pun word ("weight" and "wait"), the possible transcriptions are intended to be a superset—it is up to the LLM to decide which of the alternatives are relevant.

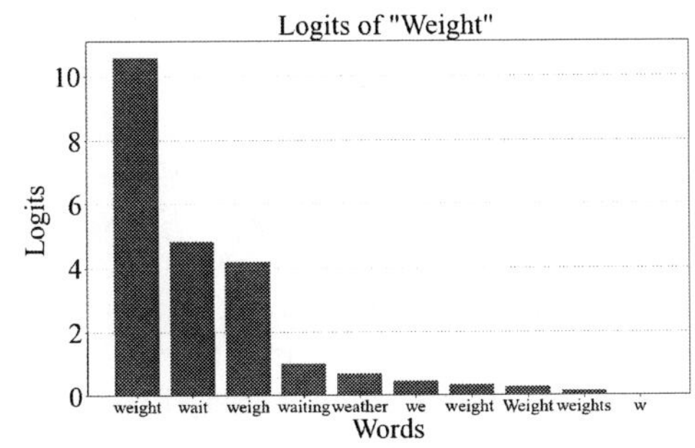

Figure 4: Logits of transcribing an audio file containing a pun, focusing on the pun-word, "Weight".

A.3 Ablation Study

To assess the impact of various prompting configurations, we conducted an ablation study (Table 4) using audio-only prompting, and no wording to prevent addressing modality in the answer. Results are shown in Table 4.

	Heterograph	Homograph
	Model Win %	Model Win %
No text, Audio Only	25.50	55.86
No aggregation wording	48.61	71.05
Our System	**51.74**	**72.59**

Table 4: Ablation results comparing results for different prompting strategies.

Additionally, we extensively tested how the separate prompting strategy shown in Figure 1-Left worked in comparison to the combined audio-text strategy employed. In every test performed, the separate strategy was significantly worse than the combined strategy.

A.4 Effects of Choice of Voice

Comedic perception may be influenced by the actual voice of the comedian. Table 5 presents a comparison of performance across different TTS voice types on the SemEval dataset using the full multimodal prompting strategy. The results show some variations in win rates, particularly for heterographs, but no clear pattern emerges that suggests a statistically significant advantage for any specific voice type. Although the androgynous voice (Alloy) slightly outperformed overall, the differences were not substantial enough to draw definitive conclusions regarding the impact of voice characteristics on the model's performance. Alloy was chosen for consistency throughout the experiments. This remains open for future study.

	Heterograph		Homograph	
	Win %	Tie %	Win %	Tie %
Nova (female)	44.59	5.25	71.48	6.30
Onyx (male)	45.44	5.65	73.33	6.42
Alloy (androgynous)	**51.74**	4.56	72.59	6.36
Onyx + Alloy	47.91	3.79	**73.09**	5.74

Table 5: Performance on SemEval for different OpenAI TTS voice types. Alloy is used throughout the experiments in this study. "Onyx + Alloy" had two different audio files, along with text, passed in to the LLM at once.

<*Definition*> Puns are a form of wordplay exploiting different meanings of a word or similar-sounding words, while non-puns are jokes or statements that don't rely on such linguistic ambiguities.
<*Instruction*> Determine whether the given text and audio is a pun. The audio provided is spoken version of the input text. It is provided in 1 different voice(s). Please see if hearing the pun aloud helps you determine whether the text is a pun, and if so, why. Give your reasons first, then make your final decision clearly. You should either say "The text input is a pun" or say "The given text is a non-pun", despite the fact that you are given both text and audio. Do not reference the fact that you are given both text and audio. Only use the most likely explanation, taking into account information from both formats. You must output the current status in a parsable JSON format. An example output looks like: "Reason": "XXX", "Choice": "The given text is a XXX"
<*Examples*> Text: When the waiter told me they were out of corn I said , ' That really shucks . ' Output: "Reason": "The text plays on the double meaning of the word 'shucks'. 'Shucks' refers to both the act of removing the husk from corn and is a homophone for 'sucks', which is used colloquially to express disappointment.", "Choice": "The given text is a pun"
Text: Desperate times call for desperate measures . Output: "Reason": "The text is an idiomatic expression meaning that one may need to take drastic actions in difficult situations. It does not exploit different meanings of a word or similar-sounding words.", "Choice": "The given text is a non-pun"
Text: A tangled bell ringer tolled himself off . Output: "Reason": "The text plays on the homophones 'tolled' and 'told', using the word 'tolled' in the context of a bell ringer (which relates to the ringing or tolling of bells) and 'told' as in scolding oneself (told sb off). This creates a humorous double meaning.", "Choice": "The given text is a pun"
Text: Don't bite the hand that feeds you . Output: "Reason": "The text is an idiomatic expression meaning one should not act ungratefully towards those who provide for them. It does not rely on a play on words or different meanings of the same word.", "Choice": "The given text is a non-pun"
Text: An illiterate fisherman was lost at c . ... "Reason": "The text is an idiomatic expression that suggests it's better to be cautious than to get into trouble. It does not rely on the ambiguity of words or similar-sounding words for a humorous effect.", "Choice": "The given text is a non-pun"
<*Your Response*> Text: Patience is a virtue heavy in wait Audio: <audio> Output:

Figure 5: Explanation prompt for an LLM, including examples and an example input pun.

<*Definition*> Puns are a form of wordplay exploiting different meanings of a word or similar-sounding words.
<*Instruction*> Below is a pun text, double meanings of the pun and two corresponding explanations. Please carefully judge which explanation is of better quality. Any explanation that fails to indicate the correct pun, misses the potential phonetic similarity between pun-alternative word pair, misses a layer of correct meaning in the pun or contains other errors is a worse explanation. Meanwhile, explanations without the above errors are better explanations. To complete the task, you must cautiously choose from one of the three answers: "Explanation 1 is much better", "Explanation 2 is much better", "Explanation 1 and 2 are of similar quality". Additionally, You must output the current status in a parsable JSON format. An example output looks like: "Choice": "XXX"
<*Your Response*> Text: Hockey players are always terrible chess players since they arent́ handy. Double Meanings of the Pun: 1. pun word and its meaning: handy <useful and convenient>. 2. alternative word and its meaning: hand <the (prehensile) extremity of the superior limb>. Explanation 1: The text plays on the double meaning of h́andy. H́andyćan refer to being skilled with oneś hands, which is relevant to hockey players, but it can also mean ńearbyór ćonvenient, which is relevant to chess players. The joke lies in the contrast between the two meanings, suggesting that hockey players are not good at chess because they are not h́andyín the sense of being close to the chessboard. Explanation 2: The text plays on the double meaning of the word h́andy. H́andyćan refer to being skilled or useful, but in the context of hockey, it also refers to the use of oneś hands, which is not allowed in chess. Output:

Figure 6: Judging prompt for an LLM, including an example annotation and two potential explanations.

Rule-based Approaches to the Automatic Generation of Puns Based on Given Names in French

Mathieu Dehouck
Lattice, CNRS, ENS-PSL,
Université Sorbonne Nouvelle
mathieu.dehouck@cnrs.fr

Marine Delaborde
LT2D, CY Cergy Paris Université
marine.delaborde@cyu.fr

Abstract

Humor is a cornerstone of human interactions. Because puns and word plays lie in the margins of phonology, syntax and semantics, large language models struggle with their generation. In this paper, we present two versions of a tool designed to create a typical kind of French joke known as "Monsieur et Madame" jokes. We then discuss the main challenges and limitations rule-based systems face when creating this kind of puns.

1 Introduction

As of 2024, large language models are able to make jokes and explain them (Jentzsch and Kersting, 2023), but are still limited with certain types of jokes. Indeed, jokes and especially puns target a very specific aspect of language and cause a "departure from norms of usage" (Crystal, 2002) which may confuse neural models. Furthermore, some jokes are based on phonetic criteria, and most large language models are still not trained to incorporate phonetic information. This paper focuses on this kind of sound-based jokes.

Of course, jokes are plentiful on the Internet and some are even explained, for example the English Wikipedia[1] has an article about "Monsieur et Madame" jokes. Thus, large language models are likely to have encountered some jokes during their training and will likely be able to tell them back when prompted to do so. However, they have difficulties generalizing and creating new ones.

French has a templatic form of joke similar to the English "Knock-knock jokes" called the "Monsieur et Madame" jokes derived from earlier birth announcement or in memoriam jokes. In English, these jokes follow a real-life scenario (Bugheşiu, 2015) where someone knocks on a door in order to enter and when asked to identify themself, answer with a first name/family name pair that makes a punchline or the beginning of a song. In French, they also follow a fixed order but in a *one question and one answer* format. First, the punster says something along the following line: "Mr. and Mrs. X, have n children. What are their names?" where X is a made-up family name and n is a number, usually one also tells whether they are daughters or sons. Then the audience tries to solve the riddle, giving the appropriate number of first names, but often gives up eventually. The punster then reveals the actual names of the children which when said with their family name usually makes a somewhat comic sentence. The children's names must either be said independently as in (1) or in sequence as in (2). The pronunciation of the underlying sentence can be sloppy and the sloppiness is often an important part of the pun.

It is worth mentioning here that the riddle format is mostly formal and that the audience is hardly ever expected to actually find the answer. There are actually other French joke types that also rely on the riddle strategy in order to involve the audience. A side effect of this strategy, is that people who already know the answer, because they have already heard the joke before, may start to be amused before the answer is revealed.

In order to acknowledge the diversity of family structures and to make these jokes more inclusive, we actually replaced the traditional "Mr. and Mrs. X" by "Family X" in our tool. However, for the sake of simplicity, we use the traditional "Mr. and Mrs. X" in this paper.

We want to study the ability of language models to interpret, solve and then create this kind of pronunciation based jokes. However, current models are far from being able to move from written language's token space to pronunciation space and back. Even more so as French orthography is highly idiosyncratic and that French family names have broader spelling conventions than the standard

[1] https://en.wikipedia.org/wiki/Monsieur_et_Madame_jokes

Proceedings of the 1st Workshop on Computational Humor (CHum), pages 18–22
January 19, 2025.

(1) Monsieur et Madame Térieur ont deux fils. Comment s'appellent-ils ?
Mr. and Mrs. Térieur have two sons. What are their names?

Alain et Alex, car, Alain Térieur (à l'intérieur) et Alex Térieur (à l'extérieur).
[a.lɛ̃ tɛʁ.jœʁ] [a l‿ɛ̃.tɛʁ.jœʁ] [a.lɛks tɛʁ.jœʁ] [a l‿e.kstɛʁ.jœʁ]
Alain and Alex, because, Alain Térieur (inside) and Alex Térieur (outside).

(2) Monsieur et Madame Cale ont trois enfants. Comment s'appellent-ils ?
Mr. and Mrs. Cale have three children. What are their names?

Anna, Lise et Mehdi, car, Anna Lise Mehdi Cale (analyse médicale).
[a.na liz me.di kal] [a.na.liz me.di.kal].
Anna, Lise and Mehdi, because, Anna Lise Mehdi Cale (medical analysis).

written language.

So as a first step, we present a series of methods used to generate first names based sentences. The different methods have their own strengths and weaknesses. The trade-off usually lies between the amount of jokes produced and the comicalness (or even meaningfulness) of jokes.

2 Why a Rule-Based approach in the AI era?

In the age of large language models, rule-based models are no longer widely used for text generation. However, in some specific tasks they may still be relevant.

2.1 State of the art

Humor can be hard to detect even for humans, so it's not surprising that it's the same for machines. However, automatic classification systems dedicated to the detection of humor, notably with the 2017 and 2021 SemEval (Potash et al., 2017; Meaney et al., 2021) focusing on tweets in English, or the HAHA challenges focusing on tweets in Spanish (Castro et al., 2018; Chiruzzo et al., 2019, 2021). Morales and Zhai (2017) use a generative language model to predict humoristic online reviews.

As for automatic generation of humor, this task is still relatively unexplored. Amin and Burghardt (2020) have produced a state-of-the-art for this task, listing 12 systems published between 1994 and 2020.

2.2 Automatic generation of puns based on names

There are currently two versions of our tool[2](Dehouck and Delaborde, 2023). The first version of the generator is based on phonetic criteria to automatically generate simple puns. The list of French terms from the English Wiktionary[3] and their pronunciation(s) (in IPA, the International Phonetic Alphabet) are used to align with a list of French names[4] and their pronunciation(s), also taken from the Wiktionary. This list of names is progressively enriched as users can enter their own name with an IPA keyboard. Alignments are made using tries (prefix trees) to find the terms whose pronunciation is compatible with the pronunciation of a name. Figure 1 shows an example of trie with pronunciations along the branches and written forms at the leaves. To find the puns, our generator identifies and shows the first names whose pronunciation in French matches the rest of the term. Then, the puns are displayed in the canonical form: a question with an answer in first(s) name(s) + last name format. This version only displays lemmas in order to avoid too much results for one pun.

The puns thus generated are displayed on a website[5]. The current version of the tool generate puns based on one first name, such as (1). Two more playful features are also being proposed. The first

[2]The first version is downloadable at the following address: https://github.com/MathieuDehouck/AliGator

[3]https://en.wiktionary.org/wiki/Category:French_terms_with_IPA_pronunciation

[4]https://en.wiktionary.org/wiki/Category:French_given_names

[5]https://tools.lattice.cnrs.fr/aligator/main.html

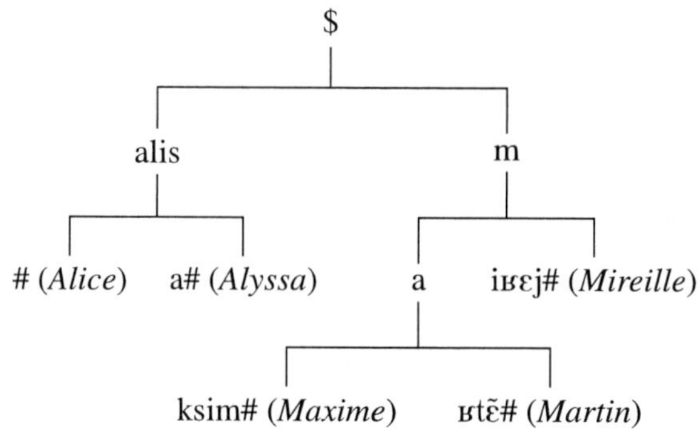

Figure 1: A trie for the given names Alice, Alyssa, Maxime, Martin and Mireille. $ represents the beginning of a string, # the end of a string and the remaining characters are plain characters. To each leaf, whose internal string contains a # character, we also associate orthographic representations for the name whose pronunciation corresponds to the path from the root to this leaf.

one, which is already available, is the generation of puns from randomly picked names. The second one is a list of the funniest puns. This one is mostly ready, but we wait to have received enough feedback from users before making it actually available.

2.3 Generation of French proper names

On our website, the user can enter a first name and ask to generate puns containing that first name[6]. If the proposed first name is not found in our database, the user can add it in IPA with its spelling variant, and thus obtain any puns that contain this name.

To display the pun in its canonical form, we created a finite-state-transducer that reads an IPA strings from the end to the beginning, applying a list of phonological rules, specific to the French language[7], that generate surnames with different levels of complexity.

For the example (1), here are some of the proper names generated: *Téryœur, Téryœurs, Théryœurt, Thérryœurd* or *Thérryœurre.* The pun generator currently uses the first form returned by the transducer, which is usually not too complex, here it would be *Théryœur*, but we are working on a process to add more diversity while avoiding forms with too many silent and double letters.

3 V2: work in progress

The first version of the tool already generates a great number of puns, but it is limited in several aspects. It is limited in term of phonological variations. And it can only generate jokes based on a fixed stock of words and expressions. In this section, we present how we plan on tackling these limitations.

3.1 Phonological relaxation

There are several reasons to allow imperfections in the phonological alignments in our tool.

As is the case for many languages, spoken and written French are quite different. At the phonological level, written French preserves a number of distinctions that are not maintained in many accents, such as the [e/ɛ] distinction in open syllables. Likewise, the close-mid/open-mid vowel distinction is strongly linked to the presence of a following coda, which leads to vowel alternation[8] in many French verbal or adjectival paradigms.

We also would like to point out that we used the transcriptions from descriptive resources as a starting point. For some of the words or first names, several pronunciations are proposed but they do not always represent all possible realizations in French. In the case of several variants, we have chosen to use the first transcription and to relax the phonological constraints in order to compensate for the absence of some variations.

To give the reader an idea of the impact of phonological relaxation, we have computed the number of puns generated by the fixed-vocabulary rule-based generator with and without the close-mid/open-mid vowel distinction. With the mid-vowel distinction enforces, out system generates 2093 puns representing 1922 lemma[9]. When the mid-vowel dis-

[6]For the moment, we only display 5 of them, for further annotation and because there are sometimes too many outputs

[7]`https://fr.wiktionary.org/wiki/Annexe:Prononciation/français`

[8]X-Sampa even has a dedicated / character to represent the archiphonemic status of vowels involved in this phenomenon.

[9]Note that a few lemma can appear with different first names. For example, *anaphore* can lead to *Anne Afaure* or

tinction is relaxed, the system generates 2728 puns (a 30% increase) representing 2382 lemma (a 24% increase). Some first names, such as *Eve* even go from generating 0 puns to 51 after the relaxation.

By taking this approach a step further, the release of constraints could also enable the production of more puns, such as: *Gordon Zola* [gɔʁ.dɔn zo.la], for *gorgonzola* [gɔʁ.gɔn'(d)zo.la].

As expected, relaxing phonological constraints increases the number of generated puns. However, if the pronunciations are so different that the audience has no chance of guessing the actual answer, the pun has to be really funny for the joke to work. There is a strong trade-off between the quality of the pun and the divergence from the expected pronunciation. This is in fact a place where users' feedback will indeed be valuable.

3.2 Ups and Downs of Syntax

For the second version of the generator, we want to go beyond the Wiktionary's words and expressions with IPA pronunciation and create new pun phrases using morphosyntax.

We use the Morphalou lexicon (ATILF, 2023) as a source for pronunciation and morphological information. This lexicon consists of french word forms annotated with pronunciation (in X-SAMPA) and morphological information. In this version, puns are no longer restricted to a single lemma, but span whole phrases (such as determiner + noun + adjective) and must thus respect gender and number agreement rules (using the information from Morphalou). First names are still extracted from the Wiktionary in this version.

We create morphologically annotated tries (prefix trees), associating their pronunciation with orthographic forms. In this way, we can find words whose pronunciation is compatible with the pronunciation of a given name while controlling for part-of-speech and morphological features.

Morphosyntactic backbones, that are sequences of parts-of-speech with agreement information, are extracted from Universal Dependencies treebanks (Zeman et al., 2022) in order not to generate purely random strings of words.

This method indeed generates many syntactically correct sentences which start with strings of sounds matching given names. However, they are often far from semantically acceptable, if meaningful at all, and therefore rarely make for funny jokes. For example, we generate puns such as the one in figure (3) which, while being syntactically correct, does not really make sense.

Implementing semantic consistency by using only rules is inconceivable. Lists of well-known movies, songs or expressions can also be useful, but seem insufficient.

This is the stage where large language models can actually be very useful. As they have been trained to mimic human language, they can produce semantically consistent sentences.

3.3 Annotation

Visitors are already invited to rate the puns directly on the website. They can also annotate these puns with tags such as "explicit content", "unintelligible" or a degree of humor (from *not funny* to *very funny*). For example, this is also the case on the JokerJudger platform used by Winters et al. (2018) to evaluate their system. In the future, a formal annotation campaign is envisioned for this task.

4 Conclusion

The first version of our generator uses rules to automatically produce puns based on one given name and one word or locution, respecting a well-known canonical form in French. This version is accessible online and the code is available on Github under MIT license.

We then consider three improvements for the second version. First, the phonological constraints relaxation in order to cover different variants of spoken French. Secondly, the use of a large language model for the semantic consistency of the sentence generation. Third, the annotation campaign for the degree of humor.

Limitations

Humor generation is a complex task and as we have discussed earlier in this paper our tools have a number of limitations.

The first version of our tool uses a fixed vocabulary of words and expressions, so it is limited in this direction.

The second version generates new phrases and is thus less limited, but has a semantic consistency problem.

Ethical Considerations

We do not see any direct way this work could be used unethically.

Anna Faure.

(3) Monsieur et Madame Golaux ont deux enfants. Comment s'appellent-ils ?
Mr. and Mrs. Golaux have two children. What are their names?

Laura et Valérie, car, Laura Valérie Golaux (l'or avalé rigolo).
[lo.ʁa va.le.ʁi go.lo] [l ɔʁ a.va.le ʁi.go.lo].
Laura and Valérie, because, Laura Valérie Golaux (the swallowed funny gold).

We actually work on making our website and tools more inclusive as we mentioned in the introduction, by removing the pun presentation from its traditional family setting.

However, we should mention that both versions of our tools are currently semantically unfiltered. For example, the first version uses any French word or expression that is annotated with its pronunciation in the Wiktionary, as source for puns. This could include all sorts of offensive terms, including and not limited to, racial, sexual or disability based slurs.

We are working on this problem. One way would be to parse the whole Wiktionary article to see if any indication is given about the offensive or derogatory nature of a word.

Since we are aware of this problem, users can actually tag puns as being offensive, if it ever was the case that our tools generated such puns.

References

Miriam Amin and Manuel Burghardt. 2020. A survey on approaches to computational humor generation. In *Proceedings of the The 4th Joint SIGHUM Workshop on Computational Linguistics for Cultural Heritage, Social Sciences, Humanities and Literature*, pages 29–41, Online. International Committee on Computational Linguistics.

ATILF. 2023. Morphalou. ORTOLANG (Open Resources and TOols for LANGuage) –www.ortolang.fr.

Alina Bugheşiu. 2015. Knock-knock jokes, proper names, and referentiality. *BAS British and American Studies*, (21):183–191.

Santiago Castro, Luis Chiruzzo, and Aiala Rosá. 2018. Overview of the haha task: Humor analysis based on human annotation at ibereval 2018. In *IberEval@ SEPLN*, pages 187–194.

Luis Chiruzzo, Santiago Castro, Mathias Etcheverry, Diego Garat, Juan José Prada, and Aiala Rosá. 2019. Overview of haha at iberlef 2019: Humor analysis based on human annotation. In *IberLEF@ SEPLN*, pages 132–144.

Luis Chiruzzo, Santiago Castro, Santiago Góngora, Aiala Rosá, JA Meaney, and Rada Mihalcea. 2021. Overview of haha at iberlef 2021: Detecting, rating and analyzing humor in spanish. *Procesamiento del Lenguaje Natural*, 67:257–268.

David Crystal. 2002. *The English Language*. London: Penguin Books.

Mathieu Dehouck and Marine Delaborde. 2023. Génération automatique de jeux de mots à base de prénoms. In *Actes de CORIA-TALN 2023. Actes de la 30e Conférence sur le Traitement Automatique des Langues Naturelles (TALN)*, page 1.

Sophie Jentzsch and Kristian Kersting. 2023. Chatgpt is fun, but it is not funny! humor is still challenging large language models. *Preprint*, arXiv:2306.04563.

Julie-Anne Meaney, Steven Wilson, Luis Chiruzzo, Adam Lopez, and Walid Magdy. 2021. SemEval 2021 task 7: HaHackathon, detecting and rating humor and offense. In *Proceedings of the 15th International Workshop on Semantic Evaluation (SemEval-2021)*, pages 105–119, Online. Association for Computational Linguistics.

Alex Morales and Chengxiang Zhai. 2017. Identifying humor in reviews using background text sources. In *Proceedings of the 2017 Conference on Empirical Methods in Natural Language Processing*, pages 492–501, Copenhagen, Denmark. Association for Computational Linguistics.

Peter Potash, Alexey Romanov, and Anna Rumshisky. 2017. SemEval-2017 task 6: #HashtagWars: Learning a sense of humor. In *Proceedings of the 11th International Workshop on Semantic Evaluation (SemEval-2017)*, pages 49–57, Vancouver, Canada. Association for Computational Linguistics.

Thomas Winters, Vincent Nys, and Daniel De Schreye. 2018. Automatic joke generation: Learning humor from examples. In *Distributed, Ambient and Pervasive Interactions: Technologies and Contexts*, pages 360–377, Cham. Springer International Publishing.

Daniel Zeman, Joakim Nivre, and al. 2022. Universal dependencies 2.11. LINDAT/CLARIAH-CZ digital library at the Institute of Formal and Applied Linguistics (ÚFAL), Faculty of Mathematics and Physics, Charles University.

Homophonic Pun Generation in Code Mixed Hindi English

Yash Sarrof
Saarland University
ysarrof@lst.uni-saarland.de

Abstract

In this study, we investigate Hinglish—a blend of Hindi and English commonly found in informal online communication—with a particular focus on automated pun generation. Our work [1] examines the applicability and adaptability of existing English pun generation pipelines to Hinglish. We assess the pun generation capabilities of Large Language Models (LLMs), particularly GPT-3.5. By employing Chain of Thought prompting and Self-Refine techniques, we identify cross-linguistic homophone detection as a central difficulty. To address this, we propose a novel algorithm for cross-lingual homophone identification and develop a Latin-to-Devanagari transliteration module to leverage the widespread use of Latin-script Hindi in online settings. Building on existing frameworks for pun generation, we incorporate our homophone and transliteration modules to improve output quality. Crowd-sourced human evaluations validate the effectiveness of our approach.

1 Introduction

Code-mixing has become widespread in written digital communication, evolving from a phenomenon primarily seen in spoken language (Winata et al., 2022). Similarly, the blend of Hindi and English, commonly known as Hinglish, is now prevalent across both spoken and written mediums.

While computational humor generation receives extensive attention in monolingual settings, especially in English, existing methods often struggle in code-mixed contexts. Puns based on homographs, for instance, tend to lose their impact when applied across languages. Homophonic puns, however, hold unique potential in code-mixed settings, as identical sounds can convey entirely different meanings in different languages.

Large Language Models (LLMs), such as those in the GPT series, demonstrate proficiency in generating English puns, largely due to their training on extensive datasets like Common Crawl. However, as noted by Jentzsch and Kersting (2023), while GPT-4 can produce puns, it frequently lacks diversity in its outputs—a challenge further amplified in code-mixed environments.

This work examines the performance of **GPT-3.5** in generating homophonic puns within the Hinglish context. Using Chain of Thought prompting (Wei et al., 2023) and the Self-Refine framework (Madaan et al., 2024)—techniques designed to enhance creative text generation—we find that a key difficulty in pun generation lies in reliably identifying cross-linguistic homophones. To address this, we propose an algorithm that detects homophones across languages.

Native Hindi speakers, who often use English as a second language, prefer the Latin script for online communication due to the complexities of the Devanagari script, which includes conjunct consonants, vowel diacritics, and a large character set. This, combined with the familiarity of the QWERTY keyboard, has led to the widespread adoption of Latin script for Hindi (Wolf-Sonkin et al., 2019). To quantify this shift, we compare Hindi word counts in Devanagari and Latin scripts across datasets like The Pile and C4, finding a substantial preference for Latin script. This discrepancy underscores the need for transliteration to leverage phonetic similarities across scripts, essential for generating homophonic puns in Hinglish. Therefore we introduce a lightweight Latin-to-Devanagari transliteration module to take advantage of this fact.

Building on He et al. (2019)'s hybrid pipeline for pun generation, we adapt it to integrate our homophone generation and transliteration modules. Results show that providing these homophones as input markedly enhances the quality of generated puns. A crowd-sourced evaluation validates these findings, providing robust evidence of the improvements.

[1] Code: https://github.com/yashYRS/HinglishPun

Proceedings of the 1st Workshop on Computational Humor (CHum), pages 23–31
January 19, 2025.

Vanilla Prompting Example

Input: Generate a Hindi English mixed pun.
Output: Why did the Hindi teacher bring a ladder to class?
Because he wanted to teach बंदर [bən̪d̪ər] (bandar), how to climb the बांस [bã:s] (bamboo).

Figure 1: Vanilla Prompting leads to grammatical but incoherent statements. The IPA provided in all prompts from hereon is only for the paper readability and they are not a part of the prompt.

Finally, we discuss the limitations of our approach and suggest directions for future research to advance humor generation in code-mixed languages further.

2 Related Work

The field of computational humor has long explored the creation and understanding of puns. Early work by Lessard and Levison (1992) focused on generating humor through an antonym-based system designed to create Tom Swifties. The Joke Analysis and Production Engine (JAPE), a pun generator, produced novel outputs and was later formalized (Ritchie, 2003). Researchers have called for more formal computational models of humor, emphasizing the need for experimental validation and advocating for the formalization of humor theories (Brône et al., 2006).

Over time, approaches to computational humor have evolved. Modern methods now include neural models (Yu et al., 2018), surprisal-based techniques (He et al., 2019), and generative adversarial networks (Luo et al., 2019). The exploration of code-mixed puns, particularly those combining Hindi and English, is a more recent development in the field. Efforts to create datasets for code-mixed Hindi-English include notable contributions from Singh et al. (2018), who curated a POS-tagged Hinglish corpus by scraping Twitter. Aggarwal et al. (2018) made pioneering efforts in identifying Hindi-English code-mixed puns. Utilizing advertisement datasets, they determined the language of each word, then identified potential pun locations using a combination of n-gram models, smoothing techniques, and phonetic similarity. Their goal was to minimize contextual differences between the word altered to create the pun and the original word, thereby maximizing contextual appropriateness. Agarwal and Narula (2021) focused on generating jokes in code-mixed Hindi-English using Hinglish word embeddings. They used deep learning approaches to generate jokes in English, which were then transformed into code-mixed Hindi-English by converting selective parts of the text or using a pre-trained encoder and transfer learning method. Their work primarily focused on general joke generation. However, to the best of our knowledge, our work on generating homophonic puns in code-mixed English-Hindi is novel.

Criteria for SelfRefine

Pun Present: Does the text have a pun?
Algorithm followed: Was the algorithm described, if any followed?
Coherence: Is the text coherent?
Funny: Is the text funny?

Figure 2: Criteria used to apply the SelfRefine framework to each of our designed prompts.

3 CoT prompting to generate puns reveals problems with finding Homophones

Chain of Thought prompting (Wei et al., 2023) has proven to be a simple yet effective technique for enhancing outputs and identifying where LLMs struggle most in performing a given task.

Post-hoc refinement is a common strategy to fix mistakes, and some popular strategies suggested recently focus on automated feedback that tries to self-critique (Xu et al., 2024; Madaan et al., 2024; Akyürek et al., 2023) and improve its output iteratively. The SelfRefine (Madaan et al., 2024) framework has been shown to be effective in various settings and has been adapted to various contexts to improve performance (Wadhwa et al., 2024; Tian et al., 2024; Shridhar et al., 2023). The idea is to assess the generated output by the same LLM with certain criterion (see Figure : 2), and then feed the assessment back to the LLM to refine the prompt, and keep doing this iteratively. For all our generated puns, we report our final answers after going through each stage iteratively at least 3 times. We stop early in case, the pun generated does not differ in terms of Levenshtein distance from the previously generated pun or if a positive automated assessment is made by the LLM.

LLMs struggling to find homophones

Step 1: EN: **pen**, HI: पेन (pen) [pɛn], HIToEN: **pen**
Step 2: Since **pen** == **pen**, go back to step 1.

Step 1 (redo): EN: **apple**, HI: एप्पल (apple) ['æpəl], HIToEN: **apple**
Step 2: Since **apple** == **apple**, go back to step 1.

Step 1 (redo): EN: **ball**, HI: बॉल (ball) [bɔl], HIToEN: **ball**
Step 2: Since **ball** == **ball**, go back to step 1.
...

Figure 3: Model output stuck in a recursive loop, repeating steps due to failure in finding distinct homophones. While the model detects incorrect homophones, it fails to correct them, leading to repeated attempts. This excerpt illustrates the pattern; the full trace included 70 retries. Most cases where HIToEN equals EN occur due to loan words in Hindi.

Step 1: EN: **doctor**, HI: डाक्टर (doctor) ['dɒktə], HIToEN: **doctor**
Step 2: Since **doctor** == **doctor**, go back to step 1.

Step 1 (redo): EN: **dude**, HI: दूध (milk) [d̪ud̪ʱɐ], HIToEN: **milk**
Step 2: Since **milk** != **dude**, proceed to step 3.

Figure 4: Illustrative trace showing rejected homophones and the selection process for acceptable ones.

When using vanilla prompting to generate code-mixed puns, the outputs typically result in grammatically correct but incoherent sentences that do not attempt to make puns (see Figure 1). To further understand this, we provided instructions based on the algorithm suggested by He et al. (2019) for creating puns, and tested the model in zero-shot, one-shot, and few-shot settings (with 2, 4, and 6 examples). Across all settings, the prompt included instructions to encourage CoT reasoning to help identify the bottleneck. The generation temperature was varied, and between 10 to 20 samples were generated and manually analysed for each configuration.

The general framework of the prompts designed is illustrated in Figure 5. This framework forced the model to regenerate its output until it successfully identified homophones. In zero-shot and one-shot learning settings, the model often incorrectly identified homophones, resulting in statements rather than actual attempts at puns.

Prompt for confirming the homophone before proceeding

Instruction: Construct a code-mixed Hindi-English pun based on the steps below.

Steps:
Step 1. Create a triplet of:
a. English word **EN**
b. Hindi word **HI**, homophone to **EN**
c. **HI** translated to English, labeled **HIToEN**
Step 2. If **HIToEN** == **EN**, redo step 1. Otherwise, proceed to step 3
Step 3. Construct short sentences (less than 10 words) with **EN** as the object of the sentence.
Step 4. Replace **EN** with **HI**.
Step 5. Replace the noun phrase at the start of the sentence with a contextualized phrase that is closely related to the **HIToEN** word.

Example:
Step 1: EN: **dude**, HI: दूध [d̪ud̪ʱɐ] (milk), HIToEN: **milk**
Step 2: Since **milk** != **dude**, proceed to step 3.
Step 3: Construct sentence with **EN** as the object: "Jack asked - What's up dude?"
Step 4: Replace **EN** with **HI**: "Jack asked - What's up दूध [d̪ud̪ʱɐ] (dude)?"
Step 5: Replace the noun phrase with a contextualized phrase: "The cow asked - What's up दूध [d̪ud̪ʱɐ] (dude)?"

Figure 5: Prompt structure to guide the model to confirm the homophone before proceeding. This input prompt contains instructions that are modeled on the basis of the algorithm suggested by He et al. (2019) to generate puns in English with necessary modifications to fit the current context

However, the few-shot settings included examples with negative samples of homophones, followed by the rejection of these negative homophones to focus on actual homophones. A sample of this approach is shown in Figure 4. Including such examples in few-shot settings led to interesting cases where the model got stuck in a recursive loop, unable to progress beyond the initial step of identifying homophones. This often resulted in the maximum token limit being reached, with the API output oscillating between the first two steps for up to 70 turns. A portion of these recursive outputs is shown in Figure 3. We hypothesize that one of the reasons these models struggle to create convincing puns is their inability to move beyond the initial step of even identifying homophones.

4 Homophone Identification

The Epitran package [2] available in Python can be used to convert orthographic text into their International Phonetic Alphabet (IPA) forms, and its efficacy has been well studied and reported in this regard (Mortensen et al., 2018). The most common words found in English as well as Hindi are collected from various sources, and these words are converted into their IPA forms using Epitran. The resulting values are compared with each other and by using Minimum edit distance as a measure, similar IPAs (lower minimum edit measures) across the 2 languages are grouped with each other. This simple yet effective technique can be used to get homophones between any of the 61 languages that are supported at the moment by Epitran. However, it must be noted that some post processing is required to remove unnecessary and extra matches that might occur. Borrowed words from the same language need to be weeded out so that we are not left with simple inflections of the same word in the 2 languages. Therefore, the Hindi words are translated as well as transliterated into English. If the minimum edit distance of the translation and transliteration is low as well, then that implies that the word in Hindi was in all likelihood a borrowed word from English, and hence that word is discarded. Words with less than 3 characters are discarded as well, since they are most likely to be filler words and would not be interesting candidates for pun generation.

[2]https://github.com/dmort27/epitran

5 Transliteration from Devanagari Script to Latin Script

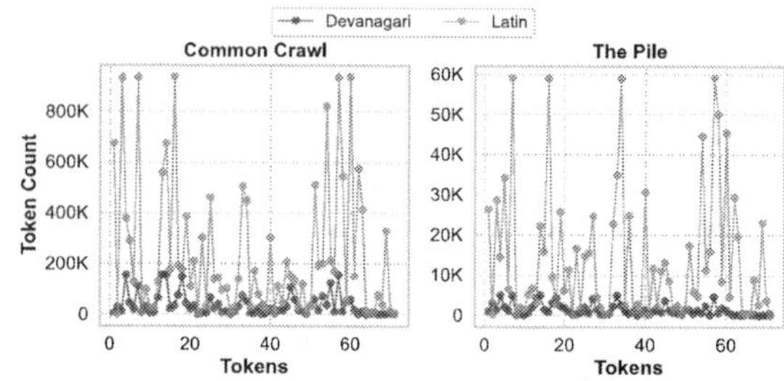

Figure 6: Comparing the count of tokens in the Devanagari script vs the same token in the Latin script for the 100 most common words in Hindi across both the Common Crawl and the Pile

To understand the prevalence and distribution of Hindi words in Devanagari and Latin scripts, we applied the What's In My Big Data? (WIMBD) framework (Elazar et al., 2024) to systematically analyze two large datasets: C4 (used to train T5 (Raffel et al., 2020)) and The Pile (Gao et al., 2020), both commonly used to train large language models (LLMs). WIMBD provides an accessible suite of tools designed to facilitate exploration and analysis of large language datasets. We specifically used the count functionality to compare the exact occurrences of Hindi words in both the scripts and found a substantially higher representation of the Latin script (see Figure: 6). This discrepancy likely results from a combination of factors, such as the dominance of Latin script in informal communication, presence of the same homographic English word, all of which align with our goal of finding homophones for pun generation. The Latin script's higher token counts increase the likelihood of identifying phonetically similar words, thus facilitating effective pun creation. Therefore to support our homophone generation step, we propose a rule-based transliteration algorithm.

The algorithm involves individual character mappings for the 42 extended consonants, 12 vowels, and 12 vowel markers of the Devanagari script to their Latin script counterparts. These mappings are stored locally. For any given word in Devanagari script, the algorithm iterates over each character. If a character is a raw vowel (not a vowel marker), the corresponding Latin equivalent is added directly from the stored mappings. If the next character is a vowel marker, it is combined with the current character. The subsequent character is then checked,

```
Data: devng: Word in Devanagari script
Result: latin: Word in Latin script
Initialize latin as an empty string; for each character c in devng do
    if c has a following vowel marker then
        c = c + vowel marker
    end
    if c is a vowel then
        Append the Latin equivalent to latin;
    end
    if c is a consonant then
        if there is a consonant following c and it also has a vowel marker then
            Append the Latin equivalent of c to latin;
        end
        else
            Append the Latin equivalent along with 'a' to handle the schwa sound to latin;
        end
    end
end
```

Algorithm 1: Transliteration Algorithm for Devanagari to Latin

effectively creating a lookahead of 2.

If the following character is a consonant with a vowel marker, the current character's mapping is appended with an "a" to denote the schwa sound typically associated with Hindi consonants. This process accounts for the rule in Hindi where a consonant is assumed to end with a schwa unless followed by another vowel. However, since two schwas do not appear consecutively in natural language, this lookahead prevents unnecessary additions of the schwa sound. If the subsequent character lacks a vowel marker, the "a" is omitted.

Word	IPA	Variation 1	Variation 2
भूख	[bʱu:kʰ]	bhook	bhuk
बिजली	[bɪd͡ʒlɪ]	bijli	bijlee

Table 1: Examples of Variations that are considered acceptable by native speakers owing to a lack of transcription standard

The proposed transliteration system achieves 64% accuracy on the Dakshina dataset (Roark et al., 2020), which, while lower than the 72.4% accuracy of the current state-of-the-art (Madhani et al., 2023) which are based on neural architectures, offers a computationally efficient alternative. Through error analysis, we identified issues within the dataset itself, including errors in ground annotations (see Table 2).

Word	IPA	Present	Actual
इनके	[ɪnkɛ]	unke	inke
में	[me:n]	be	mein
है	[hɛ]	ahai	hai

Table 2: Examples of Mistakes in the annotation of Google's Dakshina dataset, along with the correct transliterations

Additionally, the lack of standard spellings in the Latin script for transliterated Hindi poses a challenge. Since the script isn't native, multiple correct spellings often exist, yet most datasets, including those available today, only account for one variation. This results in perfectly acceptable alternative spellings being incorrectly marked as errors (see Table 1).

In conclusion, while transliteration significantly aids in processing Hinglish datasets and is crucial for the post-processing needed in homophone generation for Hinglish pun creation, its development is not without fundamental challenges. Addressing these challenges, such as handling spelling variations and inaccuracies in datasets, would make it easier to integrate transliteration systems into models like ours more effectively.

6 Modifying Pun Generation with Surprise

A stripped down version of the methodology suggested in He et al. (2019) is recreated for the current context. Given a pair of homophones (w_1, w_2), candidate sentences are found from a corpus (Brown corpus found in the NLTK chosen in our case). Sentences where the w_1 appears at the end is retained, since puns are generally considered funnier if there is an element of surprise, and the pun word appearing at the end increases the likelihood of the same. In the candidate sentences, we replace the w_1 with w_2 and subsequently try to replace the noun phrase at the start of the sentence with a topic that is related to the w_2 word instead of the w_1 word. The modified phrase results in a pun after post processing that checks for grammaticality. Since, in our case the w_2 is from a different language, we translate w_2 into English, before trying to find an appropriate topic for the same (through GLoVe Embeddings or other such distributional semantic similarity mechanisms).

A sample execution

- Homophone pairs: *city* , *seeti* (whistle)
- Find short candidate sentences from the Brown corpus where *city* appears at the end. *The man lives in the heart of the city*
- Replace *city* with the homophonic pair *The man lives in the heart of the seeti*
- Find apt topic to replace the subject. *The referee lives in the heart of the seeti*

Although the resulting phrase can lead to a pun, a filtration mechanism is required that can remove phrases / puns that don't make sense due to the change in language and can handle the grammaticality requirements of both the languages in question. This is a major limitation of this method while applying it in Code-Mixed Settings which will need to be improved upon in future extensions of this work.

7 Prompting LLMs by appending pregenerated list of Homophones

Since the cause of failure in GPT3.5 during pun generations was shown to be identification of homophones, the modules introduced in Sections 3 & 4 are leveraged and locally generated transliterated homophones are appended to the end of standardised prompts. A standard prompt structure is created for Zero shot, one shot, 4 shot (see Figure 7 as an example), 8 shot and finally 16 shot settings. In all cases, the input homophones are always appended at the end, and each input is run in a separate session without any history except for the examples in the few shot settings. This modified hybrid prompt setting improves the output drastically with many of the outputs generated fulfilling all criterion of being qualified as puns. Even, when the outputs generated are not funny, they are at least attempts at making a pun out of the given inputs.

Survey to Evaluate Hybrid Approach

A small survey was conducted to assess the quality of puns generated by our system across various settings. Fifty-six participants volunteered to rate the puns on a scale of 1 (not funny) to 5 (extremely funny). Given the voluntary nature of the survey, we evaluated 4-5 random samples per category. To ensure data integrity and prevent biased participation, we included human-generated puns from joke websites.

Example Prompt for Hybrid Approach

Task: Generate a code-mixed Hindi-English pun based on the homophones provided as input. Some example input-output pairs are provided as reference.

Input: 'Submit', 'Sab Mit' (everything gets erased)
Output: "Exam ki answer sheet return karte hi SUBMIT jata hai"

Input: <EnWord>, <HiTransliteratedHomophone><(EnglishTranslation)>

Figure 7: Example prompt for the hybrid approach. This sample has been truncated to show the most relevant parts of the prompt. The final line of input is dynamically modified at runtime.

Each participant received the puns in a random order, presented via Google Forms. To minimize bias, participants were unaware of the pun's origin. All participants were bilingual in Hindi and English, aged 20-30.

After the survey concluded, we calculated the mean ratings for each category: Human, Zero Shot, One Shot, 4 Shot, 8 Shot, and 16 Shot. Submissions with a mean rating below 1 for human-generated puns were discarded, as they likely indicated a lack of engagement. Additionally, submissions with all puns rated 5 were removed to eliminate potentially casual or insincere participation. Following this filtration, 39 submissions remained. The results presented in all graphs are based on these 39 submissions.

Mean Ratings per Category

Since humour is subjective, even the human generated puns do not always get a full score, and the mean ratings across all the samples and participants turned out to 4.32 (see Figure 8). Compared to the same, the ratings of all the other categories were pretty decent, with even Zero shot getting an average of 3.31 with slight increase in averages resulting in a 3.61 for 16 shot settings. Although these means

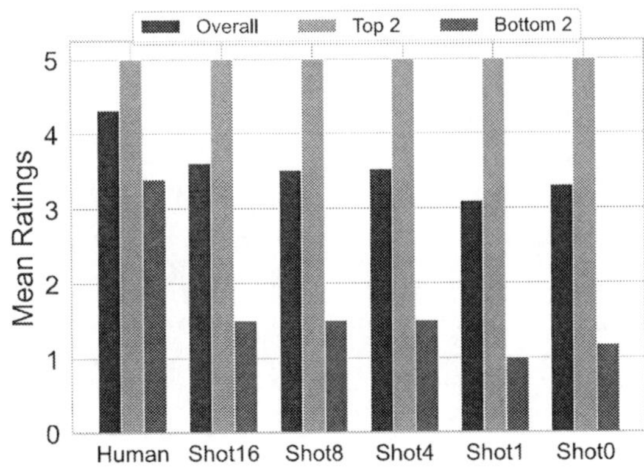

Figure 8: Mean ratings given overall, achieved by top 2 and achieved by bottom 2 puns per category of prompts

are high, the reason for the differences in the mean with the human ratings was analysed. The top 2 puns that got the highest mean scores in each category were taken, and for each category this mean turned out to be a perfect score (see Figure 8). Conversely, while trying to plot the same thing for the puns with the lowest scores, the main difference between the human generated ones get highlighted. The mean rating for Humans drops to a 3.4 which can still be considered a pretty decent score. However, for the generated puns, the score drops down significantly (see Figure 8). Thus, although our model can generate good puns, there is a lack of consistency in the generation.

7.1 Comparing Against Human Benchmarks

A box plot (see Figure 9) is created to show the variability between different samples and participants in each category. When raw ratings are considered, the scores Shot 16, Shot 4 show lower variance in their scores compared to the variances shown by the one shot and zero shot settings. As shown from the survey, it is unlikely for the mean to be a perfect 5 even for a set of human generated puns due to the subjectivity of humour. Therefore we compare the scores generated automatically against the benchmarks set by human performance. We calculate the mean rating given by each participant to the human generated jokes and per participant, we normalise the scores for all other categories based on this value. The resulting normalised scores are plotted as a box plot in Figure 10. It can be seen that Shot4, Shot8 and Shot16 perform the best. Zero Shot setting performs better than One shot settings, although they are both clearly inferior to the Few shot settings. All in all, the performance of such models in such hybrid settings is encouraging and further proves that LLMs can perform exceedingly well on highly specialised tasks such as generating puns in code mixed settings, provided they are leveraged aptly and their weaknesses are well understood.

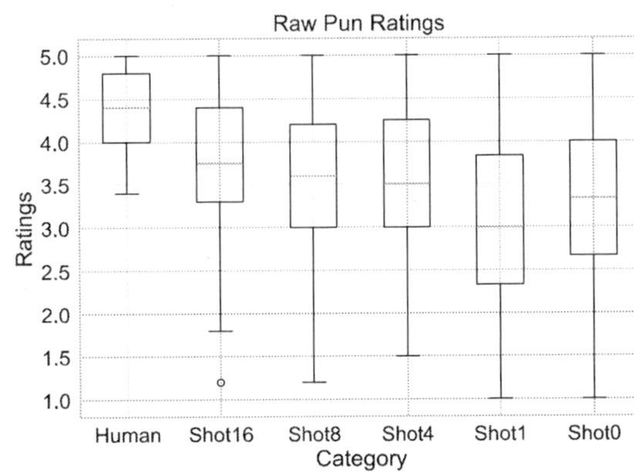

Figure 9: Box Plot with Mean Scores Per category of Prompts

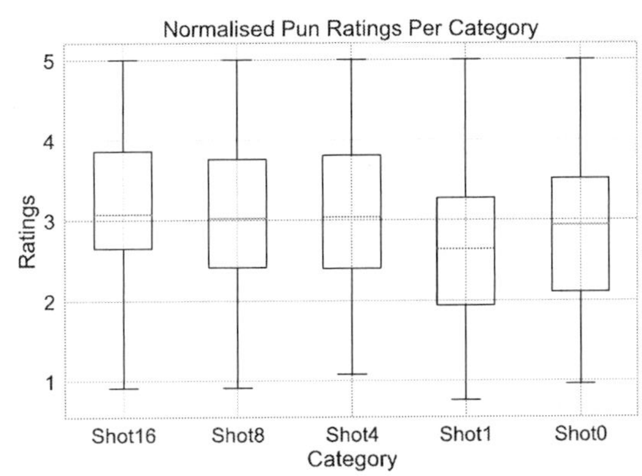

Figure 10: Box Plot with Normalised ratings according to Human Benchmarks

8 Limitations and Future Work

- Our homophone generation is constrained to single whole words. *I will see* vs *Aalsi* (lazy) are homophonic but span multiple words. Leveraging such multi word homophones could enhance the creativity of the generated content.
- The prompting experiments were conducted exclusively using $gpt-3.5-turbo$. Our current strategies do not cover the full range of possible prompts, and future work could expand on this.

- Our pun generation using Surprisal focuses on replacing individual nouns, rather than entire noun phrases. This may result in contextually weaker replacements. Fine-tuning embeddings on Hinglish data to better handle the semantics of noun phrases could lead to more contextually appropriate and higher-quality puns.

- The survey included only a small number of samples per method, as participants volunteered without compensation. A larger sample size would be needed to draw more robust conclusions.

- The pun generation methodology is not language-specific. Future work could apply the framework to other code-mixed languages, such as Spanglish (Spanish-English) or Arabizi (Arabic-English), to assess its broader applicability.

Additionally, it must be mentioned that publicly available datasets of Hinglish often suffer from various shortcomings, including inadequate maintenance, annotation issues, and insufficient scale. These limitations hinder their suitability for training and evaluating AI models effectively. Addressing these challenges and improving their quality, availability and out of the box usability is essential.

9 Conclusion

This study presents a novel exploration of homophonic pun generation within the code-mixed Hinglish context. By analyzing and adapting English-based humor generation techniques, particularly through hybrid prompting approaches with Large Language Models (LLMs), we demonstrate the feasibility of creating Hinglish puns that align with native humoristic nuances. Feeding cross-lingual homophones as well as incorporating transliteration techniques improved the pun generation capability of LLMs in the given setting, making the outputs more contextually relevant. Our findings, supported by crowd-sourced evaluations, suggest that while hybrid prompting strategies can generate engaging Hinglish puns, challenges remain, especially in achieving consistently high humor quality. Future work will benefit from expanding homophone recognition to multi-word phrases, refining the selection of humor-optimized LLMs, and developing more robust code mixed datasets to enhance the accuracy and cultural relevance of computational humor in multilingual contexts.

Ethical Statement

The evaluation survey was conducted anonymously and no private data of any individual was collected. External datasets, packages used have been attributed to the original authors and were used only after confirming that they were distributed under licenses that permit research work.

Acknowledgments

I thank Michael Hahn, Alexander Koller and the anonymous reviewers for helpful comments.

References

Kaustubh Agarwal and Rhythm Narula. 2021. Humor generation and detection in code-mixed hindi-english. In *Proceedings of the Student Research Workshop Associated with RANLP 2021*, pages 1–6.

Srishti Aggarwal, Kritik Mathur, and Radhika Mamidi. 2018. Automatic target recovery for hindi-english code mixed puns. *arXiv preprint arXiv:1806.04535*.

Afra Feyza Akyürek, Ekin Akyürek, Aman Madaan, A. Kalyan, Peter Clark, D. Wijaya, and Niket Tandon. 2023. Rl4f: Generating natural language feedback with reinforcement learning for repairing model outputs. In *Annual Meeting of the Association for Computational Linguistics*.

Geert Brône, Kurt Feyaerts, and Tony Veale. 2006. Introduction: Cognitive linguistic approaches to humor.

Yanai Elazar, Akshita Bhagia, Ian Helgi Magnusson, Abhilasha Ravichander, Dustin Schwenk, Alane Suhr, Evan Pete Walsh, Dirk Groeneveld, Luca Soldaini, Sameer Singh, et al. 2024. What's in my big data? In *The Twelfth International Conference on Learning Representations*.

Leo Gao, Stella Biderman, Sid Black, Laurence Golding, Travis Hoppe, Charles Foster, Jason Phang, Horace He, Anish Thite, Noa Nabeshima, et al. 2020. The pile: An 800gb dataset of diverse text for language modeling. *arXiv preprint arXiv:2101.00027*.

He He, Nanyun Peng, and Percy Liang. 2019. Pun generation with surprise. In *Proceedings of the 2019 Conference of the North American Chapter of the Association for Computational Linguistics: Human Language Technologies, Volume 1 (Long and Short Papers)*, pages 1734–1744, Minneapolis, Minnesota. Association for Computational Linguistics.

Sophie Jentzsch and Kristian Kersting. 2023. Chatgpt is fun, but it is not funny! humor is still challenging large language models. *arXiv preprint arXiv:2306.04563*.

G Lessard and M Levison. 1992. Computational modelling of linguistic humour: Tom swifty. In *Paper Delivered at the ALLC/ACH Joint Annual Conference. Christ Church, Oxford.*

Fuli Luo, Shunyao Li, Pengcheng Yang, Baobao Chang, Zhifang Sui, Xu Sun, et al. 2019. Pun-gan: Generative adversarial network for pun generation. *arXiv preprint arXiv:1910.10950*.

Aman Madaan, Niket Tandon, Prakhar Gupta, Skyler Hallinan, Luyu Gao, Sarah Wiegreffe, Uri Alon, Nouha Dziri, Shrimai Prabhumoye, Yiming Yang, et al. 2024. Self-refine: Iterative refinement with self-feedback. *Advances in Neural Information Processing Systems*, 36.

Yash Madhani, Sushane Parthan, Priyanka Bedekar, Gokul Nc, Ruchi Khapra, Anoop Kunchukuttan, Pratyush Kumar, and Mitesh Khapra. 2023. Aksharantar: Open indic-language transliteration datasets and models for the next billion users. In *Findings of the Association for Computational Linguistics: EMNLP 2023*, pages 40–57, Singapore. Association for Computational Linguistics.

David R. Mortensen, Siddharth Dalmia, and Patrick Littell. 2018. Epitran: Precision g2p for many languages. In *Proceedings of the International Conference on Language Resources and Evaluation.*

Colin Raffel, Noam Shazeer, Adam Roberts, Katherine Lee, Sharan Narang, Michael Matena, Yanqi Zhou, Wei Li, and Peter J Liu. 2020. Exploring the limits of transfer learning with a unified text-to-text transformer. *Journal of machine learning research*, 21(140):1–67.

Graeme Ritchie. 2003. The jape riddle generator: technical specification. *Institute for Communicating and Collaborative Systems.*

Brian Roark, Lawrence Wolf-Sonkin, Christo Kirov, Sabrina J. Mielke, Cibu Johny, Işın Demirşahin, and Keith Hall. 2020. Processing south asian languages written in the latin script: the dakshina dataset. In *Proceedings of The 12th Language Resources and Evaluation Conference (LREC)*, pages 2413–2423.

Kumar Shridhar, Koustuv Sinha, Andrew Cohen, Tianlu Wang, Ping Yu, Ramakanth Pasunuru, Mrinmaya Sachan, Jason Weston, and Asli Celikyilmaz. 2023. The art of llm refinement: Ask, refine, and trust. In *North American Chapter of the Association for Computational Linguistics.*

Kushagra Singh, Indira Sen, and Ponnurangam Kumaraguru. 2018. A twitter corpus for hindi-english code mixed pos tagging. In *Proceedings of the sixth international workshop on natural language processing for social media*, pages 12–17.

Ye Tian, Baolin Peng, Linfeng Song, Lifeng Jin, Dian Yu, Haitao Mi, and Dong Yu. 2024. Toward self-improvement of llms via imagination, searching, and criticizing. *ArXiv*, abs/2404.12253.

Manya Wadhwa, Xinyu Zhao, Junyi Jessy Li, and Greg Durrett. 2024. Learning to refine with fine-grained natural language feedback. *ArXiv*, abs/2407.02397.

Jason Wei, Xuezhi Wang, Dale Schuurmans, Maarten Bosma, Brian Ichter, Fei Xia, Ed Chi, Quoc Le, and Denny Zhou. 2023. Chain-of-thought prompting elicits reasoning in large language models. *arXiv preprint arXiv:2201.11903*.

Genta Indra Winata, Alham Fikri Aji, Zheng-Xin Yong, and Thamar Solorio. 2022. The decades progress on code-switching research in nlp: A systematic survey on trends and challenges. *arXiv preprint arXiv:2212.09660*.

Lawrence Wolf-Sonkin, Vlad Schogol, Brian Roark, and Michael Riley. 2019. Latin script keyboards for south asian languages with finite-state normalization. In *Proceedings of the 14th International Conference on Finite-State Methods and Natural Language Processing*, pages 108–117.

Wenda Xu, Daniel Deutsch, Mara Finkelstein, Juraj Juraska, Biao Zhang, Zhongtao Liu, William Yang Wang, Lei Li, and Markus Freitag. 2024. Llmrefine: Pinpointing and refining large language models via fine-grained actionable feedback. In *Findings of the Association for Computational Linguistics: NAACL 2024*, pages 1429–1445.

Zhiwei Yu, Jiwei Tan, and Xiaojun Wan. 2018. A neural approach to pun generation. In *Proceedings of the 56th Annual Meeting of the Association for Computational Linguistics (Volume 1: Long Papers)*, pages 1650–1660.

Bridging Laughter Across Languages: Generation of Hindi-English Code-mixed Puns

Likhith Asapu **Prashant Kodali** **Ashna Dua**
Kapil Rajesh Kavitha **Manish Shrivastava**
International Institute of Information Technology Hyderabad
{likhith.a, prashant.kodali}@research.iiit.ac.in
{ashna.dua, kapil.rajesh}@students.iiit.ac.in, m.shrivastava@iiit.ac.in

Abstract

Puns, as a linguistic phenomenon, hold significant importance in both humor and language comprehension. While extensive research has been conducted in the realm of pun generation in English, there exists a notable gap in the exploration of pun generation within code-mixed text, particularly in Hindi-English code-mixed text. This study addresses this gap by offering a computational method specifically designed to create puns in Hindi-English code-mixed text. In our investigation, we delve into three distinct methodologies aimed at pun generation utilizing pun-alternate word pairs. Furthermore, this novel dataset, **HECoP**, comprising of 2000 human-annotated sentences serves as a foundational resource for training diverse pun detection models. Additionally, we developed a structured pun generation pipeline capable of generating puns from a single input word without relying on predefined word pairs. Through rigorous human evaluations, our study demonstrates the efficacy of our proposed models in generating code-mixed puns. The findings presented herein lay a solid groundwork for future endeavors in pun generation and computational humor within diverse linguistic contexts.

1 Introduction

Puns, as a form of wordplay, play a central role in humor and language comprehension by exploiting phonetic or semantic ambiguity to create humor through dual interpretations (Charina, 2017; Miller et al., 2017). Puns are a linguistic tool that boosts engagement and have a broad application in entertainment, advertising, and literature (Korák, 2011; Shanaieva-Tsymbal, 2021; Bulut and Almabrouk, 2020).

Although computational approaches have made strides in pun generation and detection in English, especially with recent advancements in Large Language Models (Tian et al., 2022; Zeng et al., 2024), pun generation remains largely unexplored in low-resource languages. Code-mixed text, a common phenomenon in bilingual communities, is one such low-resource setting that presents unique challenges. Bilingual speakers code-mix for a range of sociolinguistic and pragmatic purposes, including the expression of emotions such as anger, humor, and sarcasm, among other motivations (Viscaíno, 2011; Williams et al., 2019). Given the utility of code-mixing in expressing humor and a range of emotions, the computational analysis of code-mixed puns offers an intriguing challenge. Effective pun generation in this context requires models that can align phonetic similarities and interpret contextual cues across both languages to produce coherent and meaningful humor, making it even more challenging than pun generation in a standard multilingual setting.

Our work addresses the gap in code-mixed pun generation by presenting a novel computational approach for generating Hindi-English code-mixed puns. We propose three methodologies for generating puns in code-mixed text, each designed to create puns from phonetically similar Hindi-English word pairs. All three approaches utilize a foundational Large Language Model (LLM). Our findings reveal that: a) LLMs when directly prompted (baseline method), do not perform well for generating code-mixed puns (19.8% pun success rate); b) Our innovative method surpasses basic baseline prompting, achieving pun success rates of 38.8%, 62.6%, and 43%.

Further, leveraging these techniques our research introduces a new dataset, HECoP (**H**indi **E**nglish **Co**deMixed **P**uns), containing 2,000 machine-generated sentences designed for training and evaluating code-mixed pun generation. For every sample, we gather human assessments on whether it is a pun, along with its level of funniness and naturalness. We also tested and compared various pre-trained multilingual models, such as XLM-R and mBERT, on HECoP, highlighting their effec-

Proceedings of the 1st Workshop on Computational Humor (CHum), pages 32–57
January 19, 2025.

tiveness in detecting puns in code-mixed contexts.

Additionally, we developed a structured pun generation pipeline that creates puns from a single input word, using phonetic matching, compatibility scoring, and sentence filtering to ensure humor and contextual relevance. Human evaluations confirm that our approach significantly outperforms baseline models, delivering high-quality Hindi-English code-mixed puns.

To the best of our knowledge, this is the first study to explore pun generation in a code-mixed setting, providing a novel dataset with human annotations and a framework for detecting and creating valid code-mixed puns.[1]

2 Related Work

Pun generation has evolved from template-driven approaches to sophisticated Transformer-based models. Early systems, such as JAPE-1 (Binsted and Ritchie, 1994), used fixed templates to generate puns, leveraging phonetic or semantic similarity in structured formats, but these methods were limited by their reliance on manually crafted templates. Later approaches, like T-PEG (Agustini and Manurung, 2012) and T-Peg (Hong and Ong, 2008), automated the extraction of linguistic patterns from human-generated puns, creating templates with moderate success but still constrained by template rigidity.

Recent research has explored various neural approaches for automatic pun generation. Yu et al. 2018 proposed a neural language model to generate homographic puns without requiring pun-specific training data. He et al. 2019a applied the surprisal principle in an unsupervised model, achieving a 30% success rate in human evaluations. Luo et al. 2019 introduced Pun-GAN, an adversarial generative network designed to generate puns with multiple word senses simultaneously, improving both quality and diversity compared to template-based methods. Other works focused on generating context-situated puns, where Sun et al. 2022 proposed a pipeline system including a pun word retrieval module and a pun generation module. Mittal et al., 2022 introduced AmbiPun, an approach that generates puns by creating ambiguous contexts using dictionary search and one-shot GPT3, achieving a 52% success rate. Expanding on these methods, our work introduces pun generation in a code-mixed setting. It also moves away from the need for pre-defined pairs of alternate and pun words required in prior approaches through our proposed pipeline.

[1]The code and data proposed in this paper can be found at `https://github.com/Likhith-Asapu/Codemix-Pun-Generation`

3 Task Formulation

Given a list of *homophonic* pairs of pun word P_w and alternative word A_w across two language pairs here namely Hindi and English, we seek to generate a list of Hindi-English code-mixed puns using different methods. We follow the definition of pun presented in Miller et al. (2017) where "*A pun is a form of wordplay in which one sign (e.g., a word or a phrase) suggests two or more meanings by exploiting polysemy, homonymy, or phonological similarity to another sign, for an intended humorous or rhetorical effect.*" An example of a pun following this definition is "My watch is stuck between 2 and 2.30. It's a do or *dhai* situation" where the pun word P_w is *dhai* and the alternative word A_w is *die*. In this case, the humor arises from the phonetic similarity between the Hindi word *dhai* (which means two and a half, referencing 2:30 in this context) and the English word *die*, creating a playful twist on the phrase do or die.

4 Pun Generation

We adopt a three-step approach for generating Hindi-English code-mixed puns: 1) Identification of similar sounding words across a language pair, 2) Generation of candidate sentences with alternate word A_w, 3) Replacement of A_w with P_w within these candidate sentences.

4.1 Pun - Alternate Word List Collection

The first step in generating puns is to compile a list of English and Hindi words that are phonetically similar but semantically distinct. While this is straightforward in a monolingual setting as the words share a common phonological system, code-mixed scenarios require a novel approach to identify phonetically similar words across two distinct languages.

To achieve this, we extracted English and Hindi words from existing large-scale news monolingual corpora of both languages (Goldhahn et al., 2012). These words were subsequently converted into their respective International Phonetic Alphabet (IPA) representations using the *epitrans* library (Mortensen et al., 2018), which implements a rule-based system for phonetic transcription. However,

Hindi	IPA	English	IPA	Edit
पीपल (pīpal)	/pi:pəl/	people	/pi:pəl/	0
दिल (dil)	/dil/	deal	/di:l/	0
बिक (bik)	/bik/	big	/big/	0
शौक (shock)	/ʃɔ:k/	shack	/ʃæk/	1
गुस्से (gusse)	/gusse/	goose	/gu:s/	∞

Table 1: Examples of Hindi and English words with their IPA transcriptions and Custom Levenshtein edit distances between IPA forms.

as *epitrans* generates American English transcriptions for English words, we employed a dictionary-based mapping to convert these transcriptions into their corresponding Indian English IPA symbols, leveraging prior studies on Indian English phonology (Jain et al., 2021; Grolman et al., 2021). Using Indian English IPA symbols, which align more closely with Hindi phonology than American English, enhances the accuracy of phonetic matches between English and Hindi words, thereby improving the relevance of generated puns.

To quantify the phonetic similarity between Hindi and English words, we employed the Levenshtein edit distance (Ahmed et al., 2021). This distance measures the minimal number of operations-substitutions, insertions, and deletions required to convert one word into another. We use custom costs for these operations. The substitution cost c_{sub} is adjusted based on phonetic similarities, while the insertion and deletion costs are set to infinity (∞) to ensure comparisons are only made between words with the same number of phonemes.

We define the custom substitution cost between phones x and y as follows:

$$c_{\text{sub}}(x, y) = \begin{cases} 0, & \text{if } x \text{ and } y \text{ are same phones ,} \\ 0, & \text{if } x \text{ and } y \text{ are allophones,} \\ 0, & \text{if } x \text{ and } y \text{ are long/short vowel pairs,} \\ 0, & \text{if } x \text{ and } y \text{ are voiced/unvoiced pairs,} \\ 1, & \text{otherwise.} \end{cases}$$

Aspirated sounds (e.g., [t^{h}] and [t]) and breathy-voiced variants (e.g., [d̤] and [d]) are treated as allophones with a substitution cost of 0. Similarly, long-short vowel pairs (e.g., [i:] and [i]) are assigned a cost of 0.[2] This approach integrates linguistic features like allophonic variation, vowel length distinctions, and voicing contrasts, enabling a more nuanced comparison of phonetic similarity between Hindi and English word pairs.

[2]More examples can be found in Appendix A

We generated an initial candidate set S of Hindi-English word pairs, denoted as (P_w, A_w), using a custom edit distance, with the condition that the phonetic distance is less than or equal to 1:

$$S = \{(P_w, A_w) \mid d(p(P_w), p(A_w)) \leq 1\}$$

Here, P_w represents the Hindi pun word, A_w represents the English alternate word, and $p(w)$ is the IPA transcription of w. Subsequently, we manually filtered this set to exclude cognates such as *car* and कार (kaar) to arrive at a list of 500-word pairs with distinct meanings. This filtered list serves as the foundation for our pun generation experiments, highlighting the crucial role of phonetic alignment in creating effective puns, as emphasized in prior cross-linguistic pun studies (Zhou et al., 2020; Jaech et al., 2016).

4.2 Candidate Sentence Generation

To incorporate homophonic word pairs into code-mixed sentences, we developed three methodologies for pun generation: a) Contextually Aligned Pun Generation (Sec. 4.2.1), b) Question-Answer Pun Generation (Sec. 4.2.2), and c) Subject-Masked Pun Generation (Sec. 4.2.3). We compare these approaches against a Baseline Pun Generation method, which serves as a reference for evaluating the effectiveness of each technique. All four methods utilize GPT-4o with few-shot learning to generate puns, leveraging its ability to produce contextually relevant outputs[3]. By employing varied sentence formats, these methodologies help in generating diverse and engaging puns.

4.2.1 Contextually Aligned Pun Generation

In this approach, GPT-4o is prompted to generate five sentences, each ending with the English word A_w. Furthermore, each sentence must include a context word C_w, the English translation of P_w, serving as a contextual anchor to support the pun word placed at the sentence's end. For instance, given the tuple (A_w, P_w, C_w), the prompt is structured as follows: "Generate 5 creative Hindi-English code-mixed sentences ending with the English word $\{A_w\}$. Include the English word $\{C_w\}$ as context in each sentence." By specifying word placement and contextual inclusion, this prompt facilitates the generation of sentences that align with the desired structure.

[3]For illustrative examples of the prompts used in these methodologies, refer to Appendix B

P_w/A_w	Method	Generated Sentence	Label
भय/bye	Baseline	'When fear knocks at your door, send faith to answer. कहो भय–भय, बाई–बाई!"	0
	Contextually Aligned	'मेरी लड़की की fear of heights ने हमारे adventure plan को भय कह दिया।"	1
	Question-Answer	'What do you call it जब तुम अपने डर को अलविदा कहते हो? भय"	1
	Subject-Masked	'The डरपोक लड़की waved goodभय with a smile."	1
लाश/lush	Baseline	'The garden was so beautifully green, it was a लाश paradise!"	1
	Contextually Aligned	'जंगल में एक निर्जीव dead body मिली, surrounded by एक लाश forest"	1
	Question-Answer	'What do you call a garden जो लाशों से भरा हो? लाश garden"	1
	Subject-Masked	'The भूतिया कब्रिस्तान was filled with लाश greenery"	1

Table 2: Illustrative examples of code-mixed puns generated using four distinct methods. The table presents the word pair, method, generated sentence, and the corresponding label (0 for non-pun and 1 for pun). Detailed glosses for Hindi words are provided in Table 13 in the Appendix for reference.

We add an additional filtering phase to confirm that the sentences produced by the LLM in the previous step qualify as puns and are fluent. The filtering stage refines the outputs to identify the most appropriate candidate where P_w can replace A_w while maintaining grammatical and contextual coherence. This process involves two stages: (1) Part-of-Speech (POS)[4] compatibility: ensuring P_w and A_w share the same POS tag, which safeguards grammatical consistency and if no sentences meet this criterion, all generated sentences are retained for the subsequent stage; (2) The pun word P_w replaces A_w in the sentence, and candidates are prioritized based on the placement of P_w at the sentence's end, as puns are typically more impactful when positioned at the end of a sentence (Shahaf et al., 2015; Mittal et al., 2022). This method ensures that the final output meets both POS compatibility and optimal pun placement criteria, maximizing the effectiveness of the generated puns.

For instance, given the tuple (P_w, A_w, C_w) = (डेढ़, dead, one and a half), the process yields the following sequence of transformations to generate the pun:[5]

> **Prompt:** Generate 5 creative Hindi-English sentences ending with the word 'dead'. Have the word 'one and a half' as a context in each of these sentences.
> **Final Pun:** "मैंने one and a half litre दूध ख़रीदा, but when i opened it, it was already डेढ़."

4.2.2 Question-Answer Pun Generation

This method employs a structured approach to systematically generate puns in a question-answer format. The process consists of three key stages: generating a short phrase containing A_w, replacing A_w with P_w in the generated phrase, and formulating a question based on the transformed phrase.

The first stage involves generating a short phrase that naturally incorporates A_w. This initial phrase serves as the foundation for the subsequent transformation. In the second stage, A_w in the generated phrase is replaced by P_w. Replacement of A_w with P_w introduces the pun, leveraging the linguistic similarity or contextual contrast between the two words, enabling the generated phrase to exploit dual meanings or humor.

The third and final stage involves generating a question that corresponds to the modified phrase, completing the pun. GPT-4o is again employed for this task, using its understanding of the context to generate a question that makes the pun explicit and amusing. Additionally, to cater to the code-mixed nature of the task, a Hindi translation of the question is produced. These steps are essential for framing the pun within a question-answer format, which not only heightens the humor but also adds an element of surprise.

For instance, given the word pair (P_w, A_w) = (गाय, guy), the process yields the following sequence of transformations to generate the pun:

> **Generated Small Phrase:** A cool guy
> **Replaced Pun Word:** A cool गाय
> **Generated Question:** What do you call a cow wearing sunglasses?
> **Generated Translated Question:** Sunglasses पहने हुए cow को आप क्या कहते हैं?
> **Final Pun:** Sunglasses पहने हुए cow को आप क्या कहते हैं? A cool गाय

[4]Refer to Appendix C to see POS tagger details

[5]More detailed example provided in table 9 in Appendix

Model	Suc(%)	Fun.	Accep.
Contextually Aligned	38.8	2.32	4.32
Question-Answer	62.6	2.59	4.28
Subject-Masked	43	2.24	4.54
Baseline	19.8	2.17	4.48

Table 3: Comparison of Success percentage(Suc%), Mean Funniness score rated out of 5(Fun.), and Mean Acceptability score rated out of 5(Accep.) for different pun generation methods in Section 4.2.

4.2.3 Subject-Masked Pun Generation

This approach enhances the generation of code-mixed Hindi-English puns by incorporating a subject-masking step, which refines the contextual alignment of the sentence subject with the pun word, thereby improving coherence and humor. This approach unfolds in three key stages: sentence generation, alternate word replacement, and subject replacement.

The process begins by providing the language model with a prompt designed to generate a short sentence that ends with the alternate word A_w. Subsequently, the alternate word A_w in the generated sentence is replaced with the pun word P_w. This substitution introduces the pun, similar to the process in Section 4.2.2. The third and final stage involves modifying the subject or noun phrase of the sentence to enhance the relevance of the subject and the pun word. This is achieved by masking the original subject and replacing it with a noun phrase generated in Hindi, thus, generating a pun with a highly relevant subject. Additionally, replacing the noun phrase with a translation in the alternate language, such as Hindi, yields higher-quality code-mixed sentences as noted in prior studies (Gupta et al., 2018, 2020).

For instance, given the word pair $(P_w, A_w) =$ (लाख, luck), the process yields the following sequence of transformations to generate the pun:

> **Generated Short Sentence:** The man attributed all his success to luck
> **Replaced Alternate Word:** The man attributed all his success to लाख
> **Masked Subject:** [MASK] attributed all his success to लाख
> **Final Pun Sentence:** The lucky अमीर businessman attributed all his success to लाख

4.2.4 Baseline Pun Generation

For the baseline model, we utilized GPT-4o with few-shot prompting to generate puns based on given word pairs (P_w, A_w). This method served as a foundational approach for pun generation and provided a benchmark against which the performance of other methods could be evaluated.

5 Annotation and Dataset Analysis

To ensure the development of a high-quality dataset for pun detection, a structured annotation framework was designed, enabling human annotators to evaluate each generated pun across multiple dimensions, with particular emphasis on linguistic coherence and humor quality. Four undergraduate students participated in the annotation process. Collecting these human judgments serves two purposes: to assess and compare the performance of the pun generation methods discussed above, and to compile datasets for Pun Detection. To maintain data quality, an initial pilot annotation phase was conducted using 150 samples. During this phase, annotators engaged in discussion and consensus-building to resolve disagreements, which helped establish standardized criteria and procedures before commencing full-scale annotation.

5.1 Annotation Guidelines

Each pun was evaluated on three criteria: (1) Pun Success, (2) Funniness, and (3) Acceptability, following annotation guidelines adapted from prior research (He et al., 2019b).

- **Pun Success:** This metric evaluates whether the sentence successfully incorporates wordplay, measured on a binary scale with an additional option for instances where the intended pun is not constructed using the specified word pair. This assessment ensures that the primary objective of creating a pun is achieved.
- **Funniness:** The degree of humor elicited by the pun is measured using a 5-point Likert scale, ranging from "Not Funny" to "Hilarious." This metric captures the inherently subjective nature of humor and assesses the effectiveness of the pun in generating amusement.
- **Acceptability:** This metric evaluates the grammatical accuracy and fluency of the code-mixed text on a 5-point scale, from "Definitely

Model	Validation				Test			
	F1	Precision	Recall	Accuracy	F1	Precision	Recall	Accuracy
1. Task-Specific Fine Tuning								
XLM-R (Conneau et al., 2020)	**67.8**$_{1.18}$	**69.5**$_{1.16}$	**69.0**$_{0.96}$	**69.0**$_{0.96}$	**67.1**$_{1.12}$	**68.0**$_{1.14}$	**69.0**$_{1.25}$	**69.0**$_{1.25}$
mBERT (Devlin et al., 2019)	65.28$_{1.82}$	65.4$_{1.79}$	66.0$_{2.01}$	66.0$_{2.01}$	63.4$_{1.78}$	63.5$_{1.82}$	64.0$_{1.66}$	64.0$_{1.66}$
IndicBERT (Kakwani et al., 2020)	61.74$_{0.73}$	62.3$_{0.71}$	62.9$_{0.83}$	62.9$_{0.83}$	62.0$_{3.11}$	62.4$_{2.77}$	63.5$_{2.59}$	63.5$_{2.59}$
2. Transfer Learning + Task-Specific Fine Tuning								
Hing-mBERT (Nayak and Joshi, 2022a)	64.5$_{2.22}$	65.3$_{1.57}$	65.2$_{1.65}$	65.2$_{1.65}$	65.1$_{1.74}$	66.4$_{0.64}$	65.4$_{2.19}$	65.4$_{2.19}$
Hing-Roberta (Nayak and Joshi, 2022a)	64.10$_{0.30}$	64.5$_{0.56}$	64.4$_{0.24}$	64.4$_{0.24}$	63.9$_{1.25}$	65.0$_{0.81}$	64.1$_{1.46}$	64.1$_{1.46}$
GCM-XLMR (Kodali et al., 2024)	61.63$_{2.00}$	63.2$_{2.12}$	63.9$_{1.59}$	63.9$_{1.59}$	60.1$_{1.27}$	62.2$_{0.69}$	62.6$_{0.63}$	62.6$_{0.63}$
GCM-mBERT (Kodali et al., 2024)	62.63$_{1.22}$	63.0$_{1.56}$	62.8$_{0.71}$	62.8$_{0.71}$	61.3$_{0.70}$	61.7$_{0.98}$	61.3$_{0.48}$	61.3$_{0.48}$
ACL-XLMR (Das et al., 2023)	64.01$_{0.79}$	64.2$_{0.43}$	64.9$_{0.52}$	64.9$_{0.52}$	63.3$_{2.05}$	63.8$_{2.11}$	64.5$_{2.15}$	64.5$_{2.15}$
ACL-mBERT (Das et al., 2023)	59.97$_{3.65}$	60.4$_{3.43}$	61.6$_{3.02}$	61.6$_{3.02}$	61.3$_{2.55}$	61.7$_{2.23}$	62.6$_{1.46}$	62.6$_{1.46}$
3. NLI-Based Models								
BART-large-nli (Lewis et al., 2020)	64.90$_{1.42}$	65.5$_{1.79}$	66.2$_{1.95}$	66.2$_{1.95}$	62.0$_{1.92}$	62.5$_{2.11}$	63.6$_{2.28}$	63.6$_{2.28}$
roberta-large-nli (Liu et al., 2019)	62.73$_{2.29}$	62.7$_{2.40}$	63.3$_{2.76}$	63.3$_{2.76}$	63.1$_{1.59}$	63.1$_{1.65}$	63.6$_{1.27}$	63.6$_{1.27}$
4. Few-Shot Learning								
IndicBART (Dabre et al., 2022)	54.5$_{1.71}$	54.5$_{1.71}$	55.8$_{1.78}$	55.8$_{1.78}$	53.6$_{1.69}$	53.1$_{1.65}$	53.9$_{1.70}$	53.9$_{1.70}$
mBART (Liu et al., 2020)	55.5$_{1.81}$	55.2$_{1.74}$	54.3$_{1.73}$	54.3$_{1.73}$	54.3$_{1.73}$	54.0$_{1.71}$	54.6$_{1.74}$	54.6$_{1.74}$
Llama-3.2-1B (Touvron et al., 2023)	50.5$_{2.09}$	50.1$_{2.46}$	53.5$_{2.09}$	53.5$_{2.09}$	51.5$_{2.98}$	52.2$_{1.85}$	56.5$_{1.89}$	56.5$_{1.89}$
Airavata (Gala et al., 2024)	51.9$_{2.79}$	51.8$_{4.27}$	56.7$_{2.41}$	56.7$_{2.41}$	60.5$_{3.11}$	60.7$_{2.36}$	61.1$_{2.34}$	61.1$_{2.34}$

Table 4: Performance comparison of different models for pun detection, grouped by model type. Class Weighted Metrics (F1, Precision, Recall, Accuracy) are presented for both Validation and Test datasets, with subscripts indicating standard deviation.

Unacceptable" to "Definitely Acceptable and Very Fluent." Ensuring linguistic coherence and readability is critical particularly in the context of code-mixed text.

To ensure the reliability and consistency of the annotations, inter-annotator agreement was measured using Fleiss Kappa coefficient(Fleiss and Cohen, 1973)($\kappa = 0.487$), suggesting moderate agreement. We also calculated the Average Pair Wise Percentage Agreement to be 72.2% which shows a high degree of agreement.

5.2 Pun Generation Evaluation

In Section 4.2 we described various methods to generate Hindi-English code-mixed puns. To understand which methods fare well in generating good puns we evaluated the generated puns using three quantitative metrics: (1) Success Percentage (Percentage of successful puns generated by the method), (2) Mean Funniness Score (out of 5), and (3) Mean Acceptability Score (out of 5), as shown in Table 3.

The **Baseline** method exhibited the lowest performance, achieving a Success Percentage of 19.8% and a Mean Funniness Score of 2.17, frequently failing to effectively utilize the pun-alternate word pair and often producing nonsensical outputs. The **Question-Answer** method achieved the highest Success Percentage (62.6%) and Mean Funniness Score (2.59), due to its structured question-answer format, which naturally highlights wordplay and humor while maintaining contextual relevance. The **Subject-Masked** method scored highest in Acceptability (4.54) by ensuring contextual coherence through subject adjustment, but achieved a lower Success Percentage (43%) as it sometimes constrained humor to only the subject and pun word. The **Contextually Aligned** method, which required generating sentences with two specific words, faced complexity in maintaining coherence, leading to lower Success (38.8%) and Acceptability (4.32) scores.

Overall, our proposed methods significantly outperformed the baseline, with structured approaches like Question-Answer excelling in humor generation, while methods such as Subject-Masked, achieved superior grammatical coherence.

6 Pun Detection

Having created the dataset, we wanted to evaluate if language models can be trained to detect code-mixed pun sentences. To this end, we trained various pre-trained multilingual language models. The annotated dataset was split into training (70%), development (20%), and test (10%) sets. Each model was evaluated using standard class-weighted metrics (F1 score, precision, recall, and accuracy).

6.1 Models and Methodologies

Four principal methodologies were applied for pun detection:

- **Task-specific Fine-tuning for Encoder-based Models:** Encoder-based models, such as XLM-R and mBERT, were fine-tuned specifically for the pun detection task, leveraging their pre-trained multilingual features to distinguish pun structures effectively.

- **Transfer Learning + Task-Specific Fine-tuning:** Encoder-based models continued pre-trained on large scale code-mixed corpora presented by Nayak and Joshi, 2022b (Hing models), Das et al., 2023 (ACL Models) and Kodali et al., 2024 (GCM models) were further fine-tuned for pun detection. This approach aimed to transfer relevant linguistic and contextual knowledge to enhance the detection of code-mixed puns.

- **Natural Language Inference (NLI) for NLI-based Models:** NLI-based models, including BART-nli, were assessed for their capacity to produce sentence embeddings, which may help capture semantic nuances crucial for understanding puns, especially in code-mixed contexts.

- **Few-shot Learning for Decoder and Encoder-Decoder Models:** Both decoder-only models (e.g., Airavata, LLaMA) and encoder-decoder models (e.g., IndicBART, mBART) were employed using few-shot learning to detect puns, leveraging minimal labeled data and generative capabilities.

6.2 Performance Evaluation

Model performances were evaluated on both development and test sets, with results presented in Table 4. Each model was evaluated three times on shuffled datasets constructed from 3 random seeds, and the scores were averaged with standard deviations shown as subscripts.

The **Task-Specific Fine-tuning** approach demonstrated superior performance across most metrics, with XLM-R achieving the highest F1 scores and accuracy on both validation (67.8%) and test sets (67.1%). Transfer learning combined with task-specific fine-tuning also produced competitive results, particularly for Hing-mBERT, which achieved an F1 score of 64.5% on the validation set and 65.1% on the test set.

For NLI-based models, BART-large-nli outperformed other models in this category, with a validation F1 score of 64.9%. However, it fell slightly short on the test set (62.0%). Few-shot learning approaches, while effective in resource-scarce settings, exhibited comparatively lower performance.

7 Automating Code-Mixed Pun Generation

Methods outlined in Section 4.2 are effective for producing code-mixed puns. However, a constraint is that the procedure presumes that phonetically similar word pairs have already been identified and compiled. Such a constraint might limit the extension of this approach to additional code-mixed language pairs or multilingual contexts. Hence, to further refine and partially automate the pun generation process, we propose a pipeline that generates code-mixed Hindi-English puns given only an input Hindi pun word. This pipeline comprises three key stages: (1) Selection of phonetically similar English candidates, (2) Compatibility scoring of pun-alternate word pairs, and (3) Sentence generation and filtering.

7.1 Phonetically Similar Word Selection

The pipeline begins by identifying English words phonetically similar to the input Hindi pun word P_w, as detailed in Section 4.1. Using the custom phonetic edit distance metric described, the model retrieves the top 5 English candidates from a large-scale lexicon, selecting those with the lowest scores. This ensures that the alternate words A_w are phonetically aligned with P_w, enabling the generation of natural and contextually humorous puns.

7.2 Training a Compatibility Scoring Model

The next stage involves identifying the most compatible English alternate word A_w for a given Hindi pun word P_w. To do this we trained a scoring model to compute a *compatibility score* for pun-alternate word pairs. We trained the scoring model on the 500 pairs obtained in Section 4.1 where the *compatibility score* ranged from 0 to 4 indicating the number of methods from section 4.2 that were successful in generating a pun for a given pair.

The compatibility model employs a feature set that includes:

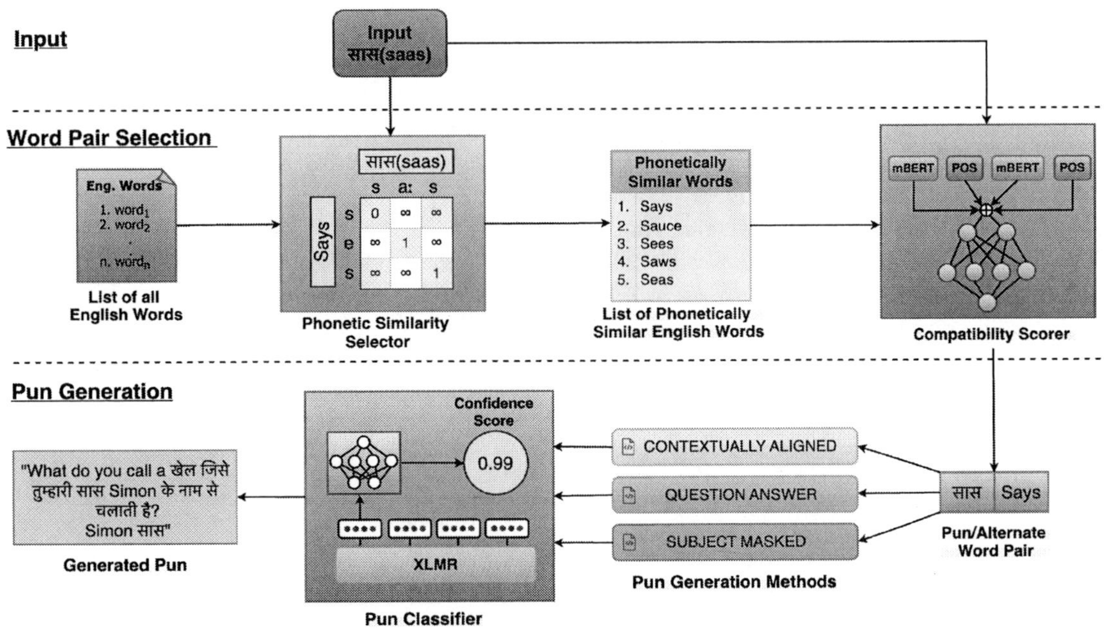

Figure 1: Overview of the proposed code-mixed pun generation pipeline, comprising of: (1) Word Pair Selection, which identifies phonetically similar English candidates for the input Hindi pun word and selects the most compatible pair (2) Pun Generation, which creates, filters, and selects the most contextually humorous sentence

- **BERT Embedding:** Contextualized word embeddings for both P_w and A_w, capturing semantic relationships essential for humor.
- **POS Compatibility:** Part-of-speech tags encoded as one-hot vectors, based on the universal POS tag set.

The outputs for the two words are concatenated and fed into a neural regression model with two hidden layers (dimensions: 512 and 256) optimized for mean squared error (MSE). This model evaluates compatibility scores to identify the most suitable English alternate word (A_w) to serve as the pun counterpart for P_w.

7.3 Sentence Generation and Filtering

Once a compatible word pair (P_w, A_w) is identified, we generate candidate sentences incorporating this pair using the methods described in Section 4.2. After generation, the candidate sentences undergo a filtering process to select the most effective pun. Specifically, we use the XLM-R model, trained on the pun classification task from section 6, to assign a confidence score to each candidate sentence, with the sentence receiving the highest confidence score chosen as the final pun candidate.

7.4 Evaluation

To assess the efficacy of our pun generation pipeline, we compared it with a baseline model in which GPT-4o is prompted directly to generate a pun using only the given pun word P_w, without additional contextual constraints. The outputs of our proposed pipeline and the baseline were directly compared in a human evaluation, where the annotators were asked to rate the funniness of each output and determine which sentence was the better pun overall.

Model	Win Rate (%)	Avg. Funniness
Proposed Model	67.65	1.79
Baseline Model	32.35	0.91

Table 5: Human evaluation results comparing the proposed pipeline with the baseline model. Average Funniness was rated out of 5.

As shown in Table 5, human evaluation demonstrates that the proposed pipeline significantly outperformed the baseline, achieving a win rate of 67.65% over 50 evaluated samples. The win rate (W_{rate}) is calculated as:

$$W_{\text{rate}} = \frac{N_{\text{model}}}{N_{\text{pun}}} \times 100$$

Where N_{model} represents the number of instances where the model's output was preferred, and N_{pun} denotes the total instances where at least one model produced a valid pun. The baseline struggles to generate quality puns even when constrained to a single pun word and often produces sentences where the pun word is not used as a pun. In contrast, our method consistently avoids such errors, ensuring humor and contextual coherence in Hindi-English code-mixed puns, further highlighting the utility of HECoP.

8 Conclusion and Future Work

This study proposed a structured approach for generating Hindi-English code-mixed puns by leveraging phonetic similarity matching between Hindi and English words. These pairs were integrated into structured sentence generation techniques, such as context-aligned, question-answer, and subject-masked prompts, embedding humor naturally in code-mixed contexts.

For pun detection, we evaluated multiple models, with encoder-based approaches like XLM-R and mBERT performing strongly, highlighting the effectiveness of fine-tuning for humor recognition. Additionally, our automated pun generation pipeline, combining phonetic matching, compatibility scoring, and sentence filtering, produced contextually relevant puns. Human evaluation confirmed that this approach significantly outperformed the baseline, demonstrating its potential for high-quality code-mixed pun generation.

Future work could explore expanding the dataset to cover additional code-mixed language pairs and incorporating advanced multilingual LLMs to further enhance pun quality and detection performance.

Limitations

The reliance on robust models like GPT-4o may be less effective for low-resource languages, and adapting the approach to other language pairs could be challenging due to issues like unavailable phonetic transcriptions or script-to-IPA mappings. Additionally, our focus on specific pun techniques does not cover subword-level puns or more complex wordplay.

References

Try Agustini and Ruli Manurung. 2012. Automatic evaluation of punning riddle template extraction. In *International Conference on Innovative Computing and Cloud Computing*.

Tafseer Ahmed, Muhammad Nizami, Muhammad Yaseen Khan, and Alessandro Bogliolo. 2021. Discovering lexical similarity using articulatory feature-based phonetic edit distance. *IEEE Access*, 10:1533 – 1544.

Kim Binsted and Graeme D. Ritchie. 1994. An implemented model of punning riddles. *ArXiv*, abs/cmp-lg/9406022.

Turkay Bulut and Najah A. Almabrouk. 2020. The functions of puns in "alice's adventures in wonderland". *The Reading Matrix : an International Online Journal*, 20:172–185.

Intan Nur Charina. 2017. Lexical and syntactic ambiguity in humor. *International Journal of Humanity Studies (IJHS)*.

Alexis Conneau, Kartikay Khandelwal, Naman Goyal, Vishrav Chaudhary, Guillaume Wenzek, Francisco Guzmán, Edouard Grave, Myle Ott, Luke Zettlemoyer, and Veselin Stoyanov. 2020. Unsupervised cross-lingual representation learning at scale. *Preprint*, arXiv:1911.02116.

Raj Dabre, Himani Shrotriya, Anoop Kunchukuttan, Ratish Puduppully, Mitesh Khapra, and Pratyush Kumar. 2022. Indicbart: A pre-trained model for indic natural language generation. In *Findings of the Association for Computational Linguistics: ACL 2022*. Association for Computational Linguistics.

Richeek Das, Sahasra Ranjan, Shreya Pathak, and Preethi Jyothi. 2023. Improving pretraining techniques for code-switched NLP. In *Proceedings of the 61st Annual Meeting of the Association for Computational Linguistics (Volume 1: Long Papers)*, pages 1176–1191, Toronto, Canada. Association for Computational Linguistics.

Jacob Devlin, Ming-Wei Chang, Kenton Lee, and Kristina Toutanova. 2019. Bert: Pre-training of deep bidirectional transformers for language understanding. *Preprint*, arXiv:1810.04805.

Joseph L. Fleiss and Jacob Cohen. 1973. The equivalence of weighted kappa and the intraclass correlation coefficient as measures of reliability. *Educational and Psychological Measurement*, 33(3):613–619.

Jay Gala, Thanmay Jayakumar, Jaavid Aktar Husain, Aswanth Kumar M, Mohammed Safi Ur Rahman Khan, Diptesh Kanojia, Ratish Puduppully, Mitesh M. Khapra, Raj Dabre, Rudra Murthy, and Anoop Kunchukuttan. 2024. Airavata: Introducing hindi instruction-tuned llm. *Preprint*, arXiv:2401.15006.

Dirk Goldhahn, Thomas Eckart, and Uwe Quasthoff. 2012. Building large monolingual dictionaries at the Leipzig corpora collection: From 100 to 200 languages. In *Proceedings of the Eighth International Conference on Language Resources and Evaluation*

(LREC'12), pages 759–765, Istanbul, Turkey. European Language Resources Association (ELRA).

Marina Borisovna Grolman, Zubayda Albertovna, Biktagirova, Olimjon Habibovich, and Kasimov. 2021. Phonetic peculiarities of the english language in india.

Deepak Gupta, Asif Ekbal, and Pushpak Bhattacharyya. 2020. A semi-supervised approach to generate the code-mixed text using pre-trained encoder and transfer learning. In *Findings of the Association for Computational Linguistics: EMNLP 2020*, pages 2267–2280, Online. Association for Computational Linguistics.

Deepak Gupta, Pabitra Lenka, Asif Ekbal, and Pushpak Bhattacharyya. 2018. Uncovering code-mixed challenges: A framework for linguistically driven question generation and neural based question answering. In *Proceedings of the 22nd Conference on Computational Natural Language Learning*, pages 119–130, Brussels, Belgium. Association for Computational Linguistics.

He He, Nanyun Peng, and Percy Liang. 2019a. Pun generation with surprise. In *North American Chapter of the Association for Computational Linguistics*.

He He, Nanyun Peng, and Percy Liang. 2019b. Pun generation with surprise. In *Proceedings of the 2019 Conference of the North American Chapter of the Association for Computational Linguistics: Human Language Technologies, Volume 1 (Long and Short Papers)*, pages 1734–1744, Minneapolis, Minnesota. Association for Computational Linguistics.

Bryan Anthony Hong and Ethel Ong. 2008. Generating punning riddles from examples. *2008 Second International Symposium on Universal Communication*, pages 347–352.

Aaron Jaech, Rik Koncel-Kedziorski, and Mari Ostendorf. 2016. Phonological pun-derstanding. pages 654–663.

Shelly Jain, Aditya Yadavalli, Ganesh Mirishkar, Chiranjeevi Yarra, and Anil Kumar Vuppala. 2021. IE-CPS lexicon: An automatic speech recognition oriented Indian-English pronunciation dictionary. In *Proceedings of the 18th International Conference on Natural Language Processing (ICON)*, pages 195–204, National Institute of Technology Silchar, Silchar, India. NLP Association of India (NLPAI).

Divyanshu Kakwani, Anoop Kunchukuttan, Satish Golla, Gokul N.C., Avik Bhattacharyya, Mitesh M. Khapra, and Pratyush Kumar. 2020. IndicNLPSuite: Monolingual corpora, evaluation benchmarks and pre-trained multilingual language models for Indian languages. In *Findings of the Association for Computational Linguistics: EMNLP 2020*, pages 4948–4961, Online. Association for Computational Linguistics.

Simran Khanuja, Sandipan Dandapat, Anirudh Srinivasan, Sunayana Sitaram, and Monojit Choudhury. 2020. GLUECoS: An evaluation benchmark for code-switched NLP. In *Proceedings of the 58th Annual Meeting of the Association for Computational Linguistics*, pages 3575–3585, Online. Association for Computational Linguistics.

Prashant Kodali, Anmol Goel, Likhith Asapu, Vamshi Krishna Bonagiri, Anirudh Govil, Monojit Choudhury, Manish Shrivastava, and Ponnurangam Kumaraguru. 2024. From human judgements to predictive models: Unravelling acceptability in code-mixed sentences. *Preprint*, arXiv:2405.05572.

Jan Korák. 2011. Word play in advertising: A linguistic analysis.

Mike Lewis, Yinhan Liu, Naman Goyal, Marjan Ghazvininejad, Abdelrahman Mohamed, Omer Levy, Veselin Stoyanov, and Luke Zettlemoyer. 2020. BART: Denoising sequence-to-sequence pre-training for natural language generation, translation, and comprehension. In *Proceedings of the 58th Annual Meeting of the Association for Computational Linguistics*, pages 7871–7880, Online. Association for Computational Linguistics.

Yinhan Liu, Jiatao Gu, Naman Goyal, Xian Li, Sergey Edunov, Marjan Ghazvininejad, Mike Lewis, and Luke Zettlemoyer. 2020. Multilingual denoising pretraining for neural machine translation. *Transactions of the Association for Computational Linguistics*, 8:726–742.

Yinhan Liu, Myle Ott, Naman Goyal, Jingfei Du, Mandar Joshi, Danqi Chen, Omer Levy, Mike Lewis, Luke Zettlemoyer, and Veselin Stoyanov. 2019. Roberta: A robustly optimized bert pretraining approach. *Preprint*, arXiv:1907.11692.

Fuli Luo, Shunyao Li, Pengcheng Yang, Lei Li, Baobao Chang, Zhifang Sui, and Xu Sun. 2019. Pun-gan: Generative adversarial network for pun generation. In *Conference on Empirical Methods in Natural Language Processing*.

Tristan Miller, Christian Hempelmann, and Iryna Gurevych. 2017. SemEval-2017 task 7: Detection and interpretation of English puns. In *Proceedings of the 11th International Workshop on Semantic Evaluation (SemEval-2017)*, pages 58–68, Vancouver, Canada. Association for Computational Linguistics.

Anirudh Mittal, Yufei Tian, and Nanyun Peng. 2022. AmbiPun: Generating humorous puns with ambiguous context. In *Proceedings of the 2022 Conference of the North American Chapter of the Association for Computational Linguistics: Human Language Technologies*, pages 1053–1062, Seattle, United States. Association for Computational Linguistics.

David R. Mortensen, Siddharth Dalmia, and Patrick Littell. 2018. Epitran: Precision G2P for many languages. In *Proceedings of the Eleventh International Conference on Language Resources and Evaluation*

(LREC 2018), Miyazaki, Japan. European Language Resources Association (ELRA).

Ravindra Nayak and Raviraj Joshi. 2022a. L3cube-hingcorpus and hingbert: A code mixed hindi-english dataset and bert language models. *Preprint*, arXiv:2204.08398.

Ravindra Nayak and Raviraj Joshi. 2022b. L3cube-hingcorpus and hingbert: A code mixed hindi-english dataset and bert language models. *ArXiv*, abs/2204.08398.

Slav Petrov, Dipanjan Das, and Ryan T. McDonald. 2011. A universal part-of-speech tagset. *ArXiv*, abs/1104.2086.

Dafna Shahaf, Eric Horvitz, and Robert Mankoff. 2015. Inside jokes: Identifying humorous cartoon captions. *Proceedings of the 21th ACM SIGKDD International Conference on Knowledge Discovery and Data Mining*.

L. Shanaieva-Tsymbal. 2021. A persuasive force of puns in british advertising. *Mìnarodnij fìlologìnij asopis*.

Jiao Sun, Anjali Narayan-Chen, Shereen Oraby, Shuyang Gao, Tagyoung Chung, Jing huan Huang, Yang Liu, and Nanyun Peng. 2022. Context-situated pun generation. *ArXiv*, abs/2210.13522.

Yufei Tian, Divyanshu Sheth, and Nanyun Peng. 2022. A unified framework for pun generation with humor principles. In *Findings of the Association for Computational Linguistics: EMNLP 2022*, pages 3253–3261, Abu Dhabi, United Arab Emirates. Association for Computational Linguistics.

Hugo Touvron, Thibaut Lavril, Gautier Izacard, Xavier Martinet, Marie-Anne Lachaux, Timothée Lacroix, Baptiste Rozière, Naman Goyal, Eric Hambro, Faisal Azhar, Aurelien Rodriguez, Armand Joulin, Edouard Grave, and Guillaume Lample. 2023. Llama: Open and efficient foundation language models. *Preprint*, arXiv:2302.13971.

María José García Viscaíno. 2011. Humor in code-mixed airline advertising. *Pragmatics*, 21:145–170.

Aya Williams, Mahesh Srinivasan, Chang Liu, Pearl Lee, and Qing Zhou. 2019. Why do bilinguals code-switch when emotional? insights from immigrant parent-child interactions. *Emotion*, 20(5):830–841.

Thomas Wolf, Lysandre Debut, Victor Sanh, Julien Chaumond, Clement Delangue, Anthony Moi, Pierric Cistac, Tim Rault, Rémi Louf, Morgan Funtowicz, Joe Davison, Sam Shleifer, Patrick von Platen, Clara Ma, Yacine Jernite, Julien Plu, Canwen Xu, Teven Le Scao, Sylvain Gugger, Mariama Drame, Quentin Lhoest, and Alexander M. Rush. 2020. Huggingface's transformers: State-of-the-art natural language processing. *Preprint*, arXiv:1910.03771.

Zhiwei Yu, Jiwei Tan, and Xiaojun Wan. 2018. A neural approach to pun generation. In *Proceedings of the 56th Annual Meeting of the Association for Computational Linguistics (Volume 1: Long Papers)*, pages 1650–1660, Melbourne, Australia. Association for Computational Linguistics.

Jingjie Zeng, Liang Yang, Jiahao Kang, Yufeng Diao, Zhihao Yang, and Hongfei Lin. 2024. barking up the right tree, a gan-based pun generation model through semantic pruning. In *International Conference on Language Resources and Evaluation*.

Yichao Zhou, Jyun-Yu Jiang, Jieyu Zhao, Kai-Wei Chang, and Wei Wang. 2020. "the boating store had its best sail ever": Pronunciation-attentive contextualized pun recognition. In *Proceedings of the 58th Annual Meeting of the Association for Computational Linguistics*, pages 813–822, Online. Association for Computational Linguistics.

A Phonetic Substitution Rules

The phonetic substitutions outlined in the three tables *American English to Indian English Substitution Table*, *Vowel Substitution Table* and *Consonant Substitution Table* were integral to the methodology described in Section 4.1. The phone pairs in the vowel and consonant table have a substitution cost of 0 as described in Section 4.1.

American English to Indian English The American English to Indian English Substitution Table (Table 6) addressed differences between American and Indian English phonologies. By converting American English IPA transcriptions into Indian English IPA symbols, which align more closely with Hindi phonology, this mapping enhanced the relevance of phonetic comparisons and ensured consistency with Indian English pronunciations.

Vowel Substitution The Vowel Substitution Table (Table 7) provided mappings for vowel variations based on shared phonetic features, such as vowel length distinctions, nasalization, and stress differences. These substitutions reduced mismatches caused by phonological variations across the two languages.

Consonant Substitution Finally, the Consonant Substitution Table (Table 8) accounted for variations in voicing and aspiration. Substitutions between voiced and unvoiced pairs (e.g., [p] and [b], [t] and [d]) and allophones (e.g., [t^h] and [t]) were assigned a substitution cost of 0. This approach allowed us to capture phonetically similar word pairs while respecting linguistic variations.

By integrating these substitution rules into the custom Levenshtein edit distance, we ensured a nuanced comparison of phonetic similarity, enabling the identification of Hindi-English word pairs suitable for pun generation.

B Implementation Details for Pun Generation Methods

The prompts and the examples of candidate sentences generated by each of the methods in Section 4.2 are given in Table 9 for Contextually Aligned Pun Generation (Section 4.2.1), Table 10 for Question-Answer Pun Generation (Section 10), Table 11 Subject-Masked Pun Generation (Section 4.2.3) and Table 12 for Baseline Pun Generation (Section 4.2.4). Refer to the System prompts in these tables to understand the pun generation process for Question-Answer and Subject-Masked Pun Generation.

For generating code-mixed text in all three methods, we initially experimented with several multilingual and code-mixed text generation models, including Airavata, LLaMA, Gemma, Gemini, and GPT-4o. Among the models evaluated, GPT-4o demonstrated superior performance in generating coherent and linguistically appropriate code-mixed text, making it the preferred choice for our experiments. This model was used for all pun generation methods in Section 4.2. The generation process used a temperature setting of 1.0 to balance creativity and coherence in the outputs.

C POS Tagger Details

To ensure grammatical consistency in our pun generation pipeline, we developed a Part-of-Speech (POS) tagger specifically tailored for Hindi-English code-mixed text. The tagger was trained on the GLUECoS benchmark dataset (Khanuja et al., 2020), which provides high-quality annotations for POS tagging in code-mixed language. For the model architecture, we employed a base XLM-RoBERTa (XLMR) model, leveraging its strong multilingual capabilities to handle the intricacies of code-mixed Hindi-English data.

The training process was conducted over five epochs, optimizing the model to recognize and classify tokens into the Universal POS tag set (Petrov et al., 2011). This tag set, with its standardized categories, ensures compatibility and consistency across linguistic resources. The trained model achieved an accuracy of 91% on the GLUECoS benchmark, demonstrating its effectiveness in accurately tagging code-mixed text.

D Annotation Guidelines

We include a screenshot of the annotation page (Figure 2) corresponding to the guidelines described in Section 5.1. Additionally, a screenshot of the annotation page (Figure 3) used for the evaluation process described in Section 7.4 is also provided.

E Pun Classifier Implementation Details

We fine-tuned multiple pre-trained multilingual language models for the task of detecting code-mixed pun sentences. The models employed in this study included XLM-R, mBERT, IndicBERT, natural language inference (NLI)-based models such as BART-large-nli and roberta-large-nli, as well as generation-based models like Airavata, LLaMA, and IndicBART. Model checkpoints were accessed and managed using the HuggingFace Transformers library (Wolf et al., 2020). All experiments were conducted using 4 NVIDIA GeForce RTX 2080 Ti GPUs to ensure computational efficiency.

Task-Specific Fine-Tuning For encoder-based models (e.g., XLM-R, mBERT, IndicBERT) and NLI-based models (e.g., BART-large-nli, roberta-large-nli), we fine-tuned the models using a batch size of 16 for training and 32 for evaluation. The training process involved a warmup phase of 500 steps, a weight decay rate of 0.01, and mixed-precision training (fp16) to optimize computational performance. Models were trained for 30 epochs, and the checkpoint with the highest accuracy on the development set was selected for inference on the test set.

Few-Shot Learning for Generative Models For decoder-only models (e.g., Airavata, LLaMA) and encoder-decoder models (e.g., IndicBART, mBART), we employed few-shot learning methodologies. The models were provided with prompts containing labeled examples as input. During inference, we utilized beam search with a beam size of 5, temperature sampling (temperature = 1.0), and nucleus sampling (top-p = 0.9) to generate predictions.

Dataset Splits and Evaluation Metrics The annotated dataset was divided into training (70%), development (20%), and test (10%) sets. Model performance was evaluated using class-weighted F1-score, precision, recall, and accuracy metrics. To address the class imbalance in the dataset, a weighted loss function was employed during training. Specifically, higher weights were assigned to the minority class (pun) by computing the weight as N_{notPun}/N_{pun}, where N_{pun} and N_{notPun} denote the number of samples in the pun and non-pun classes, respectively. Each model was evaluated on the dataset split using three different random seeds. The models were trained and tested three times, and the scores were averaged to ensure the robustness of the results. We report the mean and standard deviation of these scores in Table 4.

F Compatibility Scorer Implementation Details

The compatibility scoring model was trained to compute the *compatibility score* for pun-alternate word pairs, as detailed in Section 4.1. The training dataset comprised 500 pairs, annotated with scores ranging from 0 to 4, representing the number of methods from Section 4.2 that successfully generated a pun for the given pair.

Model Architecture The model's input features included contextualized embeddings for P_w and A_w, extracted using a pretrained BERT model. Additionally, part-of-speech (POS) tags for both P_w and A_w were encoded as one-hot vectors based on the universal POS tag set. The embeddings and POS features were concatenated into a single feature vector of size 1550 (775 dimensions for each word embedding - 768 from BERT and 7 for POS).

The neural architecture of the compatibility model consisted of two fully connected hidden layers. The first hidden layer contained 512 units, followed by a second hidden layer with 256 units, both employing ReLU activation functions. The final output layer was a single unit that predicted the compatibility score using a regression approach. Mean squared error (MSE) was used as the loss function to optimize the model's performance.

Training Hyperparameters Training was performed using a total of 100 epochs. An early stopping mechanism was employed with a patience of 5 epochs and a threshold of 0.001. The dataset was split into 90% training and 10% testing subsets, and the model was trained using the Adam optimizer with a batch size of 32.

Other Experimented Models We explored various feature representations and architectures to identify the optimal configuration for compatibility scoring. These included using BERT embeddings alone, combining static FastText word embeddings with POS tags, and employing a Siamese network architecture on BERT + POS embeddings. Among all approaches, the standard BERT + POS feature set achieved the best performance, with a minimum MSE loss of 0.82 on the validation set.

American English IPA	Indian English IPA
eɪ	eː
oʊ, ow	oː
ɑ	ɔ
ʌ	a
ð	d̪̤
ɛ	e
h	ɦ
i	iː
ɪ	i
ɹ	r
t	ʈ
θ	t^h
u	uː
ʊ	u
w	v
ŋ	ŋg

Table 6: American English to Indian English Substitutions.

Original IPA Vowel	Mapped IPA Vowel
ə, aː, ã, ãː, ɒ, ɒː, ʌ	a
æ, æː	ae
eː, ẽ, ɛ, ɛː	e
iː, ɪ, y	i
ɔː, ɔ, oː	o
ʊ, uː	u

Table 7: Vowels Mapping Table.

Original IPA	Mapped IPA
^{h}	.
ɦ	h
p	b
b̤	b
θ, t, ʈ	d
ð, ɖ, ɽ, d̤	d
k, q, x	ɡ
ɢ, ɣ, ɡ̤	ɡ
w, f	v
ʃ, ʒ̤	ʒ
d͡ʒ, d͡ʒ̤, t͡ʃ	ʒ
ɟ, ç	j
s	z
ɳ, ñ, ɲ, ŋ, ɴ	n
l, ɭ	l
ɾ, ɹ, ɻ, ɹ̩, ɾ̩	r

Table 8: Consonant Mapping Table. The first phone aspirated [^{h}] is mapped to an empty phone hence . is present in it place

Contextually Aligned Pun Generation	
Prompt for tuple (P_w, A_w, C_w)	Generate 5 creative Hindi-English code-mixed pun-style sentences ending with the english word '$\{A_w\}$'. Have the english word '$\{C_w\}$' as a context in each of these sentences. Ensure the word '$\{A_w\}$' occurs after the word '$\{C_w\}$'. Avoid providing English translations. Make sure to write the English words in roman script and Hindi words in Devanagari. Maintain a balanced 1:1 ratio between hindi and english words.
Prompt Examples for few shot generation	**User:** Generate 5 creative Hindi-English code-mixed pun-style sentences ending with the english word 'share'. Have the english word 'lion' as a context in each of these sentences. Ensure the word 'share' occurs after the word 'lion'. Avoid providing English translations. Make sure to write the English words in roman script and Hindi words in Devanagari. Maintain a balanced 1:1 ratio between hindi and english words. **Assistant:** 1. Jungle में lion का status high है, पर उसकी fame को भी एक अच्छा सा share चाहिए! 2. Lion अपने territory को protect करता है, लेकिन कभी–कभी उसको अपनी success का share भी देना पड़ता है. 3. अगर lion के साथ photo खिंचनी है, तो उसके साथ share भी करना पड़ेगा! 4. Lion की leadership को challenge करना है, तो उसका power share भी जरूरी है! 5. Lion की roar की आवाज सुनी है, तो उसका impact share करना भी तो पड़ेगा! **User:** Generate 5 creative Hindi-English code-mixed pun-style sentences ending with the english word 'bat'. Have the english word 'chair' as a context in each of these sentences. Ensure the word 'bat' occurs after the word 'chair'. Avoid providing English translations. Make sure to write the English words in roman script and Hindi words in Devanagari. Maintain a balanced 1:1 ratio between hindi and english words. **Assistant:** 1. उसने कहा, "When I have enough money in my pocket, it feels like my luck is always on my side." 2. मेरे friend ने मजाक में कहा, "Money can buy you almost everything, but you still need a bit of luck." 3. आजकल money की कमी तो सबको है, पर luck से सब कुछ मिलता है। 4. जितना भी invest करो, कभी न कभी तो मिलेगी तुम्हें money with a bit of luck! 5. अगर तुम्हारे पास money नहीं है, तो बस तुम्हें चाहिए थोड़ा सा luck! **User:** Generate 5 creative Hindi-English code-mixed pun-style sentences ending with the english word 'bat'. Have the english word 'chair' as a context in each of these sentences. Ensure the word 'bat' occurs after the word 'chair'. Avoid providing English translations. Make sure to write the English words in roman script and Hindi words in Devanagari. Maintain a balanced 1:1 ratio between hindi and english words. **Assistant:** 1. जब वह अपनी comfy chair पर बैठा, उसने सोचा, "I really need a better bat to improve my game." 2. उसने अपनी favorite chair पर बैठते हुए कहा, "This chair is perfect, but I could really use a new bat." 3. Chair पर आराम करते हुए उसने कहा, "Yaar, I wish I had a bat like that for my cricket matches." 4. उसने अपनी chair पर बैठते हुए कहा, "This chair is great for relaxing, but I'm missing a good bat." 5. जैसे ही वह chair से उठा, उसने अपने भाई से पूछा, "Have you seen my cricket bat around here? " **User:** Generate 5 creative Hindi-English code-mixed pun-style sentences ending with the english word 'book'. Have the english word 'hunger' as a context in each of these sentences. Ensure the word 'book' occurs after the word 'hunger'. Avoid providing English translations. Make sure to write the English words in roman script and Hindi words in Devanagari. Maintain a balanced 1:1 ratio between hindi and english words.

	Assistant: 1. जब भी late−night की hunger शुरू होती है, मैं तुरंत अपने favorite snack ideas book को open कर लेता हूँ। 2. Office के काम के बाद, जब hunger मुझसे मिलती है, तो मैं always अपनी comfort food recipe book देखता हूँ। 3. दिनभर की मेहनत के बाद, hunger से deal करने के लिए मैंने एक खास meal prep book खरीदी। 4. अगर weekend पर hunger strike करे, तो एक quick fixes की book मेरे पास हमेशा ready रहती है। 5. शाम की hunger को curb करने के लिए, मैंने recently एक new healthy eating book buy की है। **User:** Generate 5 creative Hindi-English code-mixed pun-style sentences ending with the english word 'deal'. Have the english word 'heart' as a context in each of these sentences. Ensure the word 'deal' occurs after the word 'heart'. Avoid providing English translations. Make sure to write the English words in roman script and Hindi words in Devanagari. Maintain a balanced 1:1 ratio between hindi and english words. **Assistant:** 1. जब भी late−night की hunger शुरू होती है, मैं तुरंत अपने favorite snack ideas book को open कर लेता हूँ। 2. Office के काम के बाद, जब hunger मुझसे मिलती है, तो मैं always अपनी comfort food recipe book देखता हूँ। 3. दिनभर की मेहनत के बाद, hunger से deal करने के लिए मैंने एक खास meal prep book खरीदी। 4. अगर weekend पर hunger strike करे, तो एक quick fixes की book मेरे पास हमेशा ready रहती है। 5. शाम की hunger को curb करने के लिए, मैंने recently एक new healthy eating book buy की है।
Example Pun Filtering Process for $(P_w, A_w, C_w) =$ (डेढ़, dead, one and a half)	**Prompt:** Generate 5 creative Hindi-English code-mixed pun-style sentences ending with the english word 'dead'. Have the english word 'one and a half' as a context in each of these sentences. Ensure the word 'dead' occurs after the word 'one and a half'. Avoid providing English translations. Make sure to write the English words in roman script and Hindi words in Devanagari. Maintain a balanced 1:1 ratio between hindi and english words. **Response after POS filtering:** "उसने one and a half ghante सोच समझकर नया laptop खरीदा, और वो बाद में एक और आधा डेढ़ हो गया।", "मैने one and a half litre दूध ख़रीदा, but when i opened it, it was already डेढ़.", "उसने one and a half ghante तक चिंता की, और फिर पता चला कि उसका plan पहले ही डेढ़ हो गया था।" **Pun:** मैने one and a half litre दूध ख़रीदा, but when i opened it, it was already डेढ़. **Rating:** 4 - Quite Funny

Table 9: Example prompts for few shot learning and Example filtering process for the Contextually Aligned Pun Generation Process, demonstrating the steps for generating Hindi-English code-mixed puns using a combination of pun words, alternate words, and contextual meanings as outlined in Section 4.2.1.

Question-Answer Pun Generation

System Prompt	Follow these steps to generate a pun: First generate a very short phrase(which can be a response to questions such as Noun Phrase) with the given alternate word. For example if the alternate word is 'guy' the generated sentence is "A cool guy". Then replace the alternate word with the pun word. For example if the pun word is 'गाय' the new sentence would become "A cool गाय". Then generate a pun question for this "What do you call a cow wearing sunglasses?". Write it in the below format ill give pairs of pun words and alternate word Generated Small Phrase: A cool guy Replace Pun Word: A cool गाय Generated Question: What do you call a cow wearing sunglasses? Generated Translated Question: What do you call a cow जो sunglasses पहनती है?
Prompt for tuple (P_w, A_w, C_w)	The pair is Pun Word = '$\{P_w\}$'(meaning $\{C_w\}$) and Alternate Word = '$\{A_w\}$'
Prompt Examples for few shot generation	**User:** The pair is Pun Word = 'लाख'(meaning lakh) and Alternate Word = luck **Assistant:** Generated Small Phrase: A stroke of luck Replace Pun Word: A stroke of लाख Generated Question: What do you call a huge fortune that strikes suddenly? Generated Translated Question: What do you call a huge fortune जो suddenly हासिल होता हे? Pun: What do you call a huge fortune जो suddenly हासिल होता हे? A stroke of लाख **User:** The pair is Pun Word = 'पीपल'(meaning tree) and Alternate Word = people **Assistant:** Generated Small Phrase: A group of people Replace Pun Word: A group of पीपल Generated Question: What do you call a gathering under a sacred tree? Generated Translated Question: What do you call a समूह under a sacred पेड़? Pun: What do you call a समूह under a sacred पेड़? A group of पीपल **User:** The pair is Pun Word = 'बिक'(meaning sold) and Alternate Word = big **Assistant:** Generated Small Phrase: A big sale Replace Pun Word: A बिक sale Generated Question: What do you call a huge sale where everything is sold out? Generated Translated Question: What do you call a huge sale जहां सब कुछ बिक जाता है? Pun: What do you call a huge sale where everything is sold out? A बिक sale **User:** The pair is Pun Word = 'वन'(meaning Forest) and Alternate Word = won **Assistant:** Generated Small Phrase: He won the game Replace Pun Word: He वन the game Generated Question: What do you call it when someone conquers a forest in a game? Generated Translated Question: What do you call it जब कोई खेल में जंगल conquer करता है? Pun: What do you call it जब कोई खेल में जंगल conquer करता है? He वन the game **User:**The pair is Pun Word = 'धन'(meaning money) and Alternate Word = done

	Assistant: Generated Small Phrase: All done Replace Pun Word: All धन Generated Question: What do you call it when you've earning making a lot of money? Generated Translated Question: What do you call it जब तुमने बोहोत सारा पैसे कमा लिया हो? Pun: What do you call it जब तुमने बोहोत सारा पैसे कमा लिया हो? All धन
Example Pun Filtering Process for $(P_w, A_w, C_w) =$ **(खो, co, lost)**	**Prompt:** The pair is Pun Word = 'खो'(meaning lost) and Alternate Word = co **Response:** Generated Small Phrase: Co-worker Replace Pun Word: खो-worker Generated Question: What do you call a colleague who is often hard to find? Generated Translated Question: What do you call a सहकर्मी जो अक्सर ढूँढने में मुश्किल होता है? **Pun:** What do you call a सहकर्मी जो अक्सर ढूँढने में मुश्किल होता है? A खो-worker **Rating:** 5 - Hilarious

Table 10: System Prompt, Generic Prompt Template, Example prompts for few shot learning, and Example filtering process for the Question-Answer Pun Generation method, demonstrating the steps for generating Hindi-English code-mixed puns using a combination of pun words, alternate words, and contextual meanings as outlined in Section 4.2.2.

Subject-Masked Pun Generation

System Prompt	Given a pair of pun words and alternate words use the following steps to generate a Hindi-English codemixed pun. First generate a short sentence ending with the alternate word. Then replace the alternate word with the pun word. Then replace the subject of the sentence to add relevance to the pun. Then translate the subject to codemixed Hindi-English version. Example: The pair is Pun Word = 'लाख'(meaning lakh) and Alternate Word = luck Short Sentence: The man attributed all his success to luck Replace Alternate Word: The man attributed all his success to लाख Mask the Subject: [MASK] attributed all his success to लाख Pun Sentence: The lucky rich businessman attributed all his success to लाख Translated Sentence: The lucky अमीर businessman attributed all his सफलता to लाख.
Prompt for tuple (P_w, A_w, C_w)	The pair is Pun Word = '$\{P_w\}$'(meaning $\{C_w\}$) and Alternate Word = '$\{A_w\}$'
Prompt Examples for few shot generation	**User:** The pair is Pun Word = 'बिक'(meaning sold) and Alternate Word = big **Assistant:** Generated Small Phrase: The event was a big success. Replace Pun Word: The event was a बिक success. Mask the Subject: [MASK] was a बिक success. Pun Sentence: The sold-out concert was a बिक success. Translated Sentence: The sold-out संगीत सभा was a बिक success. **User:** The pair is Pun Word = 'सच'(meaning truth) and Alternate Word = such **Assistant:** Generated Small Phrase: She was never faced with such challenges before. Replace Pun Word: She was never faced with सच challenges before. Mask the Subject: [MASK] was never faced with सच challenges before. Pun Sentence: The dishonest lawyer was never faced with सच challenges before. Translated Sentence: The dishonest वकील was never faced with सच challenges before. **User:** The pair is Pun Word = 'पीपल'(meaning tree) and Alternate Word = people **Assistant:** Generated Small Phrase: The park was filled with people enjoying the evening. Replace Pun Word: The park was filled with पीपल enjoying the evening. Mask the Subject: [MASK] was filled with पीपल enjoying the evening. Pun Sentence: The forest was filled with पीपल enjoying the evening. Translated Sentence: The जंगल was filled with पीपल enjoying the evening. **User:** The pair is Pun Word = 'पीपल'(meaning tree) and Alternate Word = people **Assistant:** Generated Small Phrase: The park was filled with people enjoying the evening. Replace Pun Word: The park was filled with पीपल enjoying the evening. Mask the Subject: [MASK] was filled with पीपल enjoying the evening. Pun Sentence: The forest was filled with पीपल enjoying the evening. Translated Sentence: The जंगल was filled with पीपल enjoying the evening.

Example Pun Filtering Process for $(P_w, A_w, C_w) =$ (दौरा,dora, seizure)	**Prompt:** The pair is Pun Word = 'दौरा'(meaning seizure) and Alternate Word = dora **Response:** Short Sentence: The child loves watching Dora the Explorer. Replace Alternate Word: The child loves watching दौरा the Explorer. Mask the Subject: [MASK] loves watching दौरा the Explorer. Pun Sentence: The अस्पताल के मरीज loves watching दौरा the Explorer. **Pun:** The अस्पताल के मरीज loves watching दौरा the Explorer. **Rating:** 5 - Hilarious

Table 11: System Prompts, Generic Prompt Template, Example prompts for few shot learning, and Example filtering process for the Subject-Masked Pun Generation method, demonstrating the steps for generating Hindi-English code-mixed puns using a combination of pun words, alternate words, and contextual meanings as outlined in Section 4.2.3.

Baseline Pun Generation	
Prompt for tuple (P_w, A_w, C_w)	Generate a hinglish pun where the pun word is the hindi word '$\{P_w\}$' and the alternate word is english word '$\{A_w\}$'. Maintain a balanced ratio between english and hindi words. Make sure to write the English words in roman script and Hindi words in Devanagari.
Prompt Examples for Few-Shot Generation	**User:** Generate a hinglish pun where the pun word is the hindi word 'ढाई' and the alternate word is english word 'die'. Maintain a balanced ratio between english and hindi words. Make sure to write the English words in roman script and Hindi words in Devanagari. . **Assistant:** मेरा watch 2 and 2.30 के बीच stuck है. It's a do or ढाई situation. **User:** Generate a hinglish pun where the pun word is the hindi word 'दूध' and the alternate word is english word 'dude'. Maintain a balanced ratio between english and hindi words. Make sure to write the English words in roman script and Hindi words in Devanagari. . **Assistant:** American milk ने Indian milk से क्या कहा? "What's up दूध? " **User:** Generate a hinglish pun where the pun word is the hindi word 'बेटा' and the alternate word is english word 'beta'. Maintain a balanced ratio between english and hindi words. Make sure to write the English words in roman script and Hindi words in Devanagari. **Assistant:** A daughter is the perfect child. A son is just a बेटा version. **User:** Generate a hinglish pun where the pun word is the hindi word 'स्नान' and the alternate word is english word 'none'. Maintain a balanced ratio between english and hindi words. Make sure to write the English words in roman script and Hindi words in Devanagari. **Assistant:** I really don't care कि कौन प्रतिदिन bath करता है I...Its स्नान of my business...
Example Puns Filtering Process for (P_w, A_w, C_w) = (वन, one, forest)	**Prompt** Generate a hinglish pun where the pun word is the hindi word 'वन' and the alternate word is english word 'one'. Maintain a balanced ratio between english and hindi words. Make sure to write the English words in roman script and Hindi words in Devanagari. **Pun:** Why did the tree go to therapy? Because it had too many वन–sided conversations. **Rating:** 5 - Hilarious

Table 12: Generic Prompt Template, Example prompts for few-shot learning, and Example filtering process for the Baseline Pun Generation method, demonstrating the generation of Hindi-English code-mixed puns with a balanced mix of Hindi and English words, as outlined in Section 4.2.4.

P_w/A_w	Method	Generated Sentence with Gloss, Transliteration, and Translation	Label
भय (fear)/ bye	Baseline	"When fear knocks at your door, send faith to answer. कहो भय–भय, बाई–बाई! **Gloss:** कहो = say, भय–भय = fear–fear, बाई–बाई = bye–bye **Transliteration:** When fear knocks at your door, send faith to answer, Kaho bhay-bhay, bai-bai! **Translation:** When fear knocks at your door, send faith to answer. Say fear-fear bye-bye"	0
	Contextually Aligned	"मेरी लड़की की fear of heights ने हमारे adventure plan को भय कह दिया। **Gloss:** मेरी = my, लड़की = girl, की = 's, भय = fear, कह दिया = turned into **Transliteration:** Meri ladki ki fear of heights ne hamaare adventure plan ko bhay kah diyaa. **Translation:** My daughter's fear of heights turned our adventure plan into 'fear'."	1
	Question-Answer	"What do you call it जब तुम अपने डर को अलविदा कहते हो? कहो भय **Gloss:** जब = when, तुम = you, अपने = your, डर = fear, को = to, अलविदा = goodbye, कहते = say, हो = do **Transliteration:** Jab tum apne ar ko alavidaa kahte ho? Kaho bhay. **Translation:** What do you call it when you say goodbye to your fear? Say 'fear'."	1
	Subject-Masked	"The डरपोक लड़की waved goodभय with a smile. **Gloss:** डरपोक = cowardly, लड़की = girl, goodभय = good–fear **Transliteration:** The arpok ladki waved good-bhay with a smile. **Translation:** The cowardly girl waved good-fear with a smile."	1
लाश (corpse)/ lush	Baseline	"The garden was so beautifully green, it was a लाश paradise! **Gloss:** लाश = corpse, paradise = paradise **Transliteration:** The garden was so beautifully green, it was a laash paradise. **Translation:** The garden was so beautifully green, it was a corpse paradise."	1
	Contextually Aligned	"जंगल में एक निर्जीव dead body मिली, surrounded by एक लाश forest **Gloss:** जंगल = forest, में = in, एक = a, निर्जीव = lifeless, लाश = corpse, मिली = found **Transliteration:** Jangal men ek nirjiv dead body milii, surrounded by ek lash forest. **Translation:** A lifeless dead body was found in the forest, surrounded by a corpse forest."	1
	Question-Answer	"What do you call a garden जो लाशों से भरा हो? A लाश garden **Gloss:** जो = which, लाशों = corpses, से = with, भरा = full, हो = is **Transliteration:** What do you call a garden jo lashon se bhara ho? A lash garden. **Translation:** What do you call a garden full of corpses? A corpse garden."	1
	Subject-Masked	"The भूतिया कब्रिस्तान was filled with लाश greenery **Gloss:** भूतिया = haunted, कब्रिस्तान = cemetery, लाश = corpse **Transliteration:** The bhutiyaa kabristaan was filled with lash greenery. **Translation:** The haunted cemetery was filled with corpse greenery."	1

Table 13: Examples of code-mixed Hindi-English puns generated using four different methods: Baseline, Contextually Aligned, Question-Answer, and Subject-Masked. For each word pair (P_w/A_w), the table presents a generated sentence along with its gloss, transliteration, translation, and label. The label column indicates whether the generated sentence contains a pun (**0**) or not (**1**). The examples illustrate the use of alternate words (A_w) and pun words (P_w) to create humorous and contextually relevant sentences.

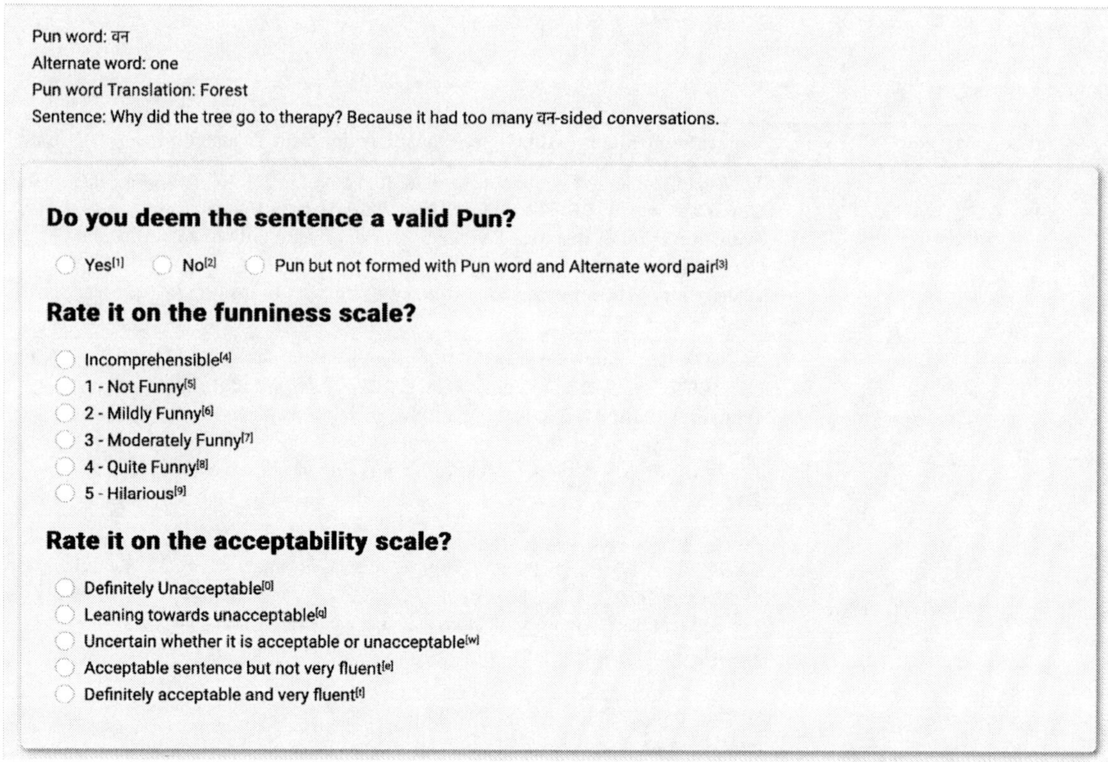

Pun word: वन

Alternate word: one

Pun word Translation: Forest

Sentence: Why did the tree go to therapy? Because it had too many वन-sided conversations.

Do you deem the sentence a valid Pun?

Yes[1] No[2] Pun but not formed with Pun word and Alternate word pair[3]

Rate it on the funniness scale?

- Incomprehensible[4]
- 1 - Not Funny[5]
- 2 - Mildly Funny[6]
- 3 - Moderately Funny[7]
- 4 - Quite Funny[8]
- 5 - Hilarious[9]

Rate it on the acceptability scale?

- Definitely Unacceptable[0]
- Leaning towards unacceptable[q]
- Uncertain whether it is acceptable or unacceptable[w]
- Acceptable sentence but not very fluent[e]
- Definitely acceptable and very fluent[r]

Figure 2: Example of the annotation interface used to evaluate puns generated by methods in Section 4.2. The evaluation focuses on three criteria: Pun Success, Funniness, and Acceptability. Annotators classify puns as successful or unsuccessful, rate humor on a 5-point Likert scale, and asses Acceptability based on sentence fluency and grammatical correctness rated on a 5-point scale, following guidelines. An additional option was given for pun success where annotators could rate if a pun was formed without the specified pun-alternate word pair.

Pun word: स्टोरी
Alternate word: storey
Pun word Translation: story

I asked the librarian for a novel, and he said, "कौन सी स्टोरी?" I replied, "Any कहानी will do!"

- Incomprehensible/ Not a pun[1]
- 1 - Not Funny[2]
- 2 - Mildly Funny[3]
- 3 - Moderately Funny[4]
- 4 - Quite Funny[5]
- 5 - Hilarious[6]

What do you call a house जिसमें हर मंजिल पर कहानियाँ होती हैं?
A two स्टोरी house

- Incomprehensible/ Not a pun[7]
- 1 - Not Funny[8]
- 2 - Mildly Funny[9]
- 3 - Moderately Funny[0]
- 4 - Quite Funny[q]
- 5 - Hilarious[w]

Which was a better Pun?

- Sentence 1[e]
- Sentence 2[t]
- None[a]

Figure 3: Example of annotation interface used to compare the funniness and quality of puns generated by the proposed pun generation pipeline (Section 7) versus the baseline model. Annotators rated each pun for funniness on a scale and selected the better pun overall.

Testing Humor Theory Using Word and Sentence Embeddings

Stephen Skalicky
Victoria University of Wellington
Wellington, New Zealand
scskalicky@gmail.com

Salvatore Attardo
East Texas A&M University
Commerce, Texas, USA
salvatore.attardo@tamuc.edu

Abstract

A basic prediction of incongruity theory is that semantic scripts in verbal humor should be in a state of incongruity. We test this prediction using a dataset of 1,182 word/phrase pairs extracted from a set of imperfect puns. Incongruity was defined as the cosine distance between their word vector representations. We compare these pun distances against similarity metrics for the pun words against their synonyms, extracted from WordNet. Results indicate a significantly lower degree of similarity between pun words when compared to their synonyms. Our findings support the basic predictions of incongruity theory and provide computational researchers with a baseline metric to model humorous incongruity.

1 Introduction

Theories such as the General Theory of Verbal Humor describe the need for incongruity between elements of jokes, puns, and other humor forms, but this theory also stipulates there must a simultaneous degree of script overlap (Attardo and Raskin, 1991). As such, computational researchers should strive to model both opposition and overlap to better connect computational algorithms to humor theory (Hempelmann, 2008). In this paper, we do so by flipping the script on prior computational research which has used incongruity as a means to generate verbal humor (e.g., Ritchie, 2004; Mihalcea et al., 2010). Instead, we aim to determine the usefulness of recent advances in word vector representations to test some aspects of humor theory with the domain of puns.

1.1 Puns and Incongruity

Puns are defined as follows:

> A pun is a textual occurrence in which a sequence of sounds must be interpreted with a formal reference to a second sequence of sounds, which may, but need not, be identical to the first sequence, for the full meaning of the text to be accessed. The perlocutionary goal or effect of the pun is to generate the perception of mirth or of the intention to do so. (Attardo, 2020, p. 177–178)

In more accessible terms, two sequences of sounds evoke two meanings, associated with the first and second sequence, respectively. These are known as the *pun* and its *target*. For example, consider this very old pun: *Why did the cookie cry? Its mother was a* ***wafer/away for*** *so long*. In this pun, we have the string text *a wafer* (the pun), which sounds like the words *away for* (the target). Note in passing that outside of context, it does not matter which is the pun and which the target. Incongruity theory makes a clear prediction: the two senses (the pun and its target) should be in a relationship of incongruity. Incongruity is defined on the basis of semantic expectations. The (non–punning) sentence "I had a peanut butter and jelly sandwich" is congruous; the sentence "I had a peanut butter and jelly suitcase" is incongruous. In the case of puns, the incongruity has to reside, ex hypothesis, in the pun/target pair (since the rest of the text is identical). Let's consider again "why did the cookie cry?" Its mother was [a wafer]/[away for] so long" since the rest of text "why did the cookie cry?" Its mother was [...] so long" is identical in either reading, the incongruity can reside only in the pair "a wafer"/"away for."

1.2 Current Study

Our goal in this paper is to test this prediction, using the metric of cosine distance between word vector representations. Word vectors (or embeddings) capture semantic relationships as a function of distributional similarity. Words which appear in similar contexts have similar meanings, and their vector representations transform these relationships

Proceedings of the 1st Workshop on Computational Humor (CHum), pages 58–62
January 19, 2025.

into a numerical, multidimensional vector space (Mikolov et al., 2013). The angle between two vectors is commonly used as a measure of the difference between them and the cosine of the angle "has the nice property that it is 1.0 for identical vectors and 0.0 for orthogonal vectors" (Singhal et al., 2001, p. 3).

Distances among vectors have previously been applied to the problem of pun generation, where it was shown that vector distance could be used to model local and global similarity of pun words, improving pun generation performance (He et al., 2019). Here we also use distances between vectors, except we seek to measure the *similarity* between words in existing puns. Cosine vector similarity has been used to compare text similarity since the 1960s (Salton, 1963), and possibly earlier, in the context of information retrieval with keywords. More recently, cosine distance has been used as a measure of semantic acceptability/deviance (Vecchi et al., 2017), as well as metaphoricity and creativity (Winter and Strik-Lievers, 2023).

2 Method

We compare the cosine similarities of vector representation of key words used in puns. Our comparisons are made using both single–word vector spaces trained with word2vec (Mikolov et al., 2013) as well as sentence embeddings using the sentence transformers architecture (Reimers and Gurevych, 2019). We further compare the degree of these cosine distances between pun words against a baseline of their synonyms, collected from WordNet (Fellbaum, 1998)[1].

2.1 Materials

We utilized a corpus of 1182 pun–target word pairs analyzed in Hempelmann (2003), which were drawn from a subset of a larger corpus of puns discussed in Sobkowiak (1991). These 1182 pairs are from imperfect, heterophonic puns, meaning that the sound of the pun and target are not the same[2]. Using these puns, Hempelmann (2003) outlined a hierarchy of phonological, syntactic, and semantic constraints which differentiated between "good" and "bad" imperfect puns. While 959 of the pun–target pairs are in the form of a word–word relationship (e.g., *frozen* and *chosen*), 223 others represent a word–phrase relationship (e.g., *fundamental* and *from the mantel*).

2.2 Measuring Pun–Target Similarity

We calculated vector representations for each word/phrase in the pun–target pairs using two methods. Firstly, we used the `sentence-transforms` (SBERT) Python module to generate vector representations for pun words using the `all-MiniLM-L6-v2 model`. This is a lightweight model provided by Hugging Face, which was fine–tuned on over 1 billion sentence pairs with a 384–multidimensional vector space[3]. This sentence embedding model allowed us to calculate vectors for the 223 targets which spanned more than one word. However, recognizing the majority of the puns were pairs of single words, we also calculated a second set of similarities using the `word2vec-google-news-300` vector representations for single words using the `word2vec` algorithm, trained on 100 billion words from Google News corpus, creating a 300–dimensional space.[4]

Cosine distances between puns and targets for SBERT and word2vec representations were measured using the `cosine_similarity` function from the `scikit-learn` Python module. In addition to the 223 puns with targets more than one word long, an additional 153 puns contained a pun or target word not in the pre–trained word2vec space, meaning their pairwise similarity could not be calculated using word2vec. The average similarity between pun–target pairs was 0.270 (*SD* = 0.109) for the SBERT vectors, and 0.143 (*SD* = 0.203) for the word2vec vectors. For word2vec, some of the cosine distances were negative, so we also calculated the absolute values to better compare the degree of similarity (positive or negative) against the SBERT values. The results were closer, with the average absolute word2vec distances at 0.198 (*SD* = 0.150). We provide more examples across the full distribution in Table 1, and plot the density of the cosine distances in Figure 2.

We interpret these results as initial confirmation of incongruity theory. The maximum possible range of the absolute values is 0.0 (no relation) to 1.0 (completely related/completely unrelated). Finding that the median/average values for the puns is near the lower quartile of possible distances suggests that the occurrence of a semantically different

[1]We have made our code and data available on an OSF Repository

[2]Contrast these with homophonic puns, such as *I used to be a banker, until I lost* ***interest.***

[3]https://huggingface.co/sentence-transformers/all-MiniLM-L6-v2

[4]https://code.google.com/archive/p/word2vec/

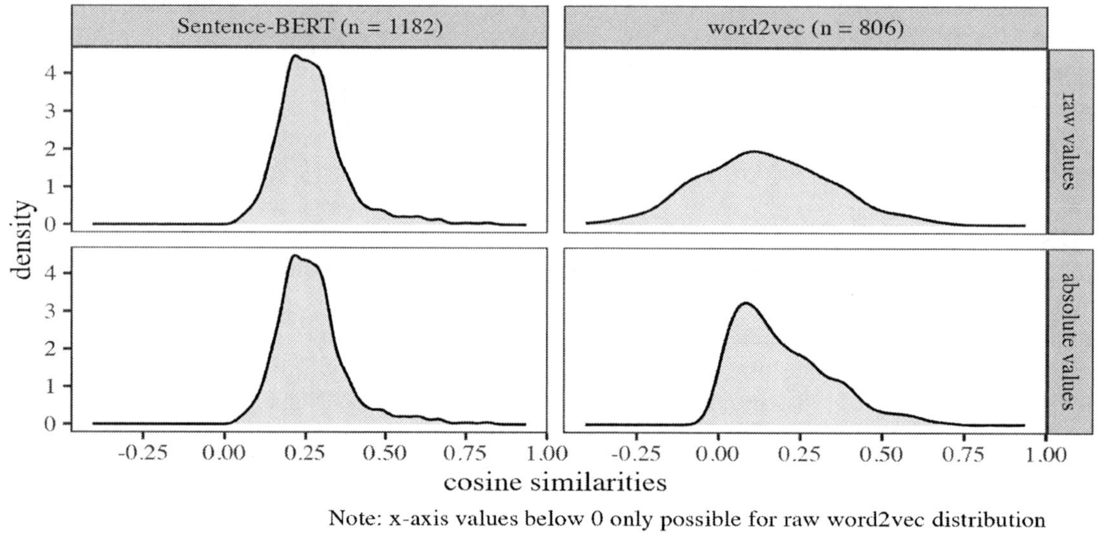

Figure 1: Distribution of cosine similarities between pun–target words using SBERT and word2vec.

	Sentence–BERT		
pun	target	sim	range
cinnamon	see a man	0.046	*min*
kitty	pity	0.161	*−1SD*
prostituting	prosecuting	0.260	*median*
tinkle	twinkle	0.379	*+1SD*
invisible	visible	0.814	*max*
	word2vec		
pun	target	sim	range
accost	cost	−0.407	*min*
salivation	salvation	−0.060	*−1SD*
pawn	upon	0.134	*median*
sheep	cheap	0.346	*+1SD*
thing	think	0.936	*max*

Table 1: Similarity values between pun and target words across distribution of similarities (minimum, median, and +/−1 standard deviation from mean), with example words.

sense will be unexpected and hence incongruous. As shown in Figure 2, most of the pun–target pairs live in this range, as indicated by the peak density values.

2.3 Establishing a Comparative Baseline

However, there is a difficulty: while in puns we can contrast the pun with its target, what should we compare that measure to? Although the resulting similarities for our pun–target pairs are relatively low on a scale from 0 to 1, a comparative baseline is needed in order to contextualise these results. We could compare a word to itself, but that only guarantees that we will get a score of approximately 0.99, or asymptotically tending to one.

As a solution, we queried WordNet, a large database of lexical meanings and connections for English words (Fellbaum, 1998). Each lexical entry in WordNet includes a list of *synsets*, which capture different semantic uses. For example, the entry *humour* has seven synsets: *temper*, *wit*, *liquid body substance*, and four different senses of *humour* (feeling humour, being humorous, sense of humour, and humorous mood). Each synset includes a list of words associated with that sense, called *lemmas*. The lemmas for *wit* are 'wit', 'humor', 'humour', 'witticism', and 'wittiness'.

We gathered the lemmas of all synsets for each pun–target word. Using the same SBERT model as we used for the puns, we then and calculated the average cosine distance between each pun word and its full set of synset lemmas. The assumption behind this approach is that punning pair words should have higher cosine similarity to their synonyms than to the pun–target words. This approach introduces a certain amount of noise — only about 2/3 of the pun words are in WordNet (again because some pun words are phrases or unorthodox spellings), and some WordNet entries are more detailed than others (meaning a greater number of synsets and lemmas for some words than others).

Specifically, of the 2,190 unique pun–target words and phrases in the pun data (some words were repeated across puns), only 1,520 words could be found in WordNet (69.41%). Using this set, results of the similarity comparisons between a word and its synonym(s) is an average of 0.422 (median = 0.385, SD = 0.156, min = 0.039, max = 0.962). This is an increase of ~56% from the average SBERT similarities and an increase of ~112% from the average of the absolute values of the word2vec similarities. Paired–sample t–tests comparing SBERT pun similarities against SBERT synonym similarities indicated these differences were significant and with large effect sizes for both pun (mean difference = 0.158, 95%CI [0.144, 0.171], t = 23.325, df = 908, Cohen's d = 1.111, $p < .001$) and target (mean difference = 0.139, 95%CI [0.128, 0.151], t = 23.704, df = 843, Cohen'd d = 1.169, $p < .001$) words found in WordNet. This comparison provides further support for the incongruity theory. Namely, the pun average similarity of 0.27 (using sentence embeddings) is capturing some degree of incongruity, in that it is much lower than the similarity to related words (0.42).

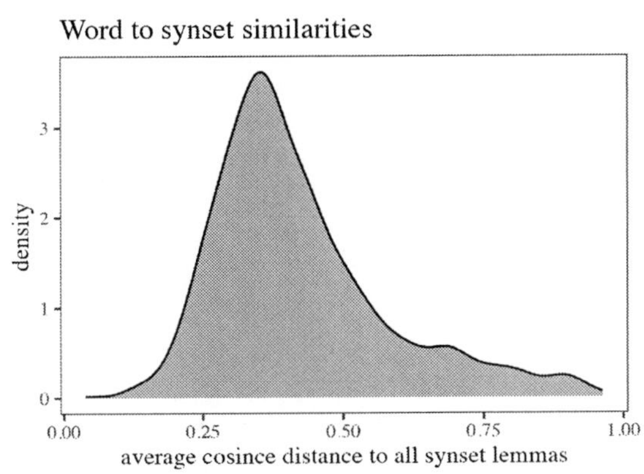

Figure 2: Distribution of cosine distance values between SBERT embeddings for pun words and their synset lemmas extracted from WordNet.

3 Discussion

The goal of our study was to test fundamental predictions of incongruity theory using computational measures of semantic distance. Using a dataset of pun–target words from 1182 imperfect, heterophonic puns, we found the cosine distances between word embeddings calculated using single–word vector spaces as well as sentence embeddings were on average significantly lower than those calculated from the pun words and their set of synonyms. In other words, pun–target words were less related to each other than they were to their own synonym entries in WordNet. As such, we find that the predictions based on the incongruity theory, that there should be a low degree of similarity between a pun and its target and that the similarity should be lower than that between a word and its synonyms, are borne out by our data.

It is noteworthy that single–word vectors from word2vec suggest less similarity between the pun words when compared to the SBERT embeddings. This likely reflects the difference in algorithms and size of training data. Nonetheless, both sets of embeddings measure the distributional probability of the target words within co–word contexts, so we have some confidence that these vectors are capturing the distributional properties of larger contexts within which the words appear. Our results thus seem to model the necessary balance for humorous incongruity — the simultaneous relationship of opposition and overlap. If the pun words were completely unrelated (e.g., cosine distances around 0), it would be unlikely that both words could be acceptable within the same sentence contexts, and thus the puns would simply not work.

We should of course point out the limitations of the study: first, we used a limited data set, collected by one scholar over 30 years ago. This may have introduced biases we are unaware of. Moreover, we used only the pun–target words from the puns — including full sentence contexts could provide more contextual information for baseline comparisons. Second, there are a growing number of different sentence embedding models, all of which will return different vector embeddings depending on their training data. More sophisticated models may be needed for future data sets and different types of humor, with the caveat that larger models comes at the expense of computational performance. Regardless, further replication of our results using other trained models and measures of similarity with puns and other datasets is necessary.

4 Conclusion

Our results provide empirical validation of theoretical assumptions related to predictions of incongruity theory. Specifically, we find incongruity between overlapping scripts of verbal humor as it occurs in puns using computational measures of semantic distance.

References

Salvatore Attardo. 2020. *The linguistics of humor: An introduction*. Oxford University Press.

Salvatore Attardo and Victor Raskin. 1991. Script theory revis(it)ed: Joke similarity and joke representation model. *Humor - International Journal of Humor Research*, 4(3-4):293–348.

Christiane Fellbaum. 1998. *WordNet: An electronic lexical database*. MIT Press, Cambridge, MA.

He He, Nanyun Peng, and Percy Liang. 2019. Pun generation with surprise. *arXiv preprint arXiv:1904.06828*.

Christian Hempelmann. 2008. Computational humor: Beyond the pun? In Victor Raskin, editor, *The primer of humor research*, pages 333–360. Mouton de Gruyter.

Christian F Hempelmann. 2003. *Paronomasic puns: Target recoverability towards automatic generation*. Ph.D. thesis, Purdue University.

Rada Mihalcea, Carlo Strapparava, and Stephen Pulman. 2010. Computational models for incongruity detection in humour. In *Computational linguistics and intelligent text processing*, pages 364–374. Springer.

Tomas Mikolov, Kai Chen, Greg Corrado, and Jeffrey Dean. 2013. Efficient estimation of word representations in vector space. *Preprint*, arXiv:1301.3781.

Nils Reimers and Iryna Gurevych. 2019. Sentence-BERT: Sentence Embeddings using Siamese BERT-Networks. *Preprint*, arXiv:1908.10084.

Graeme Ritchie. 2004. *The linguistic analysis of jokes*. Routledge, New York, NY.

Gerard Salton. 1963. Associative document retrieval techniques using bibliographic information. *J. ACM*, 10(4):440–457.

Amit Singhal et al. 2001. Modern information retrieval: A brief overview. *IEEE Data Eng. Bull.*, 24(4):35–43.

Włodzimierz Sobkowiak. 1991. *Metaphonology of English Paronomasic Puns*. P. Lang.

Eva M Vecchi, Marco Marelli, Roberto Zamparelli, and Marco Baroni. 2017. Spicy adjectives and nominal donkeys: Capturing semantic deviance using compositionality in distributional spaces. *Cognitive Science*, 41(1):102–136.

Bodo Winter and Francesca Strik-Lievers. 2023. Semantic distance predicts metaphoricity and creativity judgments in synesthetic metaphors. *Metaphor and the Social World*, 13(1):59–80.

Pragmatic Metacognitive Prompting Improves LLM Performance on Sarcasm Detection

Joshua Lee[†], Wyatt Fong[†], Alexander Le[†], Sur Shah[†], Kevin Han[†], Kevin Zhu[†*]
[†]Algoverse AI Research
{zhukevin, kevin.x.han}@berkeley.edu

Abstract

Sarcasm detection is a significant challenge in sentiment analysis due to the nuanced and context-dependent nature of verbiage. We introduce **Pragmatic Metacognitive Prompting (PMP)** to improve the performance of Large Language Models (LLMs) in sarcasm detection, which leverages principles from pragmatics and reflection helping LLMs interpret implied meanings, consider contextual cues, and reflect on discrepancies to identify sarcasm. Using state-of-the-art LLMs such as LLaMA-3-8B, GPT-4o, and Claude 3.5 Sonnet, PMP achieves state-of-the-art performance on GPT-4o on MUStARD and SemEval2018. This study demonstrates that integrating pragmatic reasoning and metacognitive strategies into prompting significantly enhances LLMs' ability to detect sarcasm, offering a promising direction for future research in sentiment analysis.

1 Introduction

Within the field of sentiment analysis, various approaches exist to improve emotion classification, from bidirectional transformers to prompt tuning for aspect-based sentiment analysis (Ataei et al., 2020; Ouyang et al., 2015; Devlin et al., 2019; Li et al., 2021; Zadeh et al., 2017; Kanakaraj and Guddeti, 2015). Yet one present limitation sentiment analysis models face is in determining sarcasm (Tan et al., 2023a).

Recent discoveries found that LLMs underperform compared to specially trained transformer encoder models in both sarcasm detection and sentiment analysis. The speculated cause of poor LLM performance is that LLMs are built on logical pipelines, which may contradict sarcasm's non-sequential nature. Regardless, studies believe improving prompting methods is a step towards the solution (Zhang et al., 2024, 2023; Tan et al., 2023b; Liu et al., 2023; Yao et al., 2024; Wei et al., 2022; Besta et al., 2024; Yao et al., 2023).

This work presents PMP[1] based on Wei et al.'s Metacognitive prompting (MP). PMP is a new approach to improving LLM sarcasm detection. Our approach incorporates linguistic principles to mimic how humans reason through emotionally complex text as well as reflection strategies commonly found in LLM reasoning and planning agents (Shinn et al., 2023). This paper presents a novel prompting approach through the use of pragmatics and reflection to improve sarcasm detection, runs its prompting method on sarcasm benchmarks, and at times exceeds the prompt results of the current state-of-the-art (SoTA) prompt for LLM sarcasm detection.

2 Background

2.1 Pragmatics

Pragmatics is a field of linguistics that goes beyond the literal meaning of a conversation. It's the social context of a statement that is needed to comprehend the subtleties of human language. (Grice, 1975; Clark, 1996; Horn and Ward, 2004). Various studies in linguistics have been conducted on the pragmatics of sarcasm. One pragmatic theory called Grice's Maxims of Conversation, poses the 4 different factors that a conversation must have to be a meaningful conversation. One study, in the field of pragmatics, analyzed Grice's Maxims. It concluded that if Grice's Maxims were exceeded, like with sarcasm in TV shows, it could be a determining factor as to whether dialogue is sarcastic (Al Anssari and Hadi, 2021).

Our method, PMP, incorporates proposed pragmatic theories on how to detect sarcasm from the field of linguistics into LLM prompting. Our

*Corresponding Author

[1]Our code can be found at: https://github.com/wyatt-fong/Pragmatic-Metacognitive-Prompting-Improves-LLM-Performance-on-Sarcasm-Detection

Proceedings of the 1st Workshop on Computational Humor (CHum), pages 63–70
January 19, 2025.

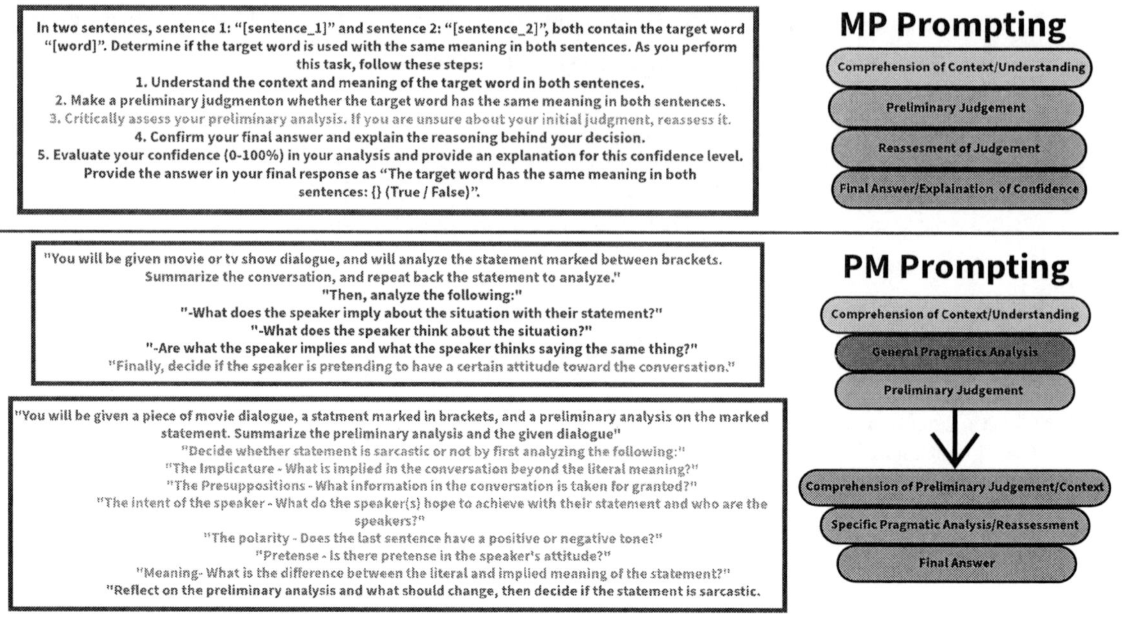

Figure 1: Metacognitive Prompt structure compared to proposed Pragmatic Metacognitive Prompt.

method encourages the LLM to analyze multiple pragmatic theories analyzing sarcasm before reaching its conclusion. A simplified explanation of the theories used in PMP is provided below.

The Standard Pragmatic Model (TSPM): Building upon the foundations of the TSPM, Gibbs and Colston, refined the understanding of sarcasm detection. His version of TSPM emphasized a process of contacting literal and non-literal meanings alongside context to determine sarcasm.

The Pretense Theory of Irony: When a speaker is ironic or sarcastic, they set up a facade to what they actually believe. (Clark and Gerrig, 1984). For instance, if someone says "Your jacket looks soooo nice" in a sarcastic tone, they are presenting an attitude that they do like the look of your jacket when they actually do not.

The Echoic Reminder Theory of Verbal Irony: This method is characterized by positive and neutral statements that ironically reference a past statement. It is often used as a critique of a scenario. An example would be the phrase "What a great idea!" which typically has a positive connotation. However, if it was used to describe a terrible plan it would take a negative connotation, conveying sarcasm. (Kreuz and Glucksberg, 1989).

Implicature: Implicatures are implicit inferences drawn automatically from the information provided in a sentence, relying on the shared context between the speaker and listener. For example, if Bob says "Do you want any cake for lunch?" and Joey responds "I don't want to get fat", the implied meaning is that Joey is declining the offer. However, inferences like these can sometimes be incorrect. For instance, Joey may have been making a completely unrelated comment. As the interpreters, we may assume that Joey's statement was relevant to the conversation, which causes us to infer his refusal.

Presupposition: The presupposition is that the information is automatically accepted as true in order for a statement to make sense. For example, in the statement "The king of France is bald", the presupposition is that there exists a King of France. This statement assumes that a king exists in France, even though there might not be one, for the sake of making sense of the statement.

3 Method

Our prompting method builds on top of Wei et al.'s Metacognitive prompting (MP). MP consists of prompting an LLM to repeat the given information, create a preliminary analysis, reflect on their preliminary analysis, and then create a final judgment (Wei et al., 2023). See Figure 1 for more details on MP. In our method, PMP, the LLM is encouraged to analyze simplified elements of pragmatic theories in the preliminary analysis and reflection stages.

Model	SemEval 2018 Acc.	SemEval 2018 Ma-F1	MUStARD Acc.	MUStARD Ma-F1
GPT-4o (IO)	64.03	63.17	67.24	65.79
GPT-4o (CoT)	58.92	51.99	58.11	55.76
GPT-4o (ToT)	63.90	63.02	69.00	68.27
GPT-4o (CoC)	70.79	70.60	69.42	68.48
GPT-4o (GoC)	74.03	74.02	70.69	69.91
GPT-4o (BoC)	62.12	61.85	69.42	68.45
GPT-4o (PMP)	**86.68**	**83.18**	**79.42**	**77.65**
GPT-4o-mini (PMP)	81.88	79.85	65.79	62.29
Claude 3.5 Sonnet (IO)	75.13	75.11	**74.78**	**74.78**
Claude 3.5 Sonnet (CoT)	71.56	71.47	73.62	73.53
Claude 3.5 Sonnet (ToT)	68.62	68.61	58.84	54.46
Claude 3.5 Sonnet (CoC)	**82.27**	**82.23**	74.20	74.16
Claude 3.5 Sonnet (GoC)	57.33	57.24	52.77	52.67
Claude 3.5 Sonnet (BoC)	65.94	65.50	59.71	56.70
Claude 3.5 Sonnet (PMP)	81.50	76.72	72.60	71.66
LLaMA-3-70B (PMP)	80.86	78.15	72.73	73.06
LLaMA-3-8B (IO)	49.36	44.47	54.64	44.99
LLaMA-3-8B (CoT)	49.36	44.55	54.20	44.86
LLaMA-3-8B (ToT)	50.64	48.63	54.35	50.56
LLaMA-3-8B (CoC)	49.23	44.36	54.93	45.66
LLaMA-3-8B (GoC)	57.33	57.24	52.7	52.67
LLaMA-3-8B (BoC)	65.94	65.50	59.71	56.70
LLaMA-3-8B (ToC)	68.88	68.21	**61.26**	**58.03**
LLaMA-3-8B (PMP)	**78.21**	**77.65**	53.48	54.69

Table 1: Comparison of PMP with Claude 3.5 Sonnet, GPT4o, GPT4o-mini, LLaMa-3-70B and LLaMA-3-8B to prompting methods. The best results are bolded.

We establish two separate LLM calls, one which analyzes the prompt from the lens of each pragmatic factor: implicature, presuppositions, intent, polarity, pretense, and potential meanings individually, and a second LLM call that reflects on the analysis and outputs a final prediction. A detailed explanation of PMP is provided in Figure 1.

4 Experimental Design

4.1 Benchmarks

We evaluated our sarcasm detection method on the same benchmarks as (Yao et al., 2024): MUStARD (Castro et al., 2019), which consists of sarcastic and non-sarcastic comments in TV and movie dialogue paired with context; and SemEval 2018 Task 3 (Van Hee et al., 2018) consisting of sarcastic and non-sarcastic twitter statements.

4.2 Models

We tested our method using models also utilized in SarcasmCue (Yao et al., 2024). The models are: GPT-4o, LLaMA 3-8B and Claude 3.5 Sonnet (Anthropic, 2024). Furthermore, we additionally tested on GPT-4o mini (OpenAI, 2023) and LLaMA 3-70B (Touvron et al., 2023).

4.2.1 SarcasmCue

Our method achieves the new SoTA in comparison to SarcasmCue. The method SarcasmCue modifies popular SoTA prompts to analyze a "cue", which is a coherent language sequence that serves as an indicator towards identifying sarcasm, from either linguistic (rhetorical devices, punctuation), contextual (topic, common knowledge), or emotional (emotional words, emojis) parts of a sentence.

SarcasmCue[2] introduces four sarcasm detection methods; three prompting techniques: Bag of Cues (BoC), Chain of Cues (CoC), and Graph of Cues (GoC), and one that requires explicit model training, Tensor of Cues (ToC). BoC removes sequential bias by treating cues independently. CoC arranges cues in a sequential order to capture the step-by-step reasoning process of sarcasm detection. GoC analyzes the relationships between cues without imposing a fixed sequence. ToC adds encoded indications through explicit training to leverage higher-order interactions among cues. For the exact prompts, please see Appendix A.

5 Results

The accuracy and Macro-F1 scores comparing PMP with prompting method baselines are compared in Table 1. The accuracy and Macro-F1 scores comparing PMP with SarcasmCue's BoC, CoC, GoC, and ToC strategies are reported in Table 1.

Comparison to Popular Prompting methods: PMP surpasses popular prompting methods such as Zero Shot, Chain of Thought, and Tree of Thought in both SemEval 2018 Task 3 and MUStARD. Across both performing well on LLaMA-3-8B and GPT-4o, with the exception of Claude 3.5 Sonnet. Zero-shot prompting still works well with Claude 3.5 Sonnet in 2 benchmarks, aligning with Yao et al.'s results. PMP's performance with LLaMA-3-70B is significantly higher than with LLaMA-3-8B.

Comparison to State of the Art (SoTA): PMP is competitive with and exceeds SarcasmCue's performance on all datasets with GPT-4o while performing well on LLaMA-3-8B on SemEval 2018. As shown in Table 2, zero-shot Claude 3.5 Sonnet achieves the highest accuracy on the MUStARD datasets, outperforming it in SarcasmCue and PMP.

Datasets: PMP performs the best on SemEval 2018 Task 3, although it falls slightly short of SarcasmCue on Claude. PMP struggles on Sarcasm Corpus V1 the most, with current SoTA and Tree of Thought outperforming it across certain models.

State of The Art and PMP: Between PMP and SarcasmCue, neither consistently achieves higher accuracies than the other across all models and datasets, excluding Claude. However, one notable factor is that for both datasets, GPT-4o utilizing PMP performs best in comparison with all other models and prompting methods. GPT-4o outperforming other LLMs aligns with previous studies such as Zhang et al.'s work, suggesting GPT-4o's performance is a common factor in sarcasm detection. Another inconsistency is that SarcasmCue underperforms some prompts in SemEval 2018 Task 3 across all models except Claude 3.5 Sonnet, while PMP outperforms prompts in SemEval 2018 Task 3 across all models but underperforms SoTA in Claude 3.5 Sonnet. Analyzing SemEval 2018 as a dataset could help explain these performance patterns.

6 Conclusion

Pragmatic Metacognitive Prompting is a novel approach for enhancing sarcasm detection in LLMs. PMP is competitive with or beats the current state-of-the-art methods for sarcasm detection with pre trained LLMs such as GPT4o and LLaMA-3-8B. It introduces various pragmatic theories into the prompt design, fosters a deeper contextual understanding that improves sarcasm identification, and incorporates a human-like reflection step for final verification and sarcasm reasoning. After testing across models like GPT-4o and LLaMA-3-8B, PMP underscores the potential of pragmatic-informed methods to outperform traditional prompting methods and points to a continued focus on linguistic theories to bridge performance gaps in sentiment analysis.

7 Limitations

While PMP represents an approach to implementing pragmatic reflection, prompting is only one implementation of pragmatics and reflection in natural language processing. A key limitation to using zero-shot prompting is that PMP does not guarantee high performance in sarcasm detection that deviates from general linguistics norms and in domain-specific contexts. Due to PMP's reliance on LLM's pretraining with data, underrepresented cultural or linguistic norms are also not accounted for with prompting. These limitations suggest PMP is a step towards improving sarcasm detection, but does not represent a comprehensive solution.

[2] At the time of the writing of this paper, Yao et al. has not published their source code. Therefore, we compare our results with the reported results from their paper.

References

R. S. Al Anssari and H. A. N. Hadi. 2021. A pragmatic study of sarcasm in selected tv shows. *International*

Journal of Linguistics, Literature and Translation, 4(7):148–153.

Anthropic. 2024. The claude 3 model family: Opus, sonnet, haiku.

T. S. Ataei, S. Javdan, and B. Minaei-Bidgoli. 2020. Applying transformers and aspect-based sentiment analysis approaches on sarcasm detection. In *Proceedings of the Second Workshop on Figurative Language Processing*.

M. Besta, N. Blach, A. Kubicek, R. Gerstenberger, M. Podstawski, L. Gianinazzi, J. Gajda, T. Lehmann, H. Niewiadomski, P. Nyczyk, and T. Hoefler. 2024. Graph of thoughts: Solving elaborate problems with large language models. In *Proceedings of the AAAI Conference on Artificial Intelligence*, volume 38, pages 17682–17690.

Santiago Castro, Devamanyu Hazarika, Verónica Pérez-Rosas, Roger Zimmermann, Rada Mihalcea, and Soujanya Poria. 2019. Reliability-aware dynamic feature composition for name tagging. In *Proceedings of the 57th Annual Meeting of the Association for Computational Linguistics (Volume 1: Long Papers)*, pages 1010–1021, Florence, Italy. Association for Computational Linguistics.

Herbert H. Clark. 1996. *Using Language*. Cambridge University Press.

Herbert H. Clark and Richard J. Gerrig. 1984. On the pretense theory of irony. *Journal of Experimental Psychology: General*, 113(1):121–126.

Jacob Devlin, Ming-Wei Chang, Kenton Lee, and Kristina Toutanova. 2019. Bert: Pre-training of deep bidirectional transformers for language understanding. *Preprint*, arXiv:1810.04805.

Raymond W. Gibbs and Herbert L. Colston. 2007. *Irony in Language and Thought*. Taylor & Francis Group, New York.

H. Paul Grice. 1975. Logic and conversation. In *Syntax and Semantics, Volume 3: Speech Acts*, pages 41–58. Academic Press.

N.A. Helal, A. Hassan, N.L. Badr, et al. 2024. A contextual-based approach for sarcasm detection. *Scientific Reports*, 14:15415.

Laurence R. Horn and Gregory L. Ward. 2004. *The Handbook of Pragmatics*. Wiley Online Library.

M. Kanakaraj and R. M. R. Guddeti. 2015. Performance analysis of ensemble methods on twitter sentiment analysis using nlp techniques. In *Proceedings of the 2015 IEEE 9th International Conference on Semantic Computing (IEEE ICSC 2015)*, pages 169–170, Anaheim, CA, USA. IEEE.

Roger J. Kreuz and Sam Glucksberg. 1989. How to be sarcastic: The echoic reminder theory of irony. *Journal of Experimental Psychology: General*, 118(4):374–386.

Chengxi Li, Feiyu Gao, Jiajun Bu, Lu Xu, Xiang Chen, Yu Gu, Zirui Shao, Qi Zheng, Ningyu Zhang, Yongpan Wang, and Zhi Yu. 2021. Sentiprompt: Sentiment knowledge enhanced prompt-tuning for aspect-based sentiment analysis. *Preprint*, arXiv:2109.08306.

Y. Liu, R. Zhang, Y. Fan, and J. Guo. 2023. Prompt tuning with contradictory intentions for sarcasm recognition. In *Proceedings of the 17th Conference of the European Chapter of the Association for Computational Linguistics*, pages 328–339.

OpenAI. 2023. Gpt-4 technical report. *arXiv preprint arXiv:2303.08774*.

X. Ouyang, P. Zhou, C. Li, and L. Liu. 2015. Sentiment analysis using convolutional neural networks. In *Proceedings of the IEEE International Conference on Computer and Information Technology*.

Noah Shinn, Federico Cassano, Edward Berman, Ashwin Gopinath, Karthik Narasimhan, and Shunyu Yao. 2023. Reflexion: Language agents with verbal reinforcement learning. *Preprint*, arXiv:2303.11366.

K. L. Tan, C. P. Lee, and K. M. Lim. 2023a. A survey of sentiment analysis: Approaches, datasets, and future research. *Applied Sciences*, 13(7).

Y. Y. Tan, C. Chow, J. Kanesan, J. H. Chuah, and Y. Lim. 2023b. Sentiment analysis and sarcasm detection using deep multi-task learning. *Wireless Personal Communications*, 129(3):2213–2237.

Hugo Touvron, Thibaut Lavril, Gautier Izacard, Xavier Martinet, Marie-Anne Lachaux, Timothée Lacroix, Baptiste Rozière, Naman Goyal, Eric Hambro, Faisal Azhar, Armand Joulin, Edouard Grave, Max Chatelain, and Hervé Jegou. 2023. Llama: Open and efficient foundation language models. *arXiv preprint arXiv:2302.13971*.

Cynthia Van Hee, Els Lefever, and Veronique Hoste. 2018. Semeval-2018 task 3: Irony detection in english tweets. In *Proceedings of The 12th International Workshop on Semantic Evaluation*, pages 39–50, New Orleans, Louisiana. Association for Computational Linguistics.

J. Wei, X. Wang, D. Schuurmans, M. Bosma, B. Ichter, F. Xia, E. Chi, Q. Le, and D. Zhou. 2022. Chain-of-thought prompting elicits reasoning in large language models. arXiv.org.

Jason Wei, Yi Tay, Shixiang Shane Gu, William Fedus, Xuezhi Wang, Dale Schuurmans, Quoc Le, Ed Chi, and Denny Zhou. 2023. Metacognitive prompting improves understanding in large language models. *Preprint*, arXiv:2308.05342.

B. Yao, Y. Zhang, Q. Li, and J. Qin. 2024. Is sarcasm detection a step-by-step reasoning process in large language models? arXiv.org.

S. Yao, D. Yu, J. Zhao, I. Shafran, T. L. Griffiths, Y. Cao, and K. Narasimhan. 2023. Tree of thoughts: Deliberate problem solving with large language models. arXiv.org.

Amir Zadeh, Minghai Chen, Soujanya Poria, Erik Cambria, and Louis-Philippe Morency. 2017. Tensor fusion network for multimodal sentiment analysis. *Preprint*, arXiv:1707.07250.

W. Zhang, Y. Deng, B. Liu, S. J. Pan, and L. Bing. 2023. Sentiment analysis in the era of large language models: A reality check. arXiv.org.

Y. Zhang, C. Zou, Z. Lian, P. Tiwari, and J. Qin. 2024. Towards evaluating large language models on sarcasm understanding. arXiv.org.

A Prompts

The prompting method we utilized in our approach guides the model through a structured reasoning process before reaching a conclusion. The prompt instructs the model to analyze a statement checking its comprehension of the given information before asking the LLM to generate an accompanying preliminary analysis analyzing basic pragmatic factors. After completing the preliminary analysis, the model then passes its generated analysis to another LLM call, where the model has a chance to reflect and comprehend the preliminary analysis originally generated. It then directs the model to refine the analysis by systematically addressing specific pragmatic aspects, including implicature, presuppositions, speaker intent, polarity, pretense, and the relationship between literal and implied meanings. The wording of our initial prompt varies per dataset to ensure that all information about the benchmark is given for the LLM to generate a proper analysis. An example of this would be with MUStARD's dataset:

"You will be given movie or TV show dialogue and will analyze the statement marked between brackets. Summarize the conversation, and repeat back the statement to analyze. Then, analyze the following:"

Decide whether the statement is sarcastic or not by first analyzing the following:

1. The Implicature – What is implied in the conversation beyond the literal meaning?

2. The Presuppositions – What information in the conversation is taken for granted?

3. The Intent of the Speaker – What do the speaker(s) hope to achieve with their statement, and who are the speakers?

4. The Polarity – Does the last sentence have a positive or negative tone?

5. Pretense – Is there pretense in the speaker's attitude?

6. Meaning – What is the difference between the literal and implied meaning of the statement?

Reflect on the preliminary analysis and what should change, then decide if the statement is sarcastic."

A.1 Cues

A.1.1 Bag of Cues

The Bag of Cues method evaluates sarcasm by treating cues and without order.

Prompt Example: "Identify if the given statement is sarcastic based on the presence of the following cues:

Rhetorical devices (e.g., irony, hyperbole, or understatement) Emotional language (e.g., frustration, happiness, or sarcasm-laden phrases) Contextual inconsistencies (e.g., contradictory meanings or unexpected word choices). Does the statement exhibit any of these cues?"

Example Application: Input: "Oh, great! Another meeting that could have been an email." Rhetorical Device: Irony Emotional Cue: Frustration Contextual Cue: Work-related sarcasm Detection: Likely sarcastic

A.1.2 Chain of Cues

The Chain of Cues method evaluates sarcasm by analyzing cues sequentially. It simulates logical reasoning to then assess the overall sarcastic nature of a statement.

Prompt Example: "Analyze the statement step-by-step: Identify any rhetorical device (e.g., hyperbole, irony). Determine if emotional cues such as frustration or humor are present. Check for contextual markers that may suggest sarcasm. Does the progression or order of these cues indicate sarcasm?"

Example Application: Input: "Thanks for breaking the printer. Really helpful." Rhetorical Device: Irony detected in "Really helpful." Emotional Cue: Frustration in the context of the statement.

Contextual Marker: Complaints about a broken printer. Detection: Sarcastic

A.1.3 Graph of Cues

The Graph of Cues method evaluates sarcasm by analyzing the relationships between cues. This method leverages interdependencies between linguistic, emotional, and contextual features.

Prompt Example: "Construct a graph where: Nodes represent sarcasm cues (e.g., rhetorical devices, emotional cues, contextual features). Edges represent relationships between these cues (e.g., reinforcement, contrast). Based on the interconnected cues, does the statement appear sarcastic?"

Example Application: Input: "Wow, you're so good at driving (said during a near accident)." Nodes: Rhetorical Device: Sarcastic praise ("so good"). Emotional Cue: Anxiety/frustration. Contextual Cue: Near accident. Edges: Reinforcement between rhetorical device and emotional cue. Contextual cue amplifies sarcasm. Detection: Sarcastic

A.1.4 Tensor of Cues

The Tensor of Cues method uses a structured, multidimensional representation of sarcasm cues to train a model explicitly. This approach captures interactions between cues in a numerical format. The implementation details include implementation details, as well as linguistic, emotional, and contextual cues to be encoded as tensors. The model is then trained to revolve around optimizing the model to learn patterns across these dimensions.

Example Tensor Encoding: Input: "Nice job ignoring me all day!" Linguistic Cue: Irony (tensor dimension 1). Emotional Cue: Frustration (tensor dimension 2). Contextual Cue: Social neglect (tensor dimension 3). Combined Tensor: Captures interrelations of cues for sarcasm prediction.

Performance Highlights: This method achieves higher accuracy by explicitly modeling multi-cue interactions compared to the prompting methods. This structured prompt ensures that the model's reasoning aligns with pragmatic analysis principles, fostering a more nuanced understanding of sarcasm detection.

B LLM Pragmatic Reasoning

Figure 2 illustrates the application of PMP and the reasoning process demonstrated by the model. As depicted, the LLM leverages various elements of the pragmatic framework to arrive at a well-considered conclusion. In the appendix, we include a detailed PMP analysis of the phrase, *"Lots of people tweeting pictures from their cars of their snowy commutes to work, whilst saying 'stay safe' Oh, the #irony!"*. In this example, PMP successfully identifies the nuanced contrast between literal and implied meanings, allowing the model to detect sarcasm effectively by contextualizing the speaker's intent, polarity, and presuppositions.

C Transformer Encoder Models

	SemEval 2018	
Model	Acc.	Ma-F1
BERT	69.60	68.40
RoBERTa	75.00	72.00
XLNet	66.00	66.00
DC-Net-RoBERTa	70.90	68.70
GPT-4o (PMP)	86.68	83.18
GPT-4o-mini (PMP)	81.88	79.85
Claude 3.5 Sonnet (PMP)	81.50	76.72
LLaMA-3-70B (PMP)	80.86	78.15
LLaMA-3-8B (PMP)	78.21	77.65

Table 2: Comparison of PMP among LLMs with reported results of Zhang et al. with transformer ecoder models on SemEval 2018 Task 3

Previous works have studied the performance of transformer encoder models in sarcasm detection with MUStARD and SemEval 2018 Task 3. The models listed in Table 2 andTable 3 are reported from Helal et al. and Zhang et al. which show their performance compared to PMP across tested LLMs. A brief explanation of each model is provided:

BERT a model built for sarcasm detection which produces context-based word em- beddings.

RoBERTa based off BERT, which removes the next-sentence predictions, utilizes larger datasets and can have larger inputs of text in training.

XLNet Uses permutation language modeling for training, which predicts the order of tokens in a random order, helping the model learn the dependencies of words better.

DC-Net-RoBERTa processes two separate inputs (DC-Net) analyzing both literal and implied sentiments of a text separately, using RoBERTa as a base.

DistilBERT Uses knowledge distillation where DistilBERT is trained on BERT data as well as mimicking the outputs of BERT while having reduced parameters.

"Lots of people tweeting pictures from their cars of their snowy commutes to work, whilst saying 'stay safe' Oh, the #irony!"
- The speaker implies that there is a contradiction in the actions of people who are driving in potentially dangerous snowy conditions while also advising others to stay safe. This irony arises from the fact that they are engaging in an activity that may compromise safety (using a phone to tweet while driving) while simultaneously promoting safety.
- The speaker likely thinks that there is hypocrisy or a lack of self-awareness in these people's actions. They find it ironic or somewhat ridiculous that the same individuals advising others to be cautious are engaging in risky behavior themselves.
- Yes, what the speaker implies and what they think are largely saying the same thing: the behavior they observe is contradictory or ironic.
Finally, the speaker is not pretending to have a certain attitude toward the conversation. Their statement expresses genuine sarcasm or criticism about the contrast between the act of tweeting while driving and the advice to "stay safe."

The preliminary analysis identifies the irony in people tweeting pictures of snowy commutes while advising others to "stay safe." Here's a summary:
- **Implicature**: By calling out the irony, the speaker highlights the contradiction in urging safety while potentially engaging in unsafe behavior (tweeting while driving).
- **Presuppositions**: It is assumed that driving in snow is risky and using a phone while driving is unsafe.
- **Intent of the Speaker**: The speaker aims to point out and criticize the perceived hypocrisy or lack of self-awareness of those tweeting from their cars, by highlighting the irony.
- **Polarity**: The tone of the last sentence is negative, as it critiques the contradiction in behavior.
- **Pretense**: There's no pretense in the speaker's attitude; they openly express criticism through sarcasm.
- **Meaning**: The literal act of tweeting "stay safe" contradicts the implied riskiness of the situation, emphasizing the irony and making the tone sarcastic.
Reflecting on the analysis, the statement is indeed sarcastic. The speaker uses sarcasm to draw attention to the irony and criticize those who are tweeting about safety while potentially compromising it themselves. No major changes are needed in the preliminary analysis.

Figure 2: PMP analysis on the phrase "Lots of people tweeting pictures from their cars of their snowy commutes to work, whilst saying 'stay safe' Oh, the #irony!".

	MUStARD	
Model	Acc.	Ma-F1
RoBERTa	86.80	87.70
DistilBERT	87.00	87.70
GPT-4o (PMP)	79.42	77.65
GPT-4o-mini (PMP)	65.79	62.29
Claude 3.5 Sonnet (PMP)	72.60	71.66
LLaMA-3-70B (PMP)	72.73	73.06
LLaMA-3-8B (PMP)	53.48	54.69

Table 3: Comparison of PMP among LLMs with reported results of Helal et al. with transformer encoder models on MUStARD

Can AI Make Us Laugh? Comparing Jokes Generated by Witscript and a Human Expert

Joe Toplyn[1], Ori Amir[2]
[1]Twenty Lane Media, LLC; [2]HaHator LLC & Pomona College
joetoplyn@twentylanemedia.com, oriacadem@gmail.com

Abstract

Evaluating the effectiveness of a joke-generating AI system ultimately comes down to one question: are its jokes as funny as those crafted by humans? Prior studies have typically relied on numerical ratings assigned by human evaluators—a method with inherent limitations—and few have directly compared the quality of AI-generated jokes to that of jokes created by professional human joke writers. In this study, we measured audience laughter—a direct and fundamental response to jokes—to assess the funniness of jokes produced by a specialized AI joke-writing system. We also compared those jokes to those written by a professional human joke writer to determine which elicited more laughter. Our findings reveal that the AI-generated jokes got as much laughter as the human-crafted ones. This suggests that the best AI joke generators are now capable of composing original, conversational jokes on par with those of a professional human comedy writer.

1 Introduction

Generating humor is often regarded as an AI-complete problem, one that requires full human intelligence to solve (Hurley, 2011; Winters, 2021). Generating original humor is even a challenge for humans (Amir, 2022; Tikhonov, 2024), and the brains of professional comedians are distinct functionally and structurally (Amir, 2016; Brawer, 2021). Witscript is one of the few AI systems that can generate contextually integrated jokes, like the jokes a human might improvise in a conversation (Toplyn, 2021b). The last time Witscript was systematically evaluated (Toplyn, 2023), human evaluators judged its responses to input sentences to be jokes 44% of the time. Since then, the Witscript system has been improved. This paper puts the current system to a more challenging test, comparing the funniness of its jokes to the funniness of jokes written by a professional human joke writer.

To determine whether Witscript is as funny as a human expert, a reliable method for evaluating the funniness of jokes is necessary. Goes et al. (2022) use an AI model, but papers on the computational generation of humor almost always evaluate the generated text using non-expert humans recruited on crowdsourcing platforms like Amazon Mechanical Turk (Loakman, 2023). This evaluation method is probably common because it is relatively low-cost and easy to carry out.

Nevertheless, using non-expert humans to rate jokes on a numerical scale has significant limitations (Amin, 2020; Hossain, 2020; Inácio, 2024; Valitutti, 2013). Evidence indicates that non-expert humans cannot appropriately evaluate the quality of creative text (Lamb, 2015). In the case of jokes, this apparent inability to judge quality may arise because jokes are designed to elicit laughter, not high numerical ratings. Indeed, a common definition of "joke" is "something said or done to provoke laughter" (`www.merriam-webster.com/dictionary/joke`). And "voiced laughter is correlated with highly amusing multimedia content" (Petridis, 2009). So, we believe that measuring the laughter elicited by a joke is a better way to measure its funniness.

Laughter is strongly influenced by social context. We laugh the most when we interact with someone in person, instead of via voice or text (Scott, 2014). Therefore, to ensure a stronger laughter signal that can be more accurately measured, a joke should be delivered to a group of people by someone in their presence. Delivering the joke to a group would also help compensate for the fact that evaluating humor is subjective: if a

Proceedings of the 1st Workshop on Computational Humor (CHum), pages 71–78
January 19, 2025.

joke elicits a big laugh from a group, that means many people thought it was funny and, therefore, that the joke can objectively be assigned a high funniness rating. We decided, then, that the most reliable way to measure the funniness of jokes like those generated by Witscript is to measure how much laughter they elicit when they are delivered by professional standup comics in front of live audiences.

2 Related Work

Other authors have tasked human evaluators with comparing the funniness of jokes written by humans to that of jokes generated by AI systems. But those authors used numerical scales, not measurements of laughter, to rate the funniness of the output (Gorenz, 2024; He, 2019; Mittal, 2022; Petrović, 2013; Tikhonov, 2024; Zhang, 2020). To the best of our knowledge, this paper represents the first time that jokes generated by an AI system have been formally evaluated in the context of standup comedy performances.

3 Description of the Witscript System

Witscript is a neural-symbolic hybrid AI system designed to work in American English (Toplyn, 2023). It's symbolic because it incorporates joke-writing algorithms created by a human expert (Toplyn, 2014). And it's neural because it executes those algorithms, and other joke-production methods, by calling on a large language model in the GPT family from OpenAI (Brown et al., 2020). The Witscript jokes used in this research were generated by the version of the Witscript app that was publicly available on October 9, 2024, from `www.witscript.com`. The algorithms are based on formulas described in Toplyn (2014) and several patents (Toplyn 2020a, 2020b, 2021a).

4 System Evaluation

4.1 Input Selection

Author OA selected 16 current news headlines for use in evaluating Witscript. Author JT, a professional comedy writer, eliminated any of those headlines that were strongly associated with events occurring after the knowledge cutoff date of the GPT model used by Witscript. That way, Witscript's performance wouldn't be adversely affected by the system's dependence on non-current training data.

From the remaining news headlines, JT selected eight that, in his expert opinion, had two characteristics that made them particularly well-suited for joke writing: (1) they were likely to capture most people's interest, as good joke topics do (Toplyn, 2014); and (2) they were relatively "evergreen"—likely to seem fresh indefinitely—so jokes based on them wouldn't get stale and unfunny before testing was completed.

Then JT edited each of the eight selected news headlines into a form that he believed, in his expert opinion, would make it a useful joke topic. Each resulting topic had the following characteristics: (1) it was one sentence; (2) it was likely to be easily understood by its intended audience of adult Americans; and (3) it was relatively simple, with only one or two attention-getting elements, which Toplyn (2014) calls "topic handles."

4.2 Joke Production

The human expert—a longtime joke writer for a well-known, U.S.-based, late-night comedy/talk show—and Witscript, operated by JT, independently generated jokes based on the eight edited topics. They were given three days to complete the task to the best of their ability, so that the speed of their joke production would not be a factor.

The human expert and JT each selected from all of their own output the one joke for each topic that they believed would elicit the most laughter from an audience of typical American adults. They submitted their eight chosen jokes to a third-party data manager without sharing them with each other. All of Witscript's selected jokes were submitted exactly as they were output by Witscript.

4.3 Laughter Measurement

Experienced standup comics performed two comedy sets in front of live audiences in comedy venues in the U.S. The comics did not reveal the sources of the jokes and did not know which jokes had been written by AI. In each set, jokes based on all of the eight topics were performed, with half of the punchlines written by the human expert and half by Witscript. Both the order of the topics and which punchline was selected for each topic were determined randomly and counterbalanced between sets. As a cover story, the comics explained that they would be performing some jokes written by a friend.

To measure the quantity of laughter elicited by each joke, the recording of each set was labeled to mark the segments in which laughter occurred. The original audio was then converted to a graph of decibels over time using Formula 1.

$$dB = 20 * log10(|s| + 1e^{-6}) \qquad (1)$$

In the formula, s is the original sound wave, and $1e^{-6}$ is the lowest sound level perceivable by humans. The area under the curve, representing the "quantity of laughter," was then computed using Simpson's numerical integration method implemented in Python (Matthews, 2004). We refer to the measure as Total Laughter; its units are decibel-seconds (see Figure 1). We believe this method best captures the quantity of laughter compared to other potential methods such as the average, median, or max, as those other methods would be poor at capturing situations in which different individuals in the audience "get the joke" at different times, resulting in the same amount of laughter spread over a longer period of time.

For the present analysis, we used the audio of two high-quality sets performed at the same North Hollywood venue by the same comedian, Mike Perkins, with audience sizes of 35 and 15. The sets were performed a month apart at the same time of day (at the end of the comedian's 10-minute set opening the 8 p.m. show). Two other sets were excluded from the analysis either because of poor venue quality or small audience size (N<10).

The audio tracks were annotated to select the segments of laughter associated with each joke. In a typical set, sounds unrelated to the laughter, such as heckling, would mix with the laughter. However, these interferences were not an issue in the sets we analyzed. Additionally, comedians might speak over the laughter to make a comment or start the next joke. But in the sets we analyzed, the comedian made an effort to let the audience laugh uninterrupted, though he often did start the next joke when he felt the laughter was dying down. We always ended the laugh segment before the comedian resumed talking, so the audio segment contained laughter only. Importantly, the comedian was not aware which jokes had been written by AI, so any such interference affected all jokes equally.

We compared the performance of Human vs. AI jokes within sets and between sets. The between-sets comparison required some form of normalization of the laughs to remove any bias resulting from the size of the audience or other

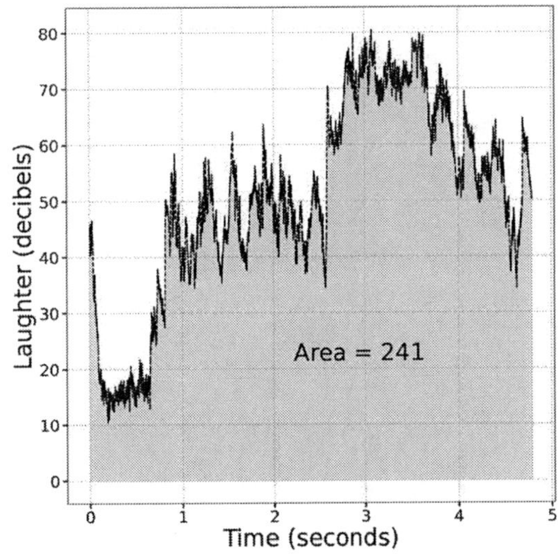

Figure 1: A demonstration of how the "Total Laughter" of a single joke is measured. The sound wave of the laughter segment following the joke is converted to dB over time. The area under the curve (here 241) is the Total Laughter in decibel-seconds.

characteristics affecting the overall loudness of its laughter. That normalization was achieved by:

1. Prior to conducting a paired t-test, we compared two joke versions across sets. The Loudness measure of all the jokes within a set was normalized by the median Loudness across all jokes in the set.
2. For the GLM the Set was included as a regressor of no interest.

4.4 The Hypothesis

Historically, the standard for demonstrating that AI had reached a certain milestone against human performance involved only a few data points. For example, Kasparov played only six games with Deep Blue (AI) in 1997 (scoring 2.5-3.5). In 2011, Watson (AI) competed only once against two human champions on *Jeopardy!*, and won. While such events would not meet the nominal standards of statistical significance required to determine that AI was "consistently" better than the human champions, they are nevertheless considered meaningful milestones, since before those events it was considered inconceivable that AI would perform at the level of those human champions even once.

If generating jokes for a comedy/talk show-style monologue, where the quality is judged by

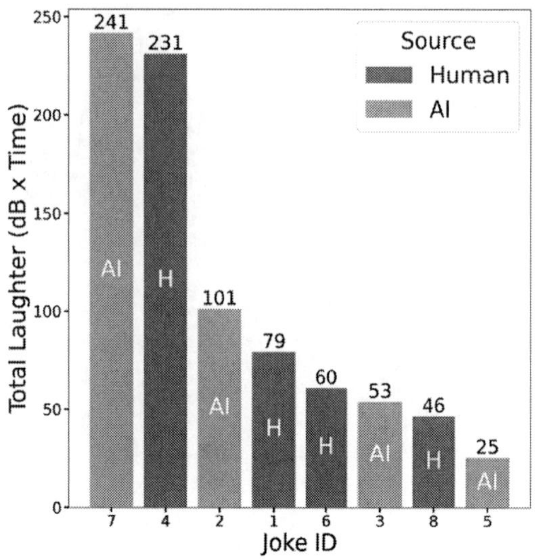

Figure 2: The jokes written by the human expert (H) and Witscript (AI) in order of the Total Laughter they elicited in Set 1. Joke ID corresponds to the actual order in which the jokes were told. The jokes are listed in the Appendix.

audience laughter, was an AI-complete problem, we would expect that:

H_0: *None* of the AI-generated jokes would perform better than *any* of the professional human writer's.

We could reject this hypothesis if:

H_1: Some of the AI-generated jokes performed better than some of the Human's.

5 Results and Discussion

5.1 Analysis Within a Set

Figure 2 displays the eight jokes performed in Set 1[1] ranked by the Total Laughter they elicited. Three of the four jokes written by AI elicited more laughter than at least one joke written by the human expert. Additionally, the joke that elicited the most laughter was AI-written.

This result is in line with H_1, in that some of the AI-written jokes did better than some of the Human's. The same pattern held true for Set 2; see the Appendix for the data. If we deem this result to be reliable, we can conclude that writing the type of humor analyzed here is not AI-complete. How can we determine this reliability?

How reliable is the measure itself? The measure captures the total laughter of an audience of N=35 and 15 in Sets 1 and 2, respectively. In a classical experiment, jokes are rated by a handful of raters. While audience members' responses are not entirely independent (e.g., laughter is contagious) whatever effect audience members had on each other was present for all jokes and presumably had the effect of signal amplification rather than of cancellation of individual differences. Additionally, unlike with raters, it is not possible to tease apart the contributions of individual raters (here, audience members). Despite these drawbacks, the number of raters/audience members is much larger than in a typical study in the field, suggesting higher reliability than the standard. The validity of the measure is arguably higher since the measure is of a natural response to jokes in a natural environment. However, there may be other forms of humor for which a traditional approach using numerical ratings would be better suited than our measurement method.

How did the Human and AI jokes compare? The funniest joke (area under the curve = 241) was written by AI. On average, AI did slightly better ($M = 106$, $SD = 96$) than the Human ($M = 104$, $SD = 86$) in Set 1, with the reverse true in Set 2 (AI: $M = 66$, $SD = 21$; Human $M = 99$, $SD = 93$). However, these differences were not significant (both sets: Mann-Whitney U(4,4) = 8.0, ns). The lack of statistical difference between the groups is not meaningful with the present sample size. Instead, as explained above (see the hypotheses), we rely on a standard similar to Deep Blue's and Watson's, that of a limited live demonstration of equivalence to human performance, which we have met.

5.2 Comparison Between the Sets

As described above, the two sets had the same eight topics, for which half of the punchlines were written by AI and half by the Human. The jokes were counterbalanced so that if a particular topic had a punchline written by the Human in Set 1 it would have a punchline written by AI in Set 2, and vice versa.

The audience size for Set 1 was bigger than for Set 2 (35 vs. 15), resulting in longer laugh times (M = 2.16 sec. vs. 1.71 sec.) and greater values on our Total Laughter metric (M = 105 vs. 83). But

[1] Set 1 had the bigger audience (N=35). It would be inappropriate to display jokes from both sets in this figure because of the difference in the Loudness baseline.

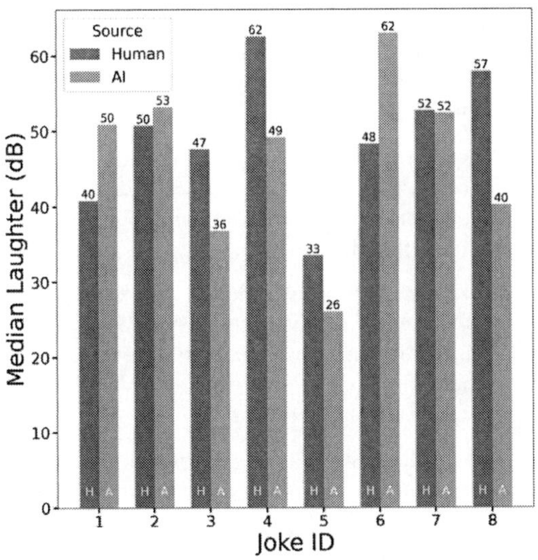

Figure 3: The Median Laughter Loudness (over the duration of the laugh) elicited by the Human (H)- vs. AI (A)-written jokes for each topic across the two sets. The lack of pattern suggests equivalent performance by the Human and AI sources.

Median Laughter Loudness showed no difference (for both sets, M = 48). Controlling for that baseline, no significant differences were observed between the AI and human-written versions of the joke for each topic. This was true for our Total Laughter metric as well as for other measures, including Mean Loudness, Median Loudness, and Length of Laugh (all paired t values < 1, ns; a GLM statistically controlling for Set effects returned the same result). Since there was no difference in the Median Laughter Loudness, that metric lends itself to a bar graph comparing the two sets which has no distortions resulting from normalization; see Figure 3.

Overall, comparing the AI and Human jokes on the same topic between sets mirrors the result of comparing the AI and Human jokes within the sets—there is no difference in the effectiveness of the jokes.

6 Contributions

This paper makes the following contributions:
1. It introduces a novel method of evaluating the funniness of jokes—measuring the laughter they elicit.
2. It demonstrates a way to compare the joke-writing ability of an AI system to that of a human expert in the real-world setting of standup comedy.
3. It provides further evidence that computational joke generation is best accomplished by taking a hybrid neural-symbolic approach.
4. It provides further evidence that at least one type of humor, generating monologue-style jokes for an American audience, is not AI-complete.

7 Conclusion

AI-written jokes, performed in front of a live audience, elicited laughter within the same range as jokes written by a professional human comedy writer.

Some AI-written jokes ranked higher than some of the human-written jokes, and the funniest joke, as measured by quantity of laughter, was written by AI.

The study provides naturalistic, real-world evidence that when it comes to generating comedy/talk show monologue-style humor, an AI system can perform at the level of a professional human comedy writer.

8 Limitations

1. Several aspects of the performances may have contributed to a joke's funniness beyond the quality of its writing. These include the comic's vocal delivery and any gestures and facial expressions he chose to make. We assume these factors influenced AI and human-written jokes equally, since the comic did not know which jokes had been written by AI. This kind of noise is the price of conducting an arguably more valid naturalistic study. It is not likely to reflect systematic bias.
2. Our measure captures the funniness ratings of the ~50 audience members for the two sets. However, the audience members cannot be considered fully independent (e.g., laughter is contagious). That acknowledged, whatever influence audience members had on each other, it was likely a constant factor of amplification affecting all jokes similarly.
3. The Witscript jokes submitted for evaluation were cherry-picked by a human expert from all of the jokes generated by Witscript on the assigned topics. However, we don't consider that to be a major limitation because the human jokes submitted for evaluation were similarly cherry-picked from multiple joke candidates crafted by the human writer.

Acknowledgments

We would like to thank the following comedians for their insights and help: Mike Perkins, Kevin Hickerson, Ajitesh Srivastava, and the comedy/talk show writer who wrote the Human jokes for the experiment.

References

Miriam Amin and Manuel Burghardt. 2020. A Survey on Approaches to Computational Humor Generation. In *Proceedings of the 4th Joint SIGHUM Workshop on Computational Linguistics for Cultural Heritage, Social Sciences, Humanities and Literature*, pages 29–41, Online. International Committee on Computational Linguistics.

Ori Amir et al. 2022. The elephant in the room: attention to salient scene features increases with comedic expertise. *Cognitive Processing,* 23(2), 203-215.

Ori Amir and Irving Biederman. 2016. The Neural Correlates of Humor Creativity. *Frontiers in Human Neuroscience, 10*(597).

Jacob Brawer and Ori Amir. 2021. Mapping the 'funny bone': neuroanatomical correlates of humor creativity in professional comedians. *Social Cognitive and Affective Neuroscience, 16*(9), 915-925.

Tom B. Brown et al. 2020. Language models are few-shot learners. arXiv preprint arXiv:2005.14165.

Fabricio Goes, Zisen Zhou, Piotr Sawicki, Marek Grzes, and Daniel G. Brown. 2022. Crowd score: A method for the evaluation of jokes using large language model AI voters as judges. arXiv preprint arXiv:2212.11214.

Drew Gorenz and Norbert Schwarz. 2024. How funny is ChatGPT? A comparison of human- and AI-produced jokes. PLoS ONE 19(7): e0305364. https://doi.org/10.1371/journal.pone.0305364.

He He, Nanyun Peng and Percy Liang. 2019. Pun Generation with Surprise. North American Chapter of the Association for Computational Linguistics.

Nabil Hossain, John Krumm, Michael Gamon, and Henry Kautz. 2020. SemEval-2020 Task 7: Assessing Humor in Edited News Headlines. In *Proceedings of the Fourteenth Workshop on Semantic Evaluation*, pages 746–758, Barcelona (online). International Committee for Computational Linguistics.

Matthew M. Hurley, Daniel C. Dennett, and Reginald B. Adams. 2011. Inside Jokes: Using Humor to Reverse-Engineer the Mind. MIT Press.

Marcio L. Inácio and Hugo G. Oliveira. 2024. Generation of Punning Riddles in Portuguese with Prompt Chaining. 15th International Conference on Computational Creativity (ICCC'24).

Carolyn Lamb, Daniel G. Brown, and Charles L.A. Clarke. 2015. Human Competence in Creativity Evaluation. Sixth International Conference on Computational Creativity.

Tyler Loakman, Aaron Maladry, and Chenghua Lin. 2023. The Iron(ic) Melting Pot: Reviewing Human Evaluation in Humour, Irony and Sarcasm Generation. Conference on Empirical Methods in Natural Language Processing.

John H. Matthews. 2004. Simpson's 3/8 Rule for Numerical Integration, Numerical Analysis-Numerical Methods Project.

Anirudh Mittal, Yufei Tian, and Nanyun Peng. 2022. AmbiPun: Generating Humorous Puns with Ambiguous Context. In *Proceedings of the 2022 Conference of the North American Chapter of the Association for Computational Linguistics: Human Language Technologies*, pages 1053–1062, Seattle, United States. Association for Computational Linguistics.

Stavros Petridis and Maja Pantic. Is this joke really funny? Judging the mirth by audiovisual laughter analysis. 2009. In *2009 IEEE International Conference on Multimedia and Expo*, New York, NY, USA, pp. 1444-1447, doi: 10.1109/ICME.2009.5202774.

Saša Petrović and David Matthews. 2013. Unsupervised joke generation from big data. In *Proceedings of the 51st Annual Meeting of the Association for Computational Linguistics (Volume 2: Short Papers)*, pages 228–232, Sofia, Bulgaria. Association for Computational Linguistics.

Sophie Scott, Nadine Lavan, Sinead Chen, and Carolyn McGettigan. 2014. The social life of laughter. *Trends in Cognitive Sciences*, 18(12), 618–620. https://doi.org/10.1016/j.tics.2014.09.002.

Alexey Tikhonov and Pavel Shtykovskiy. 2024. Humor Mechanics: Advancing Humor Generation with Multistep Reasoning. arXiv preprint arXiv:2405.07280.

Joe Toplyn. 2014. *Comedy Writing for Late-Night TV: How to Write Monologue Jokes, Desk Pieces, Sketches, Parodies, Audience Pieces, Remotes, and Other Short-Form Comedy*. Twenty Lane Media, LLC, Rye, New York.

Joe Toplyn. 2020a. Systems and Methods for Generating Jokes. U.S. Patent No. 10,642,939. Washington, DC: U.S. Patent and Trademark Office.

Joe Toplyn. 2020b. Systems and Methods for Generating Comedy. U.S. Patent No. 10,878,817. Washington, DC: U.S. Patent and Trademark Office.

Joe Toplyn. 2021a. Systems and Methods for Generating and Recognizing Jokes. U.S. Patent No. 11,080,485. Washington, DC: U.S. Patent and Trademark Office.

Joe Toplyn. 2021b. Witscript: A System for Generating Improvised Jokes in a Conversation. In *Proceedings of the 12th International Conference on Computational Creativity*, 22–31. Online: Association for Computational Creativity.

Joe Toplyn. 2023. Witscript 3: A Hybrid AI System for Improvising Jokes in a Conversation. arXiv, abs/2301.02695.

Alessandro Valitutti, Hannu Toivonen, Antoine Doucet, and Jukka M. Toivanen. 2013. "Let Everything Turn Well in Your Wife": Generation of Adult Humor Using Lexical Constraints. In *Proceedings of the 51st Annual Meeting of the Association for Computational Linguistics (Volume 2: Short Papers)*, pages 243–248, Sofia, Bulgaria. Association for Computational Linguistics.

Thomas Winters. 2021. Computers Learning Humor Is No Joke. *Harvard Data Science Review*, *3*(2). doi.org/10.1162/99608f92.f13a2337.

Hang Zhang, Dayiheng Liu, Jiancheng Lv, and Cheng Luo. 2020. Let's be Humorous: Knowledge Enhanced Humor Generation. *Annual Meeting of the Association for Computational Linguistics*.

Appendix. The Jokes

Below is a full list of the jokes and their Joke ID, which indicates the order in which they were told in the sets. Each joke has a topic that serves as a prompt/setup for both the AI- and human-written punchlines. Each set randomly includes half of the punchlines written by AI. Next to each joke, we also provide these metrics for the laughter it elicited: Total Laughter, in decibel-seconds (TL); total laugh Time, in seconds (T); and Median Laughter Loudness over the duration of the laugh, in decibels (ML).

Joke 1
Topic:
A new report says that NASA officials are worried about a leak on the International Space Station.
Human: (TL: 79, T: 2.00, ML: 40)
Will they fix it? Naw, even in space, landlords don't fix leaks.
"But Houston, we have a potty problem."
That's on them, we subcontracted to Boeing.
AI: (TL: 51, T: 1.04, ML: 50)
They're especially concerned since the leak is coming from one of their astronauts' space diapers.

Joke 2
Topic:
Why do TV stations air false political ads?
Human: (TL: 51, T: 1.04, ML: 50)
That's so after the election, we welcome the sound of "Attention, Hemorrhoid Sufferers!"
AI: (TL: 101, T: 1.96, ML: 53)
Because they want to make sure the viewers are just as confused as the candidates!

Joke 3
Topic:
A company just introduced a virtual dog leash that uses wireless technology.
Human: (TL: 73, T: 1.58, ML: 47)
Wifi can control my dog's movements? So where's his virtual pooper scooper?
AI: (TL: 53, T: 1.54, ML: 36)
But I'm pretty sure that's just a fancy way of saying 'I don't want to walk my dog.'

Joke 4
Topic:
Bob Yerkes, a stuntman who appeared in "Star Wars," died at the age of 92.
Human: (TL: 231, T: 3.92, ML: 62)
In his long career, he broke so many bones, his grave says Rest in Pieces. But true Star Wars fan to the end, he asked to be buried in his parent's basement.
AI: (TL: 48, T: 1.00, ML: 49)
He passed away surrounded by his loved ones and a strategically placed pile of mattresses.

Joke 5
Topic:
BuzzFeed put out a list of 31 things to buy when you finally decide to update your kitchen.
Human: (TL: 36, T: 1.08, ML: 33)
If you ask me, appliances are too smart already. The clock on my coffee maker flashes 12 12 12... What'll it do smarter--snicker? "Tsk tsk tsk. So much for caffeine increasing brain function."
AI: (TL: 25, T: 0.92, ML: 26)
Number 32 on the list: a new Buzzfeed article on 31 ways to use all the unnecessary gadgets you bought from the first list.

<u>Joke 6</u>
Topic:
Scientists have discovered a sixth ocean more than 400 miles below the surface of the Earth.
Human: (TL: 60, T: 1.29, ML: 48)
Great, I was just looking for a gnarly new place to surf. (mime surfing around dangers) "Stalactite! Stalagmite! Bats! Gollum!!"
AI: (TL: 94, T: 1.54, ML: 62)
Looks like Aquaman's commute just got a whole lot longer.

<u>Joke 7</u>
Topic:
Scientists are studying whether astronauts in the future could transform rocks into food.
Human: (TL: 236, T: 4.62, ML: 52)
Hey, don't give Fruity Pebbles any ideas. Rocky Road with real rocks? You could chip a tooth on Stone Ground Mustard!
AI: (TL: 241, T: 4.79, ML: 52)
Which is great news for anyone who's ever had a craving for a pebble pie.

<u>Joke 8</u>
Topic:
A new study says that young children in the UK get almost half their calories from ultra-processed food.
Human: (TL: 46, T: 0.88, ML: 57)
If you think that's bad, the other half is British cooking.
AI: (TL: 70, T: 1.79, ML: 40)
The most popular kids' meals in the UK are now the Happy Meal, the Crispy Chicken Sandwich, and Uncle Nigel's Deep-Fried Crumpets.

Evaluating Human Perception and Bias in AI-Generated Humor

Narendra Nath Joshi
Adobe Inc
San Jose, CA, USA
joshinarendranath@gmail.com

Abstract

This paper explores human perception of AI-generated humor, examining biases and the ability to distinguish between human and AI-created jokes. Through a between-subjects user study involving 174 participants, we tested hypotheses on quality perception, source identification, and demographic influences. Our findings reveal that AI-generated jokes are rated comparably to human-generated ones, with source blindness improving AI humor ratings. Participants struggled to identify AI-generated jokes accurately, and repeated exposure led to increased appreciation. Younger participants showed more favorable perceptions, while technical background had no significant impact. These results challenge preconceptions about AI's humor capabilities and highlight the importance of addressing biases in AI content evaluation. We also suggest pathways for enhancing human-AI creative collaboration and underscore the need for transparency and ethical considerations in AI-generated content.

1 Introduction

Advancements in generative artificial intelligence have opened up new avenues in creative expression. These powerful language and content generation models produce remarkably human-like text, images, audio, and code. One particularly intriguing application is its ability to generate humorous content.

Humor is a fundamental aspect of human communication and interaction. It serves various social and psychological functions, from facilitating bonding and group cohesion to reducing stress and diffusing tense situations (Martin and Ford, 2018). Psychologists have long studied the role of humor in human development, cognition, and emotional expression (Berger, 2014). Humor improves mood, enhances creativity, and fosters feelings of empathy and trust between individuals (Kuiper and Nicholl, 2004).

Humor is a uniquely human trait that has been beyond the capabilities of machines until recently. However, the latest breakthroughs in natural language processing, neural networks, and large language models challenge this assumption. Generative artificial intelligence systems can now be trained on vast repositories of human-created humor, from witty one-liners to elaborate comedic sketches. By identifying patterns, analyzing the structure of humor, and learning to mimic the creative processes of human comedians, these models can generate original humorous content that often surprises and delights its audience.

Generating, understanding, and appreciating humor requires complex cognitive processes, including pattern recognition, perspective-taking, and juxtaposing incongruous concepts (Veale, 2004). Previous research has highlighted humor's nuanced and context-dependent nature, with cultural norms, personal experiences, and social dynamics all playing a role in an individual's humorous sensibilities (Polimeni and Reiss, 2006). Exploring how generative artificial intelligence systems can capture and replicate these multifaceted elements of human humor is a fascinating and challenging area of inquiry.

However, generating high-quality humor remains a significant challenge for current systems. Humor is a complex and subjective phenomenon, often relying on cultural references, contextual understanding, and the ability to surprise and delight the audience (Ritchie, 2009). Existing generative artificial intelligence models may need help to capture the full depth and nuance of human humor, leading to humor perceived as generic or lacking in authenticity (Augello et al., 2008).

Furthermore, it is crucial to understand how human perception and biases influence the evaluation of AI-generated humor. Humans may have preconceived notions or skepticism about machines' ability to generate genuinely humorous content,

Proceedings of the 1st Workshop on Computational Humor (CHum), pages 79–87
January 19, 2025. ©2025 Association for Computational Linguistics

which could lead to biased assessments.

As generative artificial intelligence advances, it becomes increasingly important to understand its impact on various domains, including the creative arts and human-computer interaction. In this work, we explore the current state of generative artificial intelligence and its humor applications. We examine the human perception of humor created by generative artificial intelligence.

Building upon these foundational concepts and challenges, this study aims to investigate specific hypotheses and research questions regarding human perception of AI-generated humor. Our research is guided by the following hypotheses and corresponding research questions:

H1 Humans believe they can reasonably identify if humor is AI-generated. **(Reasonable Identification Hypotheses)**

- **H1a** Participants' accuracy in identifying AI-generated jokes is higher than chance.

H2 Humans have reasonable doubt in AI's abilities to generate quality humor. **(Reasonable Doubt Hypotheses)**

- **H2a** Humans rate AI-generated jokes lower in quality compared to human-generated jokes.
- **H2b** The perceived quality of AI-generated jokes improves when participants are unaware of the source.

H3 Bias towards AI-generated humor changes with exposure. **(Repeated Exposure Hypotheses)**

- **H3a** Participants' ratings of AI-generated jokes improve after repeated exposure.

H4 Demographic factors influence perception of AI-generated humor. **(Demographic Hypotheses)**

- **H4a** Younger participants rate AI-generated jokes higher than older participants.
- **H4b** Participants with a background in technology or AI are more accepting of AI-generated humor.

To investigate these hypotheses, we formulated the following research questions:

RQ1: Are participants able to accurately identify AI-generated jokes more often than by chance? *(tests Hypothesis H1a)*

RQ2: Do humans rate AI-generated jokes lower in quality compared to human-generated jokes? *(tests Hypothesis H2a)*

RQ3: Does the perceived quality of AI-generated jokes improve when participants are unaware of the source? *(tests Hypothesis H2b)*

RQ4: Do participants' ratings of AI-generated jokes improve after repeated exposure? *(tests Hypothesis H3a)*

RQ5: Do younger participants rate AI-generated jokes higher than older participants? *(tests Hypothesis H4a)*

RQ6: Are participants with a background in technology or AI more accepting of AI-generated humor? *(tests Hypothesis H4b)*

Through a carefully designed user study, we aim to address these research questions and test our hypotheses, contributing to the understanding of human perception and bias in the context of AI-generated humor.

2 Related Work

The field of computational humor has evolved from early rule-based systems to more sophisticated data-driven approaches powered by modern machine learning techniques. Researchers have increasingly focused on understanding human perception and biases towards AI-generated humor.

Previously, researchers primarily focused on rule-based systems that attempted to capture the logical structures and linguistic patterns underlying humorous expressions (Binsted, 1996 and Ritchie, 2001). These systems relied on pre-defined rules and templates to generate puns, jokes, and other forms of humor. However, they were often limited in their ability to adapt to the nuances and complexities of human humor, which can be highly context-dependent and subjective.

As the field of artificial intelligence advanced, researchers began exploring the use of machine learning algorithms to generate humor in a more data-driven manner. Mihalcea and Strapparava, 2005 developed one of the early data-driven systems, which utilized semantic relationships and linguistic features to identify and generate humorous one-liners. This approach showed promise but needed higher quality and semantically diverse training data. Valitutti et al., 2016 developed a system that could produce puns and other forms of wordplay by exploiting linguistic patterns and semantic relationships. Similarly, Winters et al., 2019 presented a general framework for computational humor that learns joke structures and parametrization from rated example jokes by learning from datasets of human-created humor. These findings suggest that modern machine learning systems can recognize and replicate the nuances of humor.

The recent advancements in large language models have further expanded the capabilities of computational humor generation. LLM-based approaches, such as those leveraging GPT-3 (Brown, 2020) or other transformer-based models, have demonstrated impressive performance in generating coherent and contextually relevant humor. These models are trained on vast amounts of text data, allowing them to capture more nuanced linguistic patterns and common-sense knowledge that can be leveraged for humor generation (Hossain, 2020).

Alongside these advancements in computational humor generation, researchers have also begun to explore the importance of understanding human perception and biases towards AI-generated humor. Humor is a highly subjective and complex phenomenon, often relying on cultural references, contextual understanding, and the ability to surprise and delight the audience (Ritchie, 2009).

3 Methodology

3.1 Study Design

We conducted a between-subjects experimental study to investigate human perception of AI-generated humor and potential biases in evaluation. The study was designed to examine how knowledge of a joke's source (human or AI) influences perception, and how different presentation contexts affect evaluation accuracy and bias.

Participants were randomly assigned to one of six experimental groups, each designed to test specific aspects of humor perception and source identification:

- **Group A (Human Baseline)** Participants evaluated only human-generated jokes, establishing a baseline for humor quality ratings and identification accuracy.
- **Group B (AI Baseline)** Participants evaluated only AI-generated jokes, allowing assessment of perceived quality and identification accuracy for AI-generated content.
- **Group C (Alternating Sequence)** Participants evaluated an alternating sequence of human and AI-generated jokes, enabling assessment of distinction abilities in a structured mixed context.
- **Group D (Mixed Presentation)** Participants evaluated a randomized set of both human and AI-generated jokes, testing identification accuracy in a naturalistic mixed context.
- **Group E (Blind AI Test)** Participants evaluated AI-generated jokes without knowledge of their source, measuring unbiased quality perception.
- **Group F (Informed AI Test)** Participants evaluated AI-generated jokes with explicit knowledge of their AI origin, enabling direct comparison with Group E to measure source-related bias.

3.2 Participant Selection and Demographics

We recruited 193 total participants from Amazon Mechanical Turk (Paolacci et al., 2010). Participating workers received a \$5.00 compensation based on an estimated work of 30 minutes for a projected wage of \$10 (US federal minimum wage is \$7.25). The workers provided informed consent before completing the study. After completing the task, participants also answered questions about demographics and prior experience with Mechanical Turk.

We performed several integrity checks for our participants. Similar to prior studies deployed on Mechanical Turk (Ashktorab et al., 2021), we excluded workers whose mean rating time was less than 3 seconds and removed workers who had uniform responses ($\sigma < 5$) in the rating responses. We also removed individuals from the study who fell outside of the mean $\pm$2SD statistic for each of the dependent variables. This process left us with 174 participants.

Demographic data was collected for:

- **Gender** (Male, Female, Non-binary, Prefer not to say, Other)
- **Age Range** (18-24, 25-34, 35-44, 45-54, 55+)
- **Experience with AI technologies** (5-point scale from "Never use it" to "Deep understanding")

3.3 Stimulus Selection and Preparation

3.3.1 Human-Generated Jokes

Human-generated jokes were sourced from (Phillips, 2013), curated by a panel of three independent raters to ensure consistent quality and appropriate content. Selected jokes represented various humor styles (wordplay, observational, situational) while controlling for potentially confounding variables such as length and complexity. The jokes were completely text-based.

3.3.2 AI-Generated Jokes

AI-generated jokes were created using Claude 3.5 Sonnet (Anthropic, 2024), with consistent prompting techniques to ensure comparable quality and style variety. The jokes underwent the same rating and filtering process as human-generated jokes to maintain experimental control. The jokes were completely text-based.

3.4 Experimental Procedure

3.4.1 Joke Presentation

Each participant evaluated twenty-five jokes in their assigned condition. In trials, we found twenty-five jokes to be appropriate as an increased number of jokes could lead to potential cognitive fatigue and a drop in study experience and quality of results. Jokes were presented individually in randomized order (except for Group C's alternating sequence) to control for order effects.

3.4.2 Rating Sessions

The experiment consisted of two phases:

1. **Initial Rating Phase**: All participants rated jokes on a 5-point scale (Very funny to Not funny at all).
2. **Source Assessment Phase**: Group E performed additional tasks:
    - Source identification (Human/AI)
    - Confidence ratings (5-point scale)

4 Results

4.1 Overall Analysis

Our analysis reveals several significant patterns in how humans perceive and evaluate AI-generated humor. We present our findings organized by research questions, incorporating both quantitative metrics and qualitative observations. The results challenge several preconceptions about AI-generated humor while confirming others, particularly regarding demographic influences and exposure effects.

4.2 Source Assessment Performance (RQ1)

Participants' ability to identify AI-generated jokes shows minimal deviation from chance:

- Accuracy: 0.43034
- Mean Confidence: 3.892

The near-chance accuracy rates suggest that distinguishing between human and AI-generated humor has become increasingly challenging. High-quality AI-generated jokes, in particular, were frequently misattributed to human authors with high confidence, indicating significant advancement in AI's ability to generate natural-seeming humor.

4.3 Quality Perception and Source Bias

4.3.1 Comparative Quality Ratings (RQ2)

Contrary to initial expectations, our analysis shows that participants do not rate AI-generated jokes significantly lower in quality compared to human-generated jokes (μ_{AI} = 2.97393, σ = 1.4137; μ_{human} = 2.94769, σ = 1.4046).

This finding is particularly noteworthy given the common assumption that AI-generated content would be perceived as inferior to human-created content. The ratings distribution shows considerable overlap between the two sources, with AI-generated jokes occasionally receiving higher scores in categories such as wordplay and situational humor.

4.3.2 Source Awareness Effects (RQ3)

The blind testing condition (Group E) demonstrates significantly different ratings compared to the informed condition (Group F):

- Blind condition: μ = 3.34064, σ = 1.1056
- Informed condition: μ = 2.92737, σ = 1.4164
- Statistical significance: [t(df) = 6.04, p = $1.78e - 09$]

The data reveals a clear pattern of bias when participants are informed about the source. In the blind condition, participants evaluated jokes primarily on their inherent humor value, leading to more favorable ratings for AI-generated content. This suggests that preconceptions about AI capabilities may influence judgment more than actual content quality.

Group	Mean Rating (First 7 Jokes)	Mean Rating (Last 7 Jokes)
A	3.02721	2.84354
B	2.88095	3.15476
C	2.90043	3.06494
D	3.21693	3.56085
E	2.99078	3.47926
F	2.91353	2.96617

Table 1: Mean Humor Ratings for First 7 and Last 7 Jokes by Group

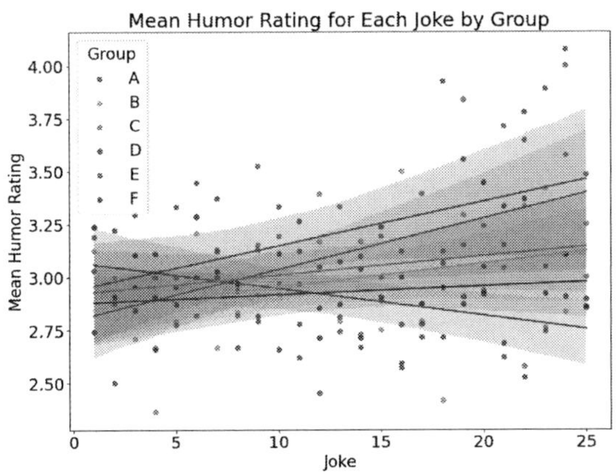

Figure 1: Mean Humor Rating for each Joke for each Group. Note that Group A is only human-generated jokes

4.4 Exposure and Learning Effects (RQ4)

Analysis of rating progression shows a significant upward linear trend in groups with AI-generated jokes (Groups B, C, D, E and F) as shown in Figure 1. The improvement in ratings over time as shown in Table 1 suggests a familiarization effect, where initial skepticism gives way to increased appreciation of AI-generated humor. This trend is particularly evident in the mixed presentation sequence group D and the blind AI test group E.

4.5 Demographic Influences

4.5.1 Age-Related Effects (RQ5)

Results reveal significant age-group differences as shown in Figure 2. The age-related differences in ratings show a clear generational pattern across different groups, with younger participants demonstrating more openness to AI-generated humor. This trend remains consistent across different joke types and presentation formats.

4.5.2 Technical Background Impact (RQ6)

Analysis of variance indicates no significant differences based on AI expertise across groups as shown in Figure 3. Participants with technical backgrounds did not provide more favorable ratings but showed a more nuanced appreciation for AI-generated humor, often mentioning technical aspects in their qualitative feedback.

4.6 Qualitative Observations

Participant feedback revealed several recurring themes. Many expressed initial skepticism, with some noting, *"It's strange to think of AI 'trying' to be funny when it doesn't actually experience humor. I'm not sure it will ever truly understand what makes people laugh"* (Participant 36) and *"The jokes were clever enough, but there's something unsettling about humor coming from a machine. It's missing the human touch"* (Participant 71). However, others were surprised by the quality of the AI-generated humor, with comments such as, *"It's impressive how well the AI captured the timing and wit usually found in human jokes. I wouldn't have guessed it was machine-generated"* (Participant 64) and *"I was genuinely surprised that an AI could come up with something this funny! I didn't expect it to pick up on such subtle humor"* (Participant 146). Finally, some participants noted recognizing patterns in the AI's humor, with one stating, *"I noticed a lot of the humor felt very structured, almost too perfect. I think the AI relies on patterns that work, but it doesn't quite get the unpredictability that human humor has"* (Participant 21), and another remarking, *"When I started paying attention, I could tell the AI was using patterns that were too precise. It didn't have the imperfections or unpredictable elements that make human humor feel fresh"* (Participant 167).

These qualitative insights provide context for the quantitative findings and highlight the complex nature of human perception of AI-generated content.

4.7 Summary of Key Findings

Our results reveal several important patterns. AI-generated jokes receive comparable ratings to human-generated ones, challenging preconceptions about AI's humor capabilities. Source blindness significantly improves perception of AI-generated humor, indicating the presence of implicit bias. Participants demonstrate poor ability to distinguish between AI and human-generated jokes despite high confidence. Repeated exposure leads to improved

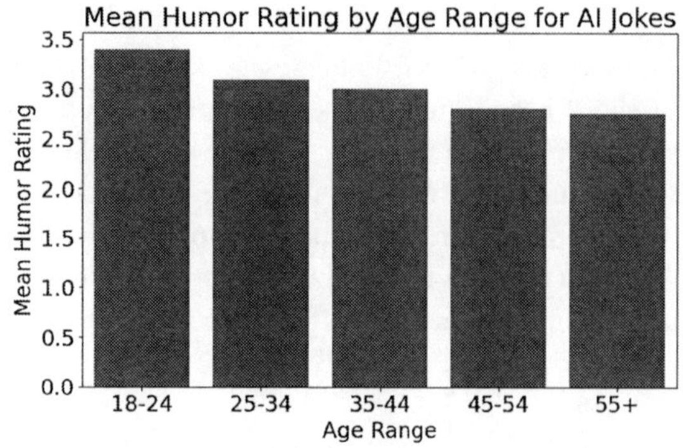

Figure 2: Mean Humor Rating by Age Range for AI-Generated Jokes

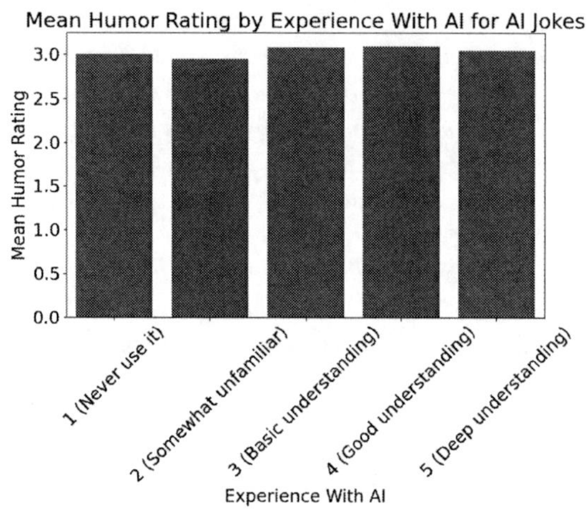

Figure 3: Mean Humor Rating by Experience with AI for AI-Generated Jokes

ratings and reduced bias. Younger participants show more favorable perceptions of AI-generated humor. Participants with technical backgrounds do not demonstrate more favorable perceptions of AI-generated humor.

5 Discussion

5.1 Human Ability to Distinguish AI Content

The inability of participants to accurately identify AI-generated jokes beyond chance levels (RQ1) has significant implications for the sophistication of current AI humor generation systems, especially when reported confidence is high. It also raises the potential need for AI disclosure in creative content, especially as the line between human and AI-generated works continues to blur. Furthermore, this finding highlights the future of human-AI creative collaboration and the ethical considerations surrounding the attribution of AI-generated content.

5.2 Evolution of AI Humor Perception

Our findings challenge the prevalent assumption that humans inherently prefer human-generated humor over AI-generated content. The comparable ratings between AI and human-generated jokes (as shown in RQ2) suggest that AI systems have reached a significant milestone in generating contextually appropriate and genuinely amusing content. This advancement reflects the sophisticated natural language processing capabilities of modern AI systems, particularly in understanding and replicating the nuanced patterns that make content humorous.

5.3 The Role of Source Bias

The improvement in perceived quality when the source is unknown (RQ3) reveals a crucial insight into human cognitive bias. This "source bias" effect demonstrates how preconceived notions about AI capabilities can influence humor appreciation. The disconnect between blind and informed ratings suggests that humans may hold unconscious biases against AI-generated content. These biases can significantly impact their evaluation of creative content, with the quality of AI-generated humor often being systematically undervalued when its source is known.

5.4 Demographic and Exposure Effects

The improvement in ratings with repeated exposure (RQ4) indicates a learning effect that could have important implications for AI content integration strategies. It suggests that public acceptance of AI-generated creative works may increase over time, as audiences become more familiar with the technology. This improvement also points to the potential for long-term shifts in perception, as repeated exposure helps individuals to better understand and appreciate AI-generated content.

5.5 Generational Differences

The observed age-related differences in humor appreciation (RQ5) reflect broader patterns in technology adoption and acceptance. Younger participants' higher ratings of AI-generated humor suggest a generational shift in attitudes toward AI-generated content. These differences may indicate potential future trends in AI acceptance, with younger generations being more open to embracing AI-driven creative works. Moreover, the role of early exposure to technology in shaping these perceptions cannot be overlooked.

5.6 Technical Literacy Impact

While technical background does not show a direct correlation with humor appreciation (RQ6), this finding still provides valuable insights into how knowledge may influence perception. It suggests that understanding AI systems could potentially reduce skepticism toward AI-generated content, even though such a relationship is not evident in the data. Additionally, education about AI capabilities may play a role in influencing public reception of AI-generated works. While no clear connection between technical literacy and humor appreciation is found, it remains a potential area for future exploration, especially in terms of how technical knowledge might shape bias against AI-generated content.

5.7 Technical Implications

Our findings suggest several key implications for the development of humor-generating AI systems. One crucial factor is the importance of context awareness in humor generation, ensuring that AI systems can understand and adapt to the nuances of different situations. The need for diverse training data is also highlighted, as it could help AI systems better appeal to various demographics, accounting for differences in humor preferences. Additionally, incorporating user feedback mechanisms into the design of AI systems may enhance their ability to tailor humor more effectively. Lastly, maintaining stylistic consistency in AI-generated humor is valuable, as it can create a more coherent and relatable experience for the audience.

5.8 Societal Implications

The study's findings also have broader societal implications, particularly in the context of AI's role in everyday life. As AI continues to integrate into various aspects of our society, it will influence not only the entertainment and media sectors but also broader cultural perceptions of creativity and originality. Understanding these dynamics can help shape policies and frameworks that govern the use and development of AI technologies in socially sensitive areas.

5.9 Creative Industry Impact

The implications of our findings extend to the future of AI in creative industries. One key aspect is the evolving role of AI in content creation, which could redefine how creative works are produced. The potential for human-AI collaborative content creation also stands out, with AI augmenting human creativity in new and innovative ways. The future of entertainment and media production will likely see a blending of human and AI-generated content, which could change how audiences consume creative works. Additionally, this shift may influence employment and skill requirements in creative fields, as new roles emerge to manage and work alongside AI systems.

5.10 Design Considerations

The study suggests several design principles that could guide future AI humor systems. Transparency in source attribution is important, ensuring users are aware of whether content is AI-generated. Adapting to user preferences and feedback is another key principle, allowing AI systems to evolve and better align with individual tastes over time. Incorporating cultural and contextual awareness will also be crucial in making AI-generated humor more relevant and relatable. Finally, a balance between novelty and familiarity is essential, as AI humor should be fresh and surprising without straying too far from what audiences find familiar and enjoyable.

5.11 Ethical Considerations

Our study raises several important ethical questions regarding AI-generated content. One of the main concerns is the need for transparency, particularly in the disclosure of AI-generated content. This disclosure is vital in maintaining trust and ensuring that audiences are informed about the nature of the material they engage with. The potential impact of AI on human creativity and expression also warrants attention, as it may alter how people perceive and value human-created art. Furthermore, the role of AI in shaping cultural narratives is a significant ethical consideration, as AI could influence societal values and perceptions. Lastly, preserving human agency in the creative process is essential, ensuring that AI serves as a tool to augment human creativity, not replace it.

5.12 Limitations and Future Research

5.12.1 Study Limitations

There are some limitations to consider in this study. First, the specific context and timing of the research may influence the findings, as perceptions of AI-generated content can evolve over time. Additionally, the limited range of humor styles tested in the study means that the findings may not fully reflect the diversity of humor types that exist. Sampling biases in participant selection could also affect the generalizability of the results. Finally, the rapid evolution of AI capabilities means that the study's conclusions may need to be revisited as new advancements emerge.

5.12.2 Future Research Directions

Future research should address several areas to further explore the impact of AI on humor appreciation and content creation. One potential direction is studying long-term changes in perception over extended exposure to AI-generated content, which could reveal how familiarity affects audience reception. Cross-cultural variations in AI humor appreciation should also be examined, as different cultures may have distinct humor preferences. Additionally, the impact of various AI disclosure methods on audience reactions warrants further investigation. Future studies could also explore the role of personalization in AI humor generation, examining how tailored content influences user satisfaction. Finally, the influence of different humor styles and contexts on AI-generated content should be explored to better understand how AI systems can cater to diverse comedic tastes.

6 Conclusion

Our findings suggest that the relationship between humans and AI-generated humor is more complex and nuanced than previously understood. As AI systems continue to evolve, the distinction between human and AI-generated content becomes increasingly subtle, challenging our preconceptions about creativity and humor. The study highlights the importance of understanding and addressing human biases in the development and deployment of AI creative systems, while also suggesting potential pathways for improving human-AI creative collaboration.

References

Anthropic. 2024. Claude. `https://www.anthropic.com`. Version 3.5 Sonnet.

Zahra Ashktorab, Michael Desmond, Josh Andres, Michael Muller, Narendra Nath Joshi, Michelle Brachman, Aabhas Sharma, Kristina Brimijoin, Qian Pan, Christine T Wolf, et al. 2021. Ai-assisted human labeling: Batching for efficiency without overreliance. *Proceedings of the ACM on Human-Computer Interaction*, 5(CSCW1):1–27.

Agnese Augello, Gaetano Saccone, Salvatore Gaglio, and Giovanni Pilato. 2008. Humorist bot: Bringing computational humour in a chat-bot system. In *2008 international conference on complex, intelligent and software intensive systems*, pages 703–708. IEEE.

Peter L Berger. 2014. *Redeeming laughter: The comic dimension of human experience*. Walter de Gruyter GmbH & Co KG.

Kim Binsted. 1996. Machine humour: An implemented model of puns.

Tom B Brown. 2020. Language models are few-shot learners. *arXiv preprint arXiv:2005.14165*.

Nabil Tarique Hossain. 2020. *Creative natural language generation: humor and beyond*. University of Rochester.

Nicholas A Kuiper and Sorrel Nicholl. 2004. Thoughts of feeling better? sense of humor and physical health.

Rod A Martin and Thomas Ford. 2018. *The psychology of humor: An integrative approach*. Academic press.

Rada Mihalcea and Carlo Strapparava. 2005. Making computers laugh: Investigations in automatic humor recognition. In *Proceedings of Human Language Technology Conference and Conference on Empirical Methods in Natural Language Processing*, pages 531–538.

Gabriele Paolacci, Jesse Chandler, and Panagiotis G Ipeirotis. 2010. Running experiments on amazon mechanical turk. *Judgment and Decision making*, 5(5):411–419.

Bob Phillips. 2013. *The World's Greatest Collection of Clean Jokes*. Harvest House Publishers.

Joseph Polimeni and Jeffrey P Reiss. 2006. The first joke: Exploring the evolutionary origins of humor. *Evolutionary psychology*, 4(1):147470490600400129.

Graeme Ritchie. 2001. Current directions in computational humour. *Artificial Intelligence Review*, 16:119–135.

Graeme Ritchie. 2009. Can computers create humor? *AI Magazine*, 30(3):71–71.

Alessandro Valitutti, Antoine Doucet, Jukka M Toivanen, and Hannu Toivonen. 2016. Computational generation and dissection of lexical replacement humor. *Natural Language Engineering*, 22(5):727–749.

Tony Veale. 2004. Incongruity in humor: Root cause or epiphenomenon?

Thomas Winters, Vincent Nys, and Danny De Schreye. 2019. Towards a general framework for humor generation from rated examples. In *ICCC*, pages 274–281.

The Theater Stage as Laboratory: Review of Real-Time Comedy LLM Systems for Live Performance

Piotr Mirowski
Improbotics
London, UK
piotr.mirowski@computer.org

Boyd Branch
Improbotics
Coventry, UK

Kory Mathewson
Improbotics
Montréal, Canada

Abstract

In this position paper, we review the eclectic recent history of academic and artistic works involving computational systems for humor generation, and focus specifically on live performance. We make the case that AI comedy should be evaluated in live conditions, in front of audiences sharing either physical or online spaces, and under real-time constraints. We further suggest that improvised comedy is therefore the perfect substrate for deploying and assessing computational humor systems. Using examples of successful AI-infused shows, we demonstrate that live performance raises three sets of challenges for computational humor generation: 1) questions around robotic embodiment, anthropomorphism and competition between humans and machines, 2) questions around comedic timing and the nature of audience interaction, and 3) questions about the human interpretation of seemingly absurd AI-generated humor. We argue that these questions impact the choice of methodologies for evaluating computational humor, as any such method needs to work around the constraints of live audiences and performance spaces. These interrogations also highlight different types of collaborative relationship of human comedians towards AI tools.

1 Introduction

Attempting to combine humor with machine intelligence is a long-standing subject of scientific enquiry and it is perceived as a fundamental challenge (Raskin, 1979). Amin and Burghardt (2020), Veale (2021) and Sharples and y Pérez (2022) provide authoritative reviews of this nascent field, which can be supplemented with examples of recent works that rely on large language models (Winters et al., 2018; Toplyn, 2023; Chen et al., 2023; Jentzsch and Kersting, 2023; Tikhonov and Shtykovskiy, 2024).

According to several computational humor researchers including Winters (2021), *"humans are the only known species that use humor for making others laugh. Furthermore, every known human civilization also has had at least some form of humor for making others laugh"* (Caron, 2002; Gervais and Wilson, 2005). This observation is often extrapolated into the assertion that humor remains an elusive goal for AI (in the same vein, researchers in computational storytelling have defined improvisational storytelling as a *grand challenge* for AI (Martin et al., 2016)). According to recent surveys (Mirowski et al., 2024), this skeptical view about AI's comedic potential is a strongly-held opinion shared by the wider comedy community, from actors and audiences to reviewers and journalists writing about comedy.

For this reason, we posit that comedy audiences and performance spaces are the ultimate environments to critically evaluate the quality of systems for the computational generation of humor. Even though some studies like (Gorenz and Schwarz, 2024) have evaluated AI-generated humor using crowd-sourced workers, human-computer interaction researchers have raised concerns about the poor quality of crowd-sourced evaluation of open-ended text generation (Karpinska et al., 2021), which can be attributed to lack of buy-in from evaluators, and to missing context. The setup of live professional comedy invites **paying audiences** expecting to have a good time, and **critical reviewers** judging the overall performance: it thus provides with a realistic and challenging testbed for computational humor systems. Moreover, the live nature of comedy performance creates rich, **interactive exchanges** between comedians and audiences, which—unlike pure online evaluation—allows comedians (and comedy generation systems) to incorporate **real-time feedback** and rich sensory and **cultural context** in the **safe** environment of theater.

At the intersection of live theater and humor sits improvisational theater and comedy (Johnstone, 1979), a complex theatrical art form that can be

Proceedings of the 1st Workshop on Computational Humor (CHum), pages 88–95
January 19, 2025.

traced back to Rhapsodes in Ancient Greece or to Commedia dell'Arte (Lea, 1934; Collins, 2001; Mathewson, 2019). Because it relies on natural human interaction and demands constant adaptation to an evolving context, theatrical improvisation (like jazz) has been qualified as *"real-time dynamic problem solving"* (Magerko et al., 2009; Johnson-Laird, 2002). According to Mathewson and Mirowski (2018) *"improv requires performers to exhibit acute listening to both verbal and non-verbal suggestions coming from the other improvisers, split-second reaction, rapid empathy towards the other performers and the audience, short- and long-term memory of narrative elements, and practiced storytelling skills"*, making it a highly interesting challenge for AI systems. Interestingly, theatrical improvisation encourages risk taking and experimentation, and it even "celebrates failure" thanks to a tacit agreement between improvisers and audiences who acknowledge the challenge of making up comedic material live on the stage. The improv stage thus provides a "safe" environment to test technological tools like artificial intelligence.

What follows is a literature and performance review of the state of the art of computational humor systems deployed in real-time in front of live audiences, whether in physical or in virtual spaces. We group these according to the type of scientific or artistic questions that they raise, starting with questions around robotic **embodiment** of chatbots, anthropomorphism and **competition** between humans and machines (Section 2), and questions around **liveness**, **timing** and utility in the artistic process (Section 3). We address the human **interpretation** and **justification** of seemingly absurd AI-generated humor (Section 4) and finish with a discussion on how the constraints of live audiences and performance spaces impact the choice of methodologies for evaluating computational humor (Section 5). We therefore suggest that the setting of live performance allows to define collaborative relationships between human comedians and AI tools.

2 Robot comedy as a test of humanity

As introduced in the previous section, a commonly held belief is that humor is seen as the last frontier of intelligence (Winters, 2021). Robot comedy can then be seen as a challenge to humanity itself[1].

[1]This prompted comedy critic Logan (2023) to unwittingly center comedy over other art forms: *"unlike music and visual art, comedy can't be easily reduced to an algorithm." (sic)*

2.1 Can robots deliver comedy on stage?

Robot embodiment presents with unique challenges of audience reception. Some robotics and theater practitioners like Hiroshi Ishiguro and Oriza Hirata took the route of anthropomorphism (Pluta, 2016) to make the robot presence as human-like as possible, whereas others like Tom Sgouros built a custom robotic arm[2] or even, like Annie Dorsen, simply staged two laptops "talking" philosophy[3].

In 2010, social roboticist Prof. Heather Knight[4] pioneered staged comedy performances with an Aldebaran Nao[5] robot delivering human-written comedy and gathering audience feedback thanks to camera sensors that track audience sentiment following each line delivered by the robot, and used this information to modify next joke selection based on audience feedback (Knight et al., 2011). Starting in 2014, Austin, Texas-based multidisciplinary artist and engineer Arthur Simone staged toy-like humanoid robots to be his partners in improvised theater performances: *Bot Party: Improv Comedy with Robots*[6], thus investigating how to improvise with a robot.

In 2016, theater improvisers and robotics researchers Dr. Piotr Mirowski and Dr. Kory Mathewson from duo *HumanMachine*[7] developed large language models (Sutskever et al., 2014) for improvisational comedy (Mathewson and Mirowski, 2017a). Unlike previous, rule-based AI methods geared at generating comedy, they trained general conversational models (Vinyals and Le, 2015) trained on OpenSubtitles (Tiedemann, 2009). The language model was coupled with speech recognition to listen to their human partner, text-to-speech and text-dependent robotic control to operate a small scale robot such as the Nao or EZ-Robot JD Humanoid[8]. Comedy derived from the human actor attempting to justify whatever the robot said.

Some of those robot performances incorporated implicit audience feedback (Knight et al., 2011; Mathewson and Mirowski, 2017a), but we hypothesize that audiences may have evaluated the novelty of the premises of those shows in addition to their comedic quality.

[2]https://sgouros.com/judy/
[3]https://anniedorsen.com/projects/hello-hi-there/
[4]https://www.ted.com/talks/heather_knight_silicon_based_comedy
[5]https://www.aldebaran.com/en/nao
[6]https://www.botparty.org/
[7]https://humanmachine.live
[8]https://www.ez-robot.com/

2.2 Computational humor presented as a competition between humans and machine

The recent rapid deployment of AI in the creative fields has raised ethical issues around the cannibalization of creative economies (Frosio, 2023) and the lack of consent in how training data for AI was obtained (Zhong et al., 2023). As a consequence, the public debate around AI is currently driven by the fear of replacement; as illustrated below, performance artists engaging AI ask the question whether AI-generated humor can ever *match* human level.

In 2023, and in the context of public releases of generative AI tools, and of their subsequent short-term impact on creative industries (contributing to the Writers Guild of America (WGA) labour action), Los Angeles-based comedians Allisson Goldberg and Brad Einstein created *Comedians vs. AI: Stage Against the Machine*[9]. Their show featured two teams of comedians, one "human" relying only on their skills, another one supported by Gen AI software like ChatGPT and DALL-E. The show evaluated AI in an adversarial context, pitting one team against another, and promising the audiences reassurance about limited capabilities of the machines; to quote one comedian, "We have the benefit of having trauma and life experience to pull from that AI doesn't have integrated yet, and that makes us more dynamic and sensitive and hilarious for now." (Jamerson, 2023).

In that same year of 2023, New York-based Comedy Bytes[10] refined this concept to focus on improvised *rap battles* and *comedy roasts* between a small cast of human performers, and cartoonish virtual avatars puppeteered by actors or text-to-speech, reading AI-generated jokes (Tett, 2023).

Other improv performances built around adversarial human-AI relationships include *The AI Improv Show* (2023) by London improv school The Free Association[11] (featuring ChatGPT-generated jokes) and Amsterdam-based Boom Chicago who produced *The Future Is Here... And It Is Slightly Annoying*[12] (2019) with improv sketches involving a tele-presence robot on wheels connected to a chatbot developed by Botnik Studios[13].

[9] https://www.comediansvsai.com/

[10] https://www.comedybytes.io/

[11] https://www.thefreeassociation.co.uk/

[12] https://boomchicago.nl/shows/the-future-is-here/

[13] https://botnik.org/

2.3 Can an AI Pass the Comedy Turing Test?

Building upon the idea of human-AI comparison, improv duo *HumanMachine* adapted in 2017 the Turing test (Turing, 1950) and introduced its comedic counterpart (Mathewson and Mirowski, 2017b). They assembled in 2018 a large-cast improv troupe, *Improbotics*[14], featuring human actors, some of whom (called *Cyborgs*) get lines from AI via headphones connected to a portable FM radio receiving lines transmitted from the AI chatbot's text-to-speech. Over hundreds of performances, the troupe has devised diverse short-form and long-form improv games featuring the Cyborg in disclosed or concealed identity. In addition to evaluating audiences' perception towards AI, the troupe evaluates audiences' perception of its language capabilities: they devised a comedy Turing test by staging non-Cyborg actors who pretend to be controlled by AI alongside the Cyborg actors. One would expect the comedy Turing test to become harder as LLM technology develops, but the comedians invented ways to "sound like an AI" to confuse the audiences, thereby demonstrating the limitations of the Turing test.

Computational humor researcher Dr. Thomas Winters designed, with comedian Lieven Schiere, a more formal Turing test performed on the stage, and aimed at evaluating advances in large language models for writing comedy ahead of the performance (Winters, 2024).

2.4 Comedic deception of audiences by AI

The idea of deception has been explored in game contexts beyond the Turing test. In 2023, filmmaker Dr. Manuel Hendry designed a dark comedic installation *The Feeling Machine*[15], where a chatbot-powered, ELIZA-inspired "psychotherapist" is embodied by an animated mask: once that "psychotherapist" establishes a rapport with an individual spectator (Hendry et al., 2023), the system provocatively shows a deep fake of that spectator making up false memories, to raise questions about misuses of technology. *The Feeling Machine* targets art museum audiences acquainted with ethical discussions around AI; at the opposite side of the spectrum sits a general audience show made by TV company Endemol Italy and presented in 2023: *Fake Show: Diffidate delle imitazioni*[16], an impro-

[14] https://improbotics.org

[15] https://www.hendry.me/

[16] https://www.raiplay.it/programmi/fakeshowdiffidatedelleimitazioni

visational game show featuring deep fakes.

Company *Improbotics* adapted that concept in 2024: they comically explore alternative life choices of a consenting audience member, acted out by different improvisers who drive live-generated deep fakes (Glennon, 2024).

3 Live performance and real-time interaction as a test for generative AI

The commonality behind the shows presented in Section 2 was that they addressed ethical interrogations about the role of AI in comedy. In this section, we review shows that investigate how to effectively deliver computational humor on stage.

3.1 AI co-creating real-time comedy dialogue

The development of large language models and conversational AI applications mostly focuses on single-user text-based dialogue. Speech recognition and dialogue systems struggle with Multi-Party Chat (MPC). Branch et al. (2024) describe how they approached this problem in *Improbotics* performances, where multiple actors interact with an AI *Cyborg* stage partner, just like in a traditional improv comedy show featuring a large cast in a lively performance. Instead of simple turn-taking in human-chatbot dialogue, the troupe resorts to human-in-the-loop curation of continuously AI-generated lines, where the most comedic or relevant lines are sent to the Cyborg performer via an earpiece; introducing a second performer who takes responsibility for selecting the AI-generated line creates a "writer's room" setup and introduces two levels of human interpretation of AI-generated material. In their 2024 performances at the Edinburgh Festival Fringe, the troupe replaced earpieces by augmented-reality glasses, delegating the role of AI line curation to the Cyborg performer, who would simultaneously read some of the AI-generated lines and try to maintain eye contact with stage partners.

Timing! The most important rule of comedy is... *Improbotics* needed to design both technology (fast speech recognition and language models, and asynchronous generation) to accelerate the robot's responses (Branch et al., 2024), and dramaturgy ("slow-burn" improv scenes relying on non-language communication to fill the time lags) (Mathewson and Mirowski, 2018). Improviser Cyborgs expressed they had struggled with AI generated lines because of slow timing and delays; their perception was that the audience preferred timely responses to higher quality but delayed responses.

In Oregon, Prof. Naomi Fitter focused on comedy timing as she has been running since 2019 regular comedy nights where her robot comedian Jon relies on audience laughter to control the timing and delivery of jokes (Srivastava and Fitter, 2021).

3.2 AI for inspiration and world building

Liveness in AI improv shows is not limited to dialogue: human actors can leverage AI-generated ideas for real-time performance. Notably, San Francisco-based Alexa Improvise[17] has used an AI assistant for game ideas since 2018; *Yes, Android* by Toronto company *Bad Dog*[18] featured actors reading LLM-generated lines in 2017; Nouméa-based *La Claque*[19] incorporated French-language AI for short-form improv suggestions in 2023; and India-UK troupe *ClimateProv* leveraged Gen AI to inspire climate-themed improvisation in 2022. Winters and Mathewson (2019) designed automatic slide generators[20] for *Powerpoint karaoke* games.

Several projects explored LLMs for long-form improvisation by supporting storytelling. Notably *Plays by Bots*, staged since 2022 by Edmonton-based *Rapid Fire Theatre*[21], rely on scripts co-written with *Dramatron* (Mirowski et al., 2023) to build the world for improvisers; and in 2021, *Improbotics* used an AI as narrator for long-form scenes (Branch et al., 2021b).

Finally, and while they do not use AI in real time during their performance, many comedians have presented material co-written with AI in front of live audiences, including Darren Walsh[22] in 2023 and Anesti Danelis[23] in 2024 at Edinburgh Fringe.

The commonality between all those shows is to employ computational humor systems as mere writing tools to support live human performance; as a consequence, audience evaluation is focused primarily on the human performers and how they engage with their audiences.

3.3 Live performance with AI in digital spaces

The development of computer-mediated communication technology has introduced a new way for humans to congregate and redefined the notion of liveness and audience interaction. Live performance

[17] https://ai.nickradford.dev/
[18] https://baddogtheatre.com/
[19] https://laclaqueimpro.com/
[20] https://talkgenerator.com/
[21] https://rapidfiretheatre.com/
[22] https://darrenwalsh.co.uk/
[23] https://www.anestidanelis.com/

no longer requires a physical space, as performers and audience can congregate virtually via teleconference and chat, overcoming long geographical distances, as proved by *Failed to Render*[24], a comedy club in virtual reality, or most improv teams performing and rehearsing online during Covid-19.

Branch et al. (2023) analysed how shared VR environments and telepresence enhance improvisational flow more than traditional teleconference; a tele-immersive environment was used in 2020-2021 for VR rehearsals and performances[25] of *Improbotics*, where the AI agent was represented by an avatar (Branch et al., 2021a). Jacob et al. (2019) used computer vision models for physical improv games in *Robot Improv Circus VR*[26]. *PORTAGING* was a humorous prompt battle with Gen AI performed on a Discord channel at NeurIPS 2022[27]. In these shows, audience engagement could be measured in chat interactions during streaming and, in some cases, laughter on live audio channels.

4 AI language and human interpretation

The remaining question about computational humor systems for live performance is how they help communicate, or how they challenge human actors to make sense of AI-generated output.

On one hand, AI can be used for meaning making: multilingual improv in *Rosetta Code* is mediated by speech recognition, machine translation, and in-ear text-to-speech (Mirowski et al., 2020). Incidently, these three tools are applications that underlie the development of language models.

On the other hand, we alluded in Section 2 to human actors trying to justify "seemingly absurd" AI-generated text. Improvisers can leverage LLMs as a creative and acting challenge (Mathewson and Mirowski, 2018), and *THEaiTRE*'s scripted production of *AI: When a Robot Writes a Play* exemplifies the glitch aesthetic of involuntarily funny absurdist LLMs (Rosa et al., 2021). Absurdist theatre, however, requires supportive audiences. The *Dramatron* system (Mirowski et al., 2023) was an attempt at making AI-generated theatrical scripts sound less "absurdist", and it aimed at supporting actors by generating more coherent narratives.

More than Human, produced in 2019 by Dr. Gunter Lösel, went in the opposite direction. Its human cast (one of whom was taking lines from an LLM) did not attempt to justify those AI-generated suggestions at all. Instead, and following the principles of Dadaism, they used AI to explore and celebrate their own "inner machine" (Loesel et al., 2020; Lösel, 2024).

5 Discussion: evaluation of live AI humor

This position paper claims that audience feedback from live performances enables a challenging testbed for computational humor systems. Arguably, some comedy material is not amenable to live or improvised formats (e.g., memes, comedic videos and films) as they are pre-written and with no live audience interaction. Nevertheless, these can be assessed by measuring audience engagement on social media, in ratings or at the box office.

Human-Computer Interaction literature provides many toolboxes for assessing live audience engagement and the creative process. Branch et al. (2024) and Mathewson and Mirowski (2018) rely on audience and performer surveys after performances. Srivastava and Fitter (2021) measure audience laughter and engagement using microphones. Mirowski et al. (2024) proposed focus groups with comedians engaging in writing tasks with LLMs and assessing AI using Creativity Support Tool metrics like (Cherry and Latulipe, 2014; Chakrabarty et al., 2024): these metrics can be applied to live and improvisational contexts as well.

The fundamental advantage of framing the evaluation of computational humor in the wider context of audience reception and feedback, is that it simultaneously defines the role that AI tools can play in the wider comedy ecosystem–as creativity support tools. Such a framing encourages a collaborative relationship between human comedians and AI tools instead of an adversarial one, and helps approach the various ethical questions around AI art (and comedy in particular) on artists (and comedians) (Epstein et al., 2023; Jiang et al., 2023).

Humans have used the technologies of their time to tell stories, from cave paintings to the internet. Generative AI is one such technology, and this paper gave examples of storytellers trying to adopt it as a writing tool for performance. Humor and comedy writers can evaluate those tools through real-time human feedback, which can be uniquely provided by live theater—an ideal experimental substrate for creative technology for storytelling.

[24] https://failedtorender.com/

[25] https://www.art-ai.io/programme/improbotics/

[26] https://gvu.gatech.edu/research/projects/robot-improv-circus-vr-installation

[27] https://neurips.cc/virtual/2022/56220

Acknowledgments

The authors wish to thank three anonymous reviewers for instrumental feedback that helped improved the paper, and the casts and guest players of Improbotics for transforming improv and the theatre stage into a laboratory.

References

Miriam Amin and Manuel Burghardt. 2020. A survey on approaches to computational humor generation. In *Proceedings of the The 4th Joint SIGHUM Workshop on Computational Linguistics for Cultural Heritage, Social Sciences, Humanities and Literature*, pages 29–41.

Boyd Branch, Christos Efstratiou, Piotr Mirowski, Kory W Mathewson, and Paul Allain. 2021a. Tele-immersive improv: Effects of immersive visualisations on rehearsing and performing theatre online. In *Proceedings of the 2021 CHI Conference on Human Factors in Computing Systems*, pages 1–13.

Boyd Branch, Piotr Mirowski, Kory Mathewson, Sophia Ppali, and Alexandra Covaci. 2024. Designing and evaluating dialogue llms for co-creative improvised theatre. In *Proceedings of the 15th International Conference on Computational Creativity*. Association for Computational Creativity.

Boyd Branch, Piotr Mirowski, and Kory W Mathewson. 2021b. Collaborative storytelling with human actors and ai narrators. In *Proceedings of the 12th International Conference on Computational Creativity*. Association for Computational Creativity.

Boyd Branch, Piotr Mirowski, Sophia Ppali, Rocio Von Jungenfeld, Paul Allain, and Christos Efstratiou. 2023. Mirror placement matters in remote collaboration. In *Extended Abstracts of the 2023 CHI Conference on Human Factors in Computing Systems*, CHI EA '23, New York, NY, USA. Association for Computing Machinery.

James E Caron. 2002. From ethology to aesthetics: Evolution as a theoretical paradigm for research on laughter, humor, and other comic phenomena. *Humor: International Journal of Humor Research*.

Tuhin Chakrabarty, Vishakh Padmakumar, Faeze Brahman, and Smaranda Muresan. 2024. Creativity support in the age of large language models: An empirical study involving professional writers. In *Proceedings of the 16th Conference on Creativity & Cognition*, pages 132–155.

Yuetian Chen, Bowen Shi, and Mei Si. 2023. Prompt to gpt-3: Step-by-step thinking instructions for humor generation. *arXiv preprint arXiv:2306.13195*.

Erin Cherry and Celine Latulipe. 2014. Quantifying the creativity support of digital tools through the creativity support index. *ACM Transactions on Computer-Human Interaction (TOCHI)*, 21(4):1–25.

Derek Collins. 2001. Improvisation in rhapsodic performance. *Helios*, 28(1):11–29.

Ziv Epstein, Aaron Hertzmann, Investigators of Human Creativity, Memo Akten, Hany Farid, Jessica Fjeld, Morgan R Frank, Matthew Groh, Laura Herman, Neil Leach, et al. 2023. Art and the science of generative ai. *Science*, 380(6650):1110–1111.

Giancarlo Frosio. 2023. Generative ai in court. *Court (September 1, 2023). in Nikos Koutras and Niloufer Selvadurai (eds), Recreating Creativity, Reinventing Inventiveness-International Perspectives on AI and IP Governance (Routledge, 2023, Forthcoming)*.

Matthew Gervais and David Sloan Wilson. 2005. The evolution and functions of laughter and humor: A synthetic approach. *The Quarterly review of biology*, 80(4):395–430.

Neave Glennon. 2024. Boti reviews | artificial intelligence improvisation. *Brighton on the inside*.

Drew Gorenz and Norbert Schwarz. 2024. How funny is chatgpt? a comparison of human-and ai-produced jokes. In *PLoS ONE*. OSF.

Manuel Flurin Hendry, Norbert Kottmann, Martin Fröhlich, Florian Bruggisser, Marco Quandt, Stella Speziali, Valentin Huber, and Chris Salter. 2023. Are you talking to me? a case study in emotional human-machine interaction. In *Proceedings of the AAAI Conference on Artificial Intelligence and Interactive Digital Entertainment*, volume 19, pages 417–424.

Mikhail Jacob, Prabhav Chawla, Lauren Douglas, Ziming He, Jason Lee, Tanuja Sawant, and Brian Magerko. 2019. Affordance-based generation of pretend object interaction variants for human-computer improvisational theater. In *Proceedings of the 10th International Conference on Computational Creativity*. Association for Computational Creativity.

Megan Jamerson. 2023. A comedian and ai walk into a bar. who was funnier? `https://www.kcrw.com/news/shows/greater-la/artificial-intel-smpd-homeless-oc/ai-comedy`. KCRW.

Sophie Jentzsch and Kristian Kersting. 2023. Chatgpt is fun, but it is not funny! humor is still challenging large language models. *arXiv preprint arXiv:2306.04563*.

Harry H Jiang, Lauren Brown, Jessica Cheng, Mehtab Khan, Abhishek Gupta, Deja Workman, Alex Hanna, Johnathan Flowers, and Timnit Gebru. 2023. Ai art and its impact on artists. In *Proceedings of the 2023 AAAI/ACM Conference on AI, Ethics, and Society*, pages 363–374.

Philip N Johnson-Laird. 2002. How jazz musicians improvise. *Music Perception*, 19(3).

Keith Johnstone. 1979. *Impro: Improvisation and the Theatre*. Faber and Faber Ltd.

Marzena Karpinska, Nader Akoury, and Mohit Iyyer. 2021. The perils of using mechanical turk to evaluate open-ended text generation. In *Proceedings of the 2021 Conference on Empirical Methods in Natural Language Processing*, pages 1265–1285.

Heather Knight, Scott Satkin, Varun Ramakrishna, and Santosh Divvala. 2011. A savvy robot standup comic: Online learning through audience tracking. In *Workshop paper (TEI'10)*.

Kathleen Marguerite Lea. 1934. Italian popular comedy: a study in the commedia dell'arte, 1560-1620 with special reference to the english stage. *(No Title)*.

Gunter Loesel, Piotr Mirowski, and Kory Wallace Mathewson. 2020. Do digital agents do dada? In *Proceedings of the 11th International Conference on Computational Creativity*, pages 488–491.

Brian Logan. 2023. Whose generated line is it anyway? ai tries to crack humour's dna. *The Guardian*.

Gunter Lösel. 2024. Theatre dialogues with machines. *Interdisciplinary Science Reviews*, 49(2):291–304.

Brian Magerko et al. 2009. An empirical study of cognition and theatrical improvisation. In *ACM Creat. & Cog.*

Lara J Martin, Brent Harrison, and Mark O Riedl. 2016. Improvisational computational storytelling in open worlds. In *Interactive Storytelling: 9th International Conference on Interactive Digital Storytelling, ICIDS 2016, Los Angeles, CA, USA, November 15–18, 2016, Proceedings 9*, pages 73–84. Springer.

Kory Mathewson and Piotr Mirowski. 2018. Improbotics: Exploring the imitation game using machine intelligence in improvised theatre. In *Proceedings of the AAAI Conference on Artificial Intelligence and Interactive Digital Entertainment*, volume 14, pages 59–66.

Kory W Mathewson. 2019. Humour-in-the-loop: Improvised theatre with interactive machine learning systems. *PhD Thesis, University of Alberta*.

Kory W Mathewson and Piotr Mirowski. 2017a. Improvised theatre alongside artificial intelligences. In *Thirteenth Artificial Intelligence and Interactive Digital Entertainment Conference*.

Kory Wallace Mathewson and Piotr Mirowski. 2017b. Improvised comedy as a turing test. *arXiv preprint arXiv:1711.08819*.

Piotr Mirowski, Juliette Love, Kory Mathewson, and Shakir Mohamed. 2024. A robot walks into a bar: Can language models serve as creativity supporttools for comedy? an evaluation of llms' humour alignment with comedians. In *The 2024 ACM Conference on Fairness, Accountability, and Transparency*, pages 1622–1636.

Piotr Mirowski, Kory W Mathewson, Boyd Branch, Thomas Winters, Ben Verhoeven, and Jenny Elfving. 2020. Rosetta code: Improv in any language. In *Proceedings of the 11th International Conference on Computational Creativity*, pages 115–122.

Piotr Mirowski, Kory W Mathewson, Jaylen Pittman, and Richard Evans. 2023. Co-writing screenplays and theatre scripts with language models: Evaluation by industry professionals. In *Proceedings of the 2023 CHI Conference on Human Factors in Computing Systems*, pages 1–34.

Izabella Pluta. 2016. Theater and robotics: Hiroshi ishiguro's androids as staged by oriza hirata. *Art Research Journal*, 3(1):65–79.

Victor Raskin. 1979. Semantic mechanisms of humor. In *Annual Meeting of the Berkeley Linguistics Society*, volume 5, pages 325–335.

Rudolf Rosa, Tomáš Musil, Ondřej Dušek, Dominik Jurko, Patrícia Schmidtová, David Mareček, Ondřej Bojar, Tom Kocmi, Daniel Hrbek, David Košt'ák, et al. 2021. When a robot writes a play: Automatically generating a theatre play script. In *Artificial Life Conference Proceedings 33*, volume 2021, page 60. MIT Press One Rogers Street, Cambridge, MA 02142-1209, USA journals-info ....

Mike Sharples and Rafael Pérez y Pérez. 2022. *Story machines: How computers have become creative writers*. Routledge.

Ajitesh Srivastava and Naomi T Fitter. 2021. A robot walks into a bar: Automatic robot joke success assessment. In *2021 IEEE International Conference on Robotics and Automation (ICRA)*, pages 2710–2716. IEEE.

Ilya Sutskever, Vinyals Oriol, and Quoc V. Le. 2014. Sequence to sequence learning with neural networks. In *Advances in Neural Information Processing Systems*, pages 3104–3112.

Gillian Tett. 2023. Can ai crack comedy? `https://www.ft.com/content/818f2cab-57ff-42c3-917b-4a83f1d87802`. Financial Times.

Jörg Tiedemann. 2009. News from opus-a collection of multilingual parallel corpora with tools and interfaces. In *Recent Advances in Natural Language Processing*, volume 5, pages 237–248.

Alexey Tikhonov and Pavel Shtykovskiy. 2024. Humor mechanics: Advancing humor generation with multistep reasoning. *arXiv preprint arXiv:2405.07280*.

Joe Toplyn. 2023. Witscript 3: A hybrid ai system for improvising jokes in a conversation. *arXiv preprint arXiv:2301.02695*.

Alan Turing. 1950. Computing machinery and intelligence. *Mind*, 59(236):433–460.

Tony Veale. 2021. *Your Wit is My Command: Building AIs with a Sense of Humor.* Mit Press.

Oriol Vinyals and Quoc Le. 2015. A neural conversational model. *arXiv preprint arXiv:1506.05869.*

Thomas Winters. 2021. Computers learning humor is no joke. *Harvard Data Science Review*, 3(2).

Thomas Winters. 2024. Evaluating humor generation in an improvisational comedy setting.

Thomas Winters and Kory W Mathewson. 2019. Automatically generating engaging presentation slide decks. In *International Conference on Computational Intelligence in Music, Sound, Art and Design (Part of EvoStar)*, pages 127–141. Springer.

Thomas Winters, Vincent Nys, and Daniel De Schreye. 2018. Automatic joke generation: Learning humor from examples. In *Distributed, Ambient and Pervasive Interactions: Technologies and Contexts: 6th International Conference, DAPI 2018, Held as Part of HCI International 2018, Las Vegas, NV, USA, July 15–20, 2018, Proceedings, Part II 6*, pages 360–377. Springer.

Haonan Zhong, Jiamin Chang, Ziyue Yang, Tingmin Wu, Pathum Chamikara Mahawaga Arachchige, Chehara Pathmabandu, and Minhui Xue. 2023. Copyright protection and accountability of generative ai: Attack, watermarking and attribution. In *Companion Proceedings of the ACM Web Conference 2023*, pages 94–98.

The Algorithm is the Message: Computing as a Humor-Generating Mode

Vittorio Marone
The University of Texas at San Antonio, USA
vittorio.marone@utsa.edu

Abstract

This position paper starts from the examination of the "Universal Handbook for Political Speeches," a satirical manual created during communist Poland as a modular tool to parody propaganda's rigid linguistic patterns and its absence of meaning, humorously revealing the absurdity of totalitarian "newspeak." Presented here in English for the first time, the "Handbook" is explored as an analog precursor to computational humor systems. More importantly, this artifact shows that humor, rather than being the product of computing, can also arise from a computationalized, combinatorial structure and process. This shifts the focus on computational algorithms and processes as a *mode* of humor generation, rather than a *tool*. That is, computing *itself*—with its processes, structure, iteration, and combinatorial logic—can be a source of humor, rather than an instrument to fabricate it. The very workings of the machine are what can make us laugh, regardless of what the machine carries or produces. The "Handbook" functions here as a spark for reflection, and hopefully a broader discussion, on how this alternative view may impact the evolution of computational humor and its applications at the dawn of the era of artificial general intelligence.

1 Introduction

The "Universal Handbook for Political Speeches" is a satirical guide distributed in Poland at the time of the Solidarity movement in the 1980s which mocked the empty, verbose, and ideologically charged rhetoric of communist propaganda (Marone, 2010). The "Handbook" seems to be a playful embodiment of "newspeak," a fictional language introduced in George Orwell's dystopian novel *1984* designed as a tool of political control to limit freedom of thought and enforce ideological conformity. The idea of recommending this mechanical approach to its users, both mimicked and lampooned the propaganda's repetitive and formulaic nature, hence unmasking its absurdity. The "Handbook" operated as a modular template that allowed users to construct endless variations of lengthy, meaningless speeches by combining prewritten phrases from four distinct categories (columns), each containing a list of interchangeable phrases (see Appendix A). These columns corresponded to different components of a sentence:

- **Column I**: Opening phrases or thematic introductions (e.g., "Dear colleagues," "On the other hand," "But let us not forget that").
- **Column II**: Descriptive or action-oriented statements related to the topic (e.g., "the execution of outlined programmatic tasks," "the scope and location of worker training," "the current organizational structure").
- **Column III**: Transitional or explanatory phrases (e.g., "compels us to analyze," "plays a crucial role in defining," "highlights the importance of appreciating").
- **Column IV**: Concluding or outcome-oriented statements (e.g., "the current administrative and financial conditions," "further directions of development," "a universal participatory system").

Proceedings of the 1st Workshop on Computational Humor (CHum), pages 96–100
January 19, 2025. ©2025 Association for Computational Linguistics

To create a speech, the user would select one phrase from each column sequentially (I → II → III → IV) and repeat this process as needed, recycling or varying combinations to extend the speech indefinitely. For example:

- **Combination 1**: "Dear colleagues, the ongoing informational and propagandistic protection of our activities plays a significant role in establishing a training system tailored to workers' needs."
- **Combination 2**: "On the other hand, the effort to strengthen and develop effective structures facilitates the preparation and construction of advanced forms of action."

This approach enables users to produce a seemingly endless series of sentences, all of which sound appropriately formal, authoritative, and ideologically consistent, while having no actual meaning. This parodied the vacuity of communist propaganda, which relied on impressive-sounding language to obscure its lack of substantive ideas.

The humor of the handbook lies in its overt mechanical sequencing, which creates the illusion of coherence regardless of content. By exposing the mechanical nature of speech construction, it highlighted how the political rhetoric of the regime was less about conveying meaning and more about projecting authority and reinforcing ideological control. Some of the key features that made the "Handbook" effective include:

- **Endless Combinations.** The modular design allowed for thousands of combinations, making the system seem both vast and methodical.
- **Parodic Authenticity.** The phrases were written in a style that closely mimicked real propaganda speeches, giving the satire its biting edge.
- **Reflection of Reality.** The mechanical relentlessness of the "Handbook" mirrored the mechanical absurdity of actual propaganda, creating a form of meta-critique.

Besides its function at the time of communism in Poland, the "Handbook" invites us to reflect on computational approaches to language and humor considering computers and algorithms not just as *tools*, but as a *mode* of generating humor. We may say that the text of the handbook was plain and not interesting in itself, but what made it fun and intriguing was its computationalization. The "satirical mechanization" of the "Handbook" demonstrates how humor can emerge from the mechanical application of language rules. This analog system anticipated computational humor systems (Amin & Burghardt, 2020) by using predefined templates and algorithms to create meaning—or its illusion. By mechanically generating discourse, it exposed propaganda's reliance on pre-fabricated rhetoric, revealing the manipulation and vacuity underlying authoritarian speech. This form of disruptive combinatorial creativity shows that humor can emerge not only from the content of the phrases, but in the very act of their arbitrary sequencing. This analog, yet computationalized form of humor exemplifies how structure, randomness, and sequencing can work to generate humor.

2 Potential Implications of Computing as a Humor-Generating Mode

2.1 Humor as Process, Not Output

Traditionally, computation in humor has been viewed as a tool—a means to achieve a predefined outcome, such as generating jokes, detecting irony, or analyzing linguistic patterns. This functional perspective treats computational processes as subservient to the end product: the humorous content itself. However, reframing computation as a humorous mode shifts the emphasis to the generative computational process instead of the outcome. From this perspective, humor emerges not from the final product (a joke or punchline) but from the structure, sequencing, and combinatorial logic inherent in computational processes. For example, in the "Universal Handbook for Political Speeches," the humor lies in its *mechanical absurdity*, as interchangeable fragments produce endless combinations of pompous, empty rhetoric. This shows that computing *itself* can embody humor when its processes are exposed.

Reframing computing as a humorous mode invites researchers to explore how structure and process—the underlying mechanics of humor generation—can themselves serve as sources of comedy. This perspective shifts attention from the *output* to the *systems and logic* driving humor, fundamentally rethinking the origins of humor in computational systems. As a result, the understanding of computational humor may evolve into a domain where the *humorous mechanics* of systems—not just their *humorous outputs*—become complementary to understanding and designing computational humor.

2.2 Meta-Humor and Human-Machine Dynamics

Meta-humor arises when a system reflects on or reveals its own mechanisms. Computational humor as a mode inherently generates meta-humor, where the system's own generative logic ignites the joke. This parallels the "Handbook," where humor arises primarily from its visible combinatorial structure rather than the semantic content of individual phrases. Similarly, the unintentionally humorous results of AI systems (Shane, 2019) often arise from their rigid adherence to structures, patterns, and system logic, and leaving them exposed may engender novel forms of meta-humor. Therefore, studying computational processes through the lens of theories of humor may provide novel understandings in the field of computer science and computational linguistics. In a sense, this would mark a shift from *computational humor* to *humorous computation*.

"Humorous computational systems" inspired by the "Handbook" could be explicitly designed to reveal or parody their algorithmic nature, generating humor through the visible mechanics of their construction and operation. This taps into the human fascination with exposed mechanisms, as seen in watches (e.g., the Swatch GK100 Jellyfish wristwatch on display at the MoMA), computers (e.g., the original translucent iMac G3, also on display at the MoMA), or car gearboxes (e.g., the visible gearchange mechanism in the Lotus Emira). Other examples include quirky musical instruments (e.g., Wintergatan's Marble Machine), Rube Goldberg machines, and Theo Jansen's Strandbeests. In all these creations, the visible systems and processes are more captivating than their final output, like the melody produced or where an object lands.

Since current computational humor systems evaluate success based on user reactions to generated content (e.g., laughter or ratings of "funny"), this new approach would require developing new metrics that assess the humor embedded in computational structures, such as incongruity levels, randomness, or structural creativity.

Superiority theories of humor (Lintott, 2016) suggest that humans may laugh at machines when their "cold" logic or mechanical limitations appear inferior to human reasoning. However, computational systems that present their own processes and mechanisms as sources of humor, as well as the inherent absurdity of their existence and their interactions with humans, could invert this dynamic, making machines appear self-aware and relatable. This would challenge understandings and desired outcomes of human-machine interaction. Rather than striving to make machines more human, exposing their inner workings and non-humanity might make people perceive them as more relatable and therefore—paradoxically—as more human. While science strives to make AI and robots as similar as possible to real humans, those that humorously expose their computational logic and "non-humanness" might make technology feel less intimidating and more accessible, particularly for non-technical users.

These forms of *machine self-deprecating humor* that point at its combinatorial mechanisms, system inefficiencies, or their programmers' biases, may change how humans perceive and interact with machines. For example, interjecting self-reflective humorous comments at random intervals may give an AI a unique personality that shows "awareness" of its inner workings by exposing them through a sort of *humorous computational transparency* (for instance, in response to a user's negative feedback on the AI's output). As another example, an AI-generated voice assistant could intentionally switch to a robot-like voice to humorously express its flawed or unsatisfactory performance as a machine. This kind of revealing and self-referential humor by AI systems could also be used as an educational tool to demystify computational processes and concepts making them less intimidating and more engaging for students, especially when introducing them to fields like computer science, robotics, and artificial intelligence.

By implementing this approach, chatbots and robotic companions that generate humor by revealing their computational processes could feel more relatable, as some people may find "replicants" intimidating, if not outright creepy. This "see-through" approach to *humorous computational thinking* could transform how people interact with AI chatbots and robotic companions, and how they integrate them into their lives.

2.3 Broader Implications

Most computational humor research aims to mimic or reproduce human humor. Treating computing as a humor-generating mode suggests that algorithmic processes need not replicate human humor. Instead, they can "embrace" their own unique, mechanical absurdity, producing humor that is distinctly computational. This has the potential to change and expand not only what we find humorous as human beings, but the very understanding of humor itself, from *human-like* to *more-than-human*.

By focusing on structure and process, researchers can identify distinctly computational forms of humor, where the logic of systems generates a unique type of comedy that does not rely on replicating human expression. Here, examining computing as a humorous mode reveals the uniquely human ability to find humor in structural absurdity and mechanical logic. This contributes to philosophical and psychological discussions about what distinguishes humans from machines and how mechanical and computational processes can expand "humanness" by broadening modes of humor generation and enjoyment. More broadly, computational humor systems can reveal how humans relate to mechanized processes. Through this lens, computational humor moves beyond *imitation* to become a tool for *exploration* of what makes us smile—of what make us human.

3 Conclusion

The "Universal Handbook for Political Speeches" is more than a historical curiosity—it is a powerful case study in how *the algorithmic structuring of language* can be used as a mode of humor generation. Its analog design anticipates the computational methods used in modern language generation while serving as a timeless reminder of the power of humor to unmask authoritarian absurdity. Building on this foundation, this paper advocates for viewing computing as a mode of humor generation, where humor emerges from the structure and process itself rather than solely from the output. The "Handbook" demonstrates how modular structures, algorithms, and processes can engender humor, offering new ways to design systems that embrace the creative potential of computing rather than striving to replicate human-like humor. Finally, this approach can deepen our understanding of human-machine dynamics by emphasizing shared experiences of absurdity and creativity, in a fragile balance between *sequencing* and *randomness*, *order* and *chaos*.

Computational humor systems challenge us to rethink the nature of humor itself and the ways in which humans and machines can collaborate in playful and meaningful ways. At the dawn of artificial general intelligence, these systems offer a glimpse of a future where algorithms are not just *functional* but also *inspiring*, especially if we let their unequivocal, mechanistic non-humanness shine through.

4 Limitations

This position paper presents a conceptual framework for understanding computational humor as a generative mode rather than a tool, using the "Universal Handbook for Political Speeches" as a case study. However, the analysis relies on a single historical artifact, which, while illustrative, may limit the generalizability of the arguments to contemporary computational humor systems. The absence of empirical testing or concrete implementation of the proposed ideas means that their practical applicability and effectiveness remain speculative. Furthermore, the paper does not extensively address how these ideas might interact with the latest advances in neural network-based language models, natural language processing, computational linguistics, or multimodal humor systems. Finally, as a position paper, it does not engage directly with broader ethical implications, such as how the use of computational humor might shape human-machine interactions in unintended ways. Of course, these limitations also represent doors open to further reflection and interdisciplinary research.

References

Amin, M., & Burghardt, M. (2020). A survey on approaches to computational humor generation. *Proceedings of the 4th Joint SIGHUM Workshop on Computational Linguistics for Cultural Heritage, Social Sciences, Humanities and Literature*, 29–41. International Committee on Computational Linguistics. https://aclanthology.org/2020.latechclfl-1.4

Lintott, S. (2016). Superiority in humor theory. *The Journal of Aesthetics and Art Criticism, 74*(4), 347–358. https://doi.org/10.1111/jaac.12321

Marone, V. (2010). *La quotidianità dell'assurdo [The everyday absurd]*. Archetipo Libri.

Shane, J. (2019). *You look like a thing and I love you: How AI works and why it's making the world a weirder place.* Voracious.

Appendix A

I	II	III	IV
Dear colleagues	the execution of outlined programmatic tasks	compels us to analyze	the current administrative and financial conditions
on the other hand	the scope and location of worker training	plays a crucial role in defining	further directions of development
similarly	the continuous quantitative growth and range of our activities	necessitates specification and clarification of	a universal participatory system
but let us not forget that	the current organizational structure	facilitates the preparation and construction of	participants' attitudes toward organizational tasks
in this way	the new organizational activity model	ensures the participation of a wide group in shaping	new proposals
because daily experience shows us that	the continuous development of various activity forms	plays a significant role in establishing	progressive educational directives
and the importance of these issues is self-evident, because	the ongoing informational and propagandistic protection of our activities	efficiently enables the creation of	a training system tailored to workers' needs
hence, the rich and varied experience of	the effort to strengthen and develop effective structures	highlights the importance of appreciating	suitable activation conditions
furthermore, the organizational focus, which includes	the consultation with a broad active base	serves as an intriguing test for the evaluation of	a new developmental model
therefore, this ideological premise expressed by	the initiation of a general process that reshapes attitudes	leads to a process of introducing and modernizing	advanced forms of action

Author Index

Association for Computational Linguistics
209 N. Eighth Street
Stroudsburg, Pennsylvania 18360

ISBN 979-8-3313-1361-6

CURRAN ASSOCIATES INC.
proceedings.com